TOM MOORE

Terence de Vere White

TOM MOORE

THE IRISH POET

HAMISH HAMILTON
LONDON

First published in Great Britain 1977
by Hamish Hamilton Ltd
90 Great Russell Street London WC1B 3PT

Copyright © 1977 by Terence de Vere White

SBN 241 89622 3

Printed in Great Britain by
Western Printing Services Ltd
Bristol

CONTENTS

LIST OF ILLUSTRATIONS

Between pages 114 *and* 115

INTRODUCTION

FIRST OF all, acknowledgments of indebtedness, beginning with those who have laboured in this (or an adjoining) field before me and thereby lightened my task. All Moore students have to go to school to Professor Wilfred S. Dowden of Rice University, Houston, Texas, the editor of Moore's letters. His work on the Journal known hitherto only in the edition by Lord John Russell, in eight volumes, after Moore's death, has brought about a reassessment of Moore, his relations with some of his friends and his manner and habits.

Lord John was intent on propriety and cut as he pleased. He grew tired and skimped the work when the Journal took so unconscionably long to come to a close. I have seen Dr Hoover H. Jordan's reassessment of Moore (*Bolt Upright*) published by the Salzburg Studies in English Literature in 1975 in two volumes. This is an excellent example of American scholarship, hugely painstaking and comprehensive. Dr Jordan has looked at the original Journal, and in consequence has been able to enlarge our knowledge considerably. His filling in of supplementary detail is exhaustive and painstaking to a degree beyond emulation. I have also benefited from the Moore research done by Howard Mumford Jones of Harvard whose biography of the poet (*The Harp That Once*) was published in America in 1937. It is a more scholarly work than L. A. G. Strong's (*The Minstrel Boy*) published in that year in England. Before these, Stephen Gwynn had written a compact and, so far as it went, extremely competent biography for the *English Men of Letters* series.

Moore's friendship with Byron and the destruction of the *Memoirs* of the latter, in which Moore played a reluctant part, is the best known incident in the Irish poet's career. I found Mrs Doris Langley Moore's *The Late Lord Byron* of enormous assistance. I think her estimate of Moore closer to my own than his American biographers'. I am grateful to her and to Mr John Grey Murray for leave to quote from that work.

A biographer is often miserably short of material; a plight which leads to such devices as imagining what his subject felt or thought on occasions when he may well have done neither; such is not the plight of anyone who writes about Moore. The problem Moore presents was posed by his erstwhile friend J. W. Croker in his savage critique of Moore's *Memoirs* in the *Quarterly*. The man, as revealed by his Journal and letters, was not the man people met in the world. Which was the real, the true Moore? If we are to judge him only on his own evidence we can find arguments to support contrary views in his own admissions. I found his very Irish character of intense interest, and recognised all his failings in myself. He had remarkable talents. Some of the *Melodies* will live as long as the language.

I have not attempted a definitive biography. Mine is an effort to pin down an elusive figure and, in the course of doing so, to give a picture of the places he frequented and the people among whom he moved.

As well as those to whom I referred at the beginning, I should like to thank here, the late Director of the National Library, Dr Patrick Henchy; his successor, Alf MacLochlainn; Dr Maurice O'Connell of Fordham University; Dr Tom Walsh of Wexford; Sir John Betjeman and Mr John Grey Murray who allowed me to quote a verse from the Poet Laureate's moving tribute to Moore; Dr Brian Boydell; Professor W. B. Stanford; Victoria Glendinning; Lord Shelburne; Mr Niall Montgomery; Miss Nora Connolly; Dr James White, Director of the National Gallery, and my co-Governors and Guardians who have kindly allowed me to reproduce some of the Gallery's collection of Moore's pictures; the Director of the National Portrait Gallery for permission to reproduce the portraits of Lord Lansdowne, J. W. Croker and Samuel Rogers.

Mr Andrew O'Connor and Mr John Hutchinson were most helpful in my research for illustrations; Miss Hilda Macdermott, as so often before, laboured gallantly at her task of deciphering and typing my illegible manuscript.

PROLOGUE

SHE CRIED when she saw Moore's death in *The Times*. Lady
Morgan hadn't cried for ages; she surprised herself because he
had tended to get on her nerves of recent years; and the last
time he came to Dublin she had been struck by how very old
and bald he looked although he retained his cock-sparrow air.
He was very pleasant, but rather egotistical and shallow, she
decided. A little mind and a brilliant imagination.

They could see through each other, Irish adventurers both;
having less genius (and being a woman) she had to fight
harder; she had sometimes resented his elusiveness and a trace
of condescension in his manner when he hesitated before accepting her invitation to dine—he had always three engagements
for each meal—but all that was so little in the face of death.
And there had been nobody like him. She sat down at once
and wrote a letter to the newspaper. There must be a public
monument.

The idea of a statue was already in the air; a meeting had
been convened at Lord Charlemont's Dublin house to form a
committee. Sir Samuel Ferguson was an excellent choice for
treasurer, a poet and married to a Guinness (nobody would feel
uneasy about the fate of their subscriptions). From Charlemont
House the party adjourned to the Castle, across the river, where
the Lord Lieutenant entertained five hundred 'friends' of
Moore to a concert of his religious songs. The choice of programme was to conciliate clergymen present who might think
it unsuitable that they should attend if there were dancing. One
of Moore's most patriotic songs was sung—but the Lord
Lieutenant took no offence. It was a most satisfactory Dublin
occasion.

There was some debate about a site for the statue; Leinster
Lawn was the first choice, but that was abandoned in favour of
one beside Trinity College. The choice of a sculptor led to

acrimony. Christopher Moore, the poet's namesake, had done a head in his lifetime; but he was a very minor figure in comparison with Hogan of Cork, Canova's pupil. There were rumours of bigotry and jobbery when Hogan was passed over, nor did he seek to disguise his chagrin. Nobody, it seems, paid any attention to Lady Morgan's letter. To have 'some regard to *financial* means', she wrote, 'is an indispensable restraint upon national enthusiasm in Ireland'. And, she reminded, 'the site and the climate should be carefully considered'.

When the statue was unveiled by the Lord Lieutenant, Lord Carlisle, in October 1857, it was apparent at once that someone had blundered.

> Botch'd at first in pedestal and base,
> Botch'd again to fit him in his place . . .

That was how a correspondent put it in *The Dublin Builder*. Lady Morgan decided that it was 'almost *grotesque* and might be anyone else than little Moore'. As if to complete the humiliation of the national bard, Dublin Corporation decided to let him preside over the largest public lavatory in the city. Mr Bloom was not likely to overlook this as he 'passed under Tommy Moore's roguish finger. They did right putting him up over a urinal; meeting of the waters. Ought to be places for women. Running into cake shops'.

Stephen Dedalus, characteristically, took a more discouraging line. 'He looked at it without anger; for, although sloth of the body and of the soul crept over it like unseen vermin, over the shuffling feet and up the folds of the cloak and around the servile head, it seemed conscious of its indignity. It was a Firbolg in the borrowed cloak of a Milesian; and he thought of his friend Davin, the peasant student.'

Moore's statue is the strongest argument for his decision to live in England. It is a libel in metal, holding him up to posterity's ridicule and contempt. So long as his distorted image stands there his bones are more worthily housed in their Wiltshire tomb with his darling Bessy, who survived him and tended his memory, and the children, who went before. He is near Bowood, where he met only courtesy, respect and kindness, where nobody sneered and the great met as equals, where

Lord Lansdowne, the most disinterested statesman of his age, was a cultivated, appreciative host.

Ireland has rejected Moore: after Daniel O'Connell, the greatest Irishman of his day. It was not always so. In the hall of the National Library, the windows are dedicated to Dante, Virgil, Shakespeare, Chaucer—the only Irishman in that gallery is Thomas Moore. Nobody would have known better than himself that was an error of judgement; but it makes up for the ignominy of the statue, erected thirty years before, and the premises over which it presides.

Moore is an intellectual Aunt Sally, the obvious target for inverted snobbery. His chosen way of life offends the spirit of an age which sees no loss of pride in dependence on the indiscriminate patronage of the public purse. Moore supported himself by his pen. He liked life in great houses where politics were discussed by Ministers of State, history by historians, and poetry by poets; if he sang for his supper, he sang as a bird sings wherever he happened to be. It was his natural form of expression. He was born to please. There was nothing shameful and nothing sad about his manner of life. Sir John Betjeman need not have sighed:

> I can but regard you neglected and poor,
> Dear bard of my boyhood, mellifluous Moore,
> That far from the land which of all you loved best
> In a village of England your bones should have rest.

He liked it there as much as he liked ever to be in one place. It was the chosen nest out of which he flew on the least pretext. Not until his final collapse and the death in life of his silent years could he resist any temptation to travel. He loved his peaceful cottage and his adoring Bessy, 'his darling girl'; he rejoiced when he returned to them the happiest and most blessed of men. Home again, he itched to be on the wing. The statue must be taken down, and somewhere in a green corner a sanctuary for singing birds be dedicated in its stead. That is where he belongs.

But he rests where he lived; there is a touching appropriateness about the simple slab under which he lies with Bessy, Anastasia and Russell close to the wall of Bromham Church, whose spire he could espy over the hedges from his pleasant house at Sloperton close at hand. There is a small door in the church wall and a miniature stairway beside the tomb, as if to allow the little Moore ghosts to go in to pray when the fancy took them. But, alas, in 1907, national piety conspired to collect money for a huge Celtic cross. It does not so much mark the grave as shut it off from its surroundings. The one wrong note, however well-intended. How Moore would have hated it!

MOORE WAS born over his father's shop in Aungier Street,
Dublin, on the 28th day of May 1779. Mrs Moore had been
Anastasia Codd; her father was described as a provision mer-
chant in Wexford.

Everything about the poet's father was subdued; and his
origins do not seem to have interested either himself or his
family. They came, apparently, from Kerry and may have in
times gone by been driven out of Leix, the O'Moore county.
In his days of fame the poet sometimes received applications for
financial assistance from namesakes in Kerry, claiming to be
poor relations. In Moyvane there is local tradition.

Mrs Moore was considerably younger than her husband and
had already borne him two daughters. Tom was the youngest
child and that most precious of all human kind—an Irish
mother's only son.

The facial resemblance between mother and son was almost
comical; and it was from his mother that he inherited his
talents. If the portrait of Moore's father in the Dublin Gallery
is at all like, he was exceptionally handsome; but he was
ineffective in business and easy-going. Mrs Moore was the
driving force, and there are many references to her charm. In
different circumstances she might well have been one of the
actresses that left Dublin to win fame in London. Her husband,
with a little cajoling, allowed her to set up a miniature salon
over the shop; she had the capacity to radiate happiness, an
example of Yeats's belief that the good are always the merry.
Because of the father's passive role, it was a woman's house.

The shop in Aungier Street still stands; but it did not look
like that in Moore's time; the old brick front has been plastered
over and a cornice of cement added. Nobody who wished to cut
a dash socially nowadays would choose to be born in that street;
but it had a certain panache when Moore was a boy. The

Dublin streets, except in the poorest quarters, were then not socially stratified; there was not the same rigid distinction between shopping and residential areas. Ten years after the Moores looked out proudly at their son passing by on the arm of a Marquess, the shop had changed hands, but there were still schools and private houses on the street; lawyers and doctors lived beside practitioners in various trades. An Aungier Street resident could educate his children; hire horses; buy jewellery; call in an accoucheur, doctor, attorney; consult an architect; hire paper-hangers, carvers, gilders, cabinet-makers; have a suit or stays fitted; buy bread, candles, hats, coal, medicines; enter a convent and attend churches of two denominations, without moving out of the street.

Aungier Street in the latter half of the eighteenth century was fashionable and prosperous. It reflected the fortunes of the city which flourished in sympathy with the growing confidence of the Irish colony which increasingly—as in the United States— began to assert its parliamentary independence. After the Act of Union of 1800, there was a gradual decline; a great deal of the city was allowed to fall into decay, and there was a growing tendency, among those who could afford it, to move out to the suburbs.

When Moore was a boy, several members of the Irish parliament lived in Aungier Street as well as various legal eminences. One of them, Francis Perry, Deputy Clerk and Keeper of the Rolls, was among the first to recognise the little genius living over the grocer's shop at No. 12. When he died the fourteen-year old poet published an ode to his memory.

He described himself as a child. 'From my natural quickness and the fond pride with which I was regarded at home, it was my lot, unluckily perhaps—though from such a source I can consider nothing unlucky—to be made at a very early age a sort of *show* child; and a talent for reciting was one of the first which my mother's own taste led her to encourage and cultivate in me.'

His father had a house at Sandymount where the family used to repair in summer time for the benefit of sea bathing. On Saturday evening Tom joined them there, and stayed over the Sunday. 'My father at that time kept a little pony for me, on

which I always rode down on those evenings; and at the hour
when I was expected, there generally came with my sister a
number of young girls to meet me, and full of smiles and
welcomes, walked by the side of my pony into the town.'

Mrs Moore may have indulged her son, but she was ambitious
for him. She examined him every day in his school studies; on
a few occasions, coming home from an evening party at one or
two o'clock in the morning, she woke him up, and he cheerfully
sat up in bed and repeated his lesson.

At school, on speech day, when the class in which he had got
first prize was stood up, the other boys, older and much taller
than Tommy, placed themselves above him to hide their
disgrace. They did not reckon with the champion's mother.
Her voice was heard ringing out from the gallery (her son had
submitted cheerfully to the *placement*) demanding that justice
be done.

She was careful about the company her darling kept. He
looked back with pleasure to visits to an elderly maiden lady,
whose name was Dodd, and who lived in a small neat house in
Camden Street. 'The class of society she moved in was somewhat of a higher level than ours; and she was the only person to
whom, during my childhood, my mother could ever trust me
for any time, away from herself.' He attributed his own taste
for good society and facility for adapting himself to that sphere
to 'her constant attention to this object'.

Miss Dodd used to invite little Tom to spend Christmas with
her. He delighted in the attentions he received from his hostess
and her guests. On one occasion he sat for hours under the tea
table with a barrel-organ in his lap waiting for the moment
when he would surprise them with his music. But when his
mother took him to visit friends with a country-house, a
carriage and other signs of wealth, he was disenchanted. 'They
left the impression of being rather vulgar people.'

He described his life at home, his bedroom—a corner,
boarded off, in the room where the two clerks in his father's
business slept. He shared his corner with an uncle, his mother's
brother, until he went to lodge elsewhere. Tom organised the
clerks into a debating and literary society, of which he constituted himself president. They met once or twice a week.

When there was no company, the clerks ate bread and cheese, washed down with beer, at the family table while the Moore parents had their 'regular meat supper', and Mr Moore never missed his tumbler of whiskey punch. After the meal, Tom and the clerks went upstairs to their meeting. They made up verses and riddles. Ennis, one of the clerks, was possibly the first person to introduce Moore to patriotic themes. He was fond of reciting Sarsfield's gallant speeches.

That the clerks were fond of their little president is indisputable; with everyone he lived a charmed life, going unwhipped at his first school, where the master, a wild, odd fellow in a cocked hat, who used to spend the greater part of his nights in drinking at public houses, rarely appeared in class before noon. He would then generally beat the boys all round for disturbing his slumbers. But Tom, the youngest boy in the school, was his favourite, and escaped. Mrs Moore may have helped to purchase immunity; it was her practice to heap 'all sorts of kindness and attentions' on anyone who was likely to assist Tom in his learning.

The key to Moore's character in later life is provided by his mother. She was determined by any means in her power to give him the opportunity that she had been denied. Her means included blandishments of every kind, but not servility. She had a keen interest in politics and her sympathies were patriotic. When Tom was not quite four years old, she taught him verses that had recently been published against Grattan, the national hero, for having accepted a tribute of £100,000 from parliament, after his triumphant assertion of its sovereignty. This led to a temporary set-back in Grattan's popularity. It seemed that he had not been sufficiently vigilant. Mrs Moore must have thought so, for she taught Tom to recite

> Pay down his price, he'll wheel about,
> And laugh like Grattan at the nation.

Tom put peculiar energy into the denunciation of one whom he was afterwards—rightly—to regard as a great and good man. But even at four years of age he was anticipating the privilege of the makers of the nation's songs—they can be revolutionary with impunity.

Moore was always given as much rope as he needed because he would never come to harm. He says that he was unaware of any difference between himself and other children, but he never forgot how a Captain Mahony, who met the Moores somewhere, asked his mother if he passed the nights with the 'little people' on the hills. At breakfast he would say—to the child's great amusement—'Well, Tom, what news from your friends on the hills?'

Once or twice he spent part of his holidays at a small country house in Dundrum, which is now a suburb of Dublin. In the middle of a field stood a ruined castle. The children he was playing with decided to make him King of the Castle. 'A day was accordingly fixed for the purpose; and I remember the pleasure with which I felt myself borne on the shoulders of the other boys to this ruin; and there crowned on its summit by the hands of some little girl of the party.'

There was a celebrated school in Dublin at this time kept by Samuel Whyte. He had pronounced another pupil 'a most incorrigible dunce'; but Richard Brinsley Sheridan was not a biddable child, and Whyte told the story against himself. He, too, found Moore irresistible. An actor *manqué*, he encouraged talents of that kind in his pupils. As in his first school, Moore was singled out for performances on public occasions. He admitted that jealousy was aroused by the preference among the other pupils' mothers.

'Oh, he's an old little crab', said one, 'he can't be less than eleven or twelve years of age.' But Moore never lacked a champion. 'Then, madam', said a gentleman sitting next her, 'if that is the case he must have been four years old before he was born.'

Whyte spent much of his time helping in theatrical productions, writing prologues, coaching actors and actresses, among them a very pretty Miss Campion, who had later success in London. One day Tommy was sent for by his schoolmaster to be introduced to her and to recite *Alexander's Feast* for her benefit. He described the rapture with which he walked through the streets afterwards, wondering if he would meet her and would she recognise him, and his delight when the encounter took place, and she did.

Whyte's theatrical passions caused anxiety among parents of some of his pupils. Mrs Moore had destined her brilliant son for the bar. She was confident that the Catholic disabilities would soon be removed (a Catholic was not allowed to take silk or become a judge). She did not want Tom to become an actor, and it was almost impossible to avoid the contagion. Even Sheridan's sister, Mrs Lefanu, married to a clergyman, was bitten by the bug. Moore described her as having 'a good deal of the talent of her family, with a large alloy of affectation'.

She played Jane Shore with considerable success at the house of a Lady Borrowes. At a repeat performance in 1790 (when Moore was eleven) Mrs Lefanu being ill, a daughter of Samuel Whyte played her part, and Moore recited the prologue.

'Besides our childish sports, we had likewise dawning within us all those vague anticipations of a mature period—those little love-makings, gallantries, ambitions, rivalries—which in the first stirrings have a romance and sweetness about them that never come again.' Moore's story is of the Dublin small grocer's son who became a famous poet in his day and an intimate of the fashionable and the great: but how magical and pleasure-filled his childhood in comparison with, say, Sheridan's at Harrow.

The argument against Moore's sort of pampered up-bringing is that it leaves the subject of it unfit to face the harshness of life. But the qualities which made everyone who met him his slave as a child were not going to fail him in the world.

His first poem was published when he was fourteen years old; it was a milestone in his life. Inscribed to 'Zelia', the verse originated in a rhyming contest with 'an old maid', Miss Hannah Byrne, who used to be a great deal at the Moore's house. Zelia was her pen-name; Moore chose the anagram 'Romeo'. She was, he said, an uninspiring object.

There was a suggestion that Tom should leave Whyte's school and study under Dr Carr in Coppinger Lane, who concentrated on Latin. But, like everyone else, the Latin usher, Donovan, had taken a 'strong fancy' to Moore ('thanks to my own quickness and teachableness') and he was roped into the family circle. In the evenings he taught Tom all the Greek and Latin that he knew and also did his best to instil 'a thorough and ardent passion for poor Ireland's liberties, and a deep and cordial hatred for those who were then lording over and trampling her down'. Moore declared himself to have been born a rebel, 'yet the strong hold which the feeling took so early, both of my imagination and heart, I owe a good deal, I think, to those conversations, during school hours with Donovan'.

The influence of Whyte was in another direction. His theatrical leanings were 'rather against his success in the way of his profession', but they were very much to Moore's advantage. Whyte saw in the little prodigy his dream pupil. Not only did he produce him for public displays, he gave him the benefit of his wide reading in English as well as imparting his enthusiasm for acting, public-speaking, poetry and music. His influence on Moore's juvenile poetry—which Byron said aroused his youthful eroticism—must have been considerable. Moore's early verse was regarded as licentious. In fact he never went far beyond his schoolmaster's model, published seven years before Tom was born; not calculated one might have thought to recommend him to anxious parents.

When first thy soft lip I but civilly pressed,
Eliza, how great was my Bliss!
The fatal contagion ran quick to my Breast;
I lost my poor Heart with a Kiss.
And now, when supremely thus blest with your Sight,
I scarce can my Transport restrain;
I wish, and I pant, to repeat the Delight;
And kiss you again, and again.

In Rapture I wish to enjoy all those Charms
Still stealing from Favour to Favour—
Now, now, o ye Gods! let me fly to your Arms,
And kiss you for ever and ever.

Whyte, the illegitimate son of the deputy governor of the Tower of London, was no ordinary pedagogue. When Moore addressed an ode to him which began: 'Hail! heaven-taught Votary of the laurel'd Nine', Whyte was so pleased he had it published. Moore, then fifteen, had no further favours to hope for from his schoolmaster; he had been entered on the books of Trinity College on June 2nd 1794.

He is there described as a Protestant; but there is no evidence to show who made the entry. Moore never pretended
to be other than a Catholic when he was in Trinity or ever
changed his religion although he ceased in early life to practise
it.

In his *Memoirs* he admits that 'it was for a short time
deliberated in our family circle whether I ought not to be
entered as a Protestant. But such an idea could hold but a brief
place in honest minds, and its transit, even for a moment,
through the thoughts of my worthy parents, only shows how
demoralising must be the tendency of laws which hold forth to
their victims such temptations to duplicity'. The Moores would
have been in some awe of Trinity, and might have left the
business to a friend such as Whyte. Moore never hid his
religion, but he took an easy-going attitude to its discipline. 'I
cannot remember exactly the age at which I first went to
confession, but it must have been some three or four years
before I went to the University; and my good mother (as
anxious in her selection of a confessor for me as she was in every
step that regarded my welfare, here or hereafter), instead of
sending me to any of our friends, the friars of Stephen Street,
committed me to the care of a clergyman of the name of
O'Halloran, who belonged to Townsend Street Chapel, and
bore a very high character.'

The part of the proceedings that Moore liked best was
breakfasting after the confession with Mrs Devereux, wife of a
West Indian captain and a relation of his mother. She provided
a splendid meal of buttered toast, eggs, beefsteak, etc. But
'notwithstanding the gentle and parental manner of the old
confessor, his position, sitting there as my judge, rendered him
awful in my eyes; and the necessity of raking up all my boyish
pecadilloes, my erring thoughts, desires, and deeds before a
person so little known to me, was both painful and humiliating.
We are told that such pain and humiliation are salutary to the
mind, and I am not prepared to deny it, the practice of confession as a moral restraint having both sound arguments and
high authority in its favour. So irksome, however, did it at last
become to me, that, about a year or two after my entrance into
college, I ventured to signify to my mother a wish that I should

no longer go to confession; and, after a slight remonstrance, she sensibly acceded to my wish.'

The Moores, on Sundays, heard Mass in the friary in Great Stephen Street. Some of the priests were frequent visitors to the house. Mrs Moore roped one of them in to teach Tom Italian. Another visitor taught him French.

Moore's skill at the piano was acquired in the same manner. 'In pursuance of the usual system of my mother, the person who instructed my sister in music—Billy Warren, as we familiarly called him—became soon an intimate in the family, and was morning and night a constant visitor. The consequence was that, though I never received from him any regular lessons in playing, yet by standing often to listen when he was instructing my sister, and endeavouring constantly to pick out tunes or *make* them—when I was alone—I became a pianoforte player (at least sufficiently so to accompany my own singing) before almost anyone was in the least aware of it.'

The getting of the piano had been quite a business. Mr Moore, 'having more present to his mind both the difficulty of getting money and the risks of losing it', shrank from the expenditure, but Mrs Moore prevailed. She was used to these contests, and won by strategy, buying two identical suits for Tom when she had met with opposition to the purchase of one.

Before the piano came to the house, efforts had been made to teach Tom to play. He had resisted strongly whether—as he said—'from shyness or hopelessness of success'. There had been a humble earlier attempt to play the harpsichord when Tom was a child, the instrument having been left on his father's hands by a bankrupt customer. Mrs Moore engaged a boy to teach Tom how to play it, but they spent their time jumping over the tables and chairs of the drawing-room. The lessons were left off. He acquired the power to play a few tunes with his right hand only. 'It was soon, however, discovered that I had an agreeable voice and taste for singing; and in the sort of gay life we led (for my mother was always fond of society), this talent of mine was frequently called upon to enliven our tea-parties and suppers.'

The arrival of the piano led to more ambitious entertainments in Aungier Street. Chief among the guests were Wesley

Doyle and Joe Kelly; the latter was a brother of Michael Kelly who, some years earlier, had left Dublin to get his voice trained, and impressed Mozart so favourably, that he gave him the chief tenor's role in the original performance of *Don Giovanni* in Vienna. In later years he sang at Drury Lane, under the management of Sheridan. In the singing after supper Mrs Moore took part. She had a clear soft voice. Tom, needless to say, used to be called on to perform.

Moore's name was entered in the books of Trinity College in June, 1794, but he did not begin his course until the following January. The interval was spent in a long holiday. 'If I were to single out the part of my life the most happy and the most *poetical* (for all was yet in fancy and in promise with me), it would be that interval of holiday.'

One of the friends Moore made at school was a son of a leading barrister, Beresford Burston. The 'acquaintance with the family', he acknowledged, 'was one of those steps in the scale of respectable society which it delighted my dear mother to see me attain and preserve'. The Burstons had a town house in York Street and a country villa near Blackrock. So far from Moore pressing the acquaintance, Burston's father encouraged the friendship, and much of the time when Moore was industriously idling was spent at the Burston's country house where he read Mrs Radcliffe's romances and listened to Haydn's music being played on the harpsichord by the Burston girls. So far from nursing social ambitions, he was 'dreaming away the time in that sort of vague happiness which a young mind conjures up for itself so easily'.

MOORE AT the University did not follow the course that his biddable disposition suggested. He was ever anxious to please his mother, but he found the routine syllabus boring. In his second year he gave up the struggle and confined himself to what appealed to his tastes. He entered a poem in English for an examination in Latin prose, but the examiner, instead of rejecting his exercise, put the verses before the Board and recommended that Moore be given a premium for them. He was awarded the *Travels of Ancharsis* in a very handsome binding. The first gain, he noted, of his pen, which was afterwards to be his sole support.

Trinity had disillusioned him. The fellows, in general, knew little more about Latin verse than their students.

Through friendship with the son of the librarian, Dean Craddock, Moore got permission to use Marsh's Library. This is a very rare collection of books, formerly owned by Archbishop Marsh, and housed in the precincts of St Patrick's Cathedral. Moore had begun as early as 1794 to translate the odes of Anacreon. He now proposed instead of his regular studies to make a translation of every ode attributed (most of them doubtfully) to the Greek poet.

Before he came to Trinity, his closest friends were Beresford Burston and Bond Hall, 'neither of them at all studious or clever'. But Hall was fun to be with and Moore observed that if he had been at all inclined to pedantic display in conversation, the society of these friends would have cured him of it.

A writer in *The Irish Quarterly Review* (1854) recalled the striking impression made by Moore's first speech in college and his increasing power as a speaker. In his debating society there were medals given for occasional prose and verse, the method was to send them in anonymously, and on the night of the awards they were read out by the members in rotation. Moore's

effort was entitled an *Ode Upon Nothing*, with Notes by Tris-
megistus Rustifustius. As is the way with triumphs of this kind,
he could not afterwards remember what he said that 'excited
roars of laughter throughout'. Whatever they were, they were
exactly suited to the occasion and he sat down amidst triumphant cheers.

But the opposition was not to be laughed away. 'Two or
three of the gravest and most eloquent of the antagonist party'
rose in succession. The first beginning 'I knew well what we
were to expect from that quarter; I was fully prepared for that
ready display of wit and playfulness which has so much amused
and diverted the attention of the Society from the serious . . .'
Moore, in his reply, acknowledged 'the serious impression'
made upon him and the sincere pains he felt at 'deliberately
offending against those laws prescribed alike by good morals
and good taste'.

His conduct disappointed those whom he considered as 'the
most ardent spirits of his own faction'; the opposition, however,
was mollified and did not press for a division. 'As soon as the
excitement of the affair had passed away, I myself, in order to
prevent any recurrence of the subject, took an opportunity of
quietly removing the composition from the books.'

No wonder his college friend, Robert Emmet, refrained from
enlisting his active support.

But he may have been far more spirited than his own account
suggests. Grattan's *Memoirs* confirm a report sent by John
Wilson Croker to T. C. Croker that when Lord Camden came
to Ireland as Viceroy in 1795 instead of Lord Fitzwilliam—a
signal that Catholic hopes were blasted—'the Provost, Fellows
and Scholars went to Dublin Castle to present a complimentary
address. On their arrival the Scholars suddenly wheeled about
and retired to Hyde's Coffee House where Thomas Moore,
since distinguished as a Poet, being called to the Chair and
W. H. Ellis being appointed Secretary an address was voted to
the Rt. Honble. Henry Grattan expressive of their approbation
of his conduct and principles during the late popular administration'.

The address begins 'We, the students of the University of
Dublin'. It is signed by Thomas Moore as Chairman and

laments 'the removal of a beloved Viceroy, *whose arrival we regarded as the promise of public reform, and his presence the pledge of general tranquility*'. And it expresses a hope '*that the harmony and strength of Ireland will be founded on the solid basis of Catholic Emancipation, and the reform of those grievances, which have inflamed public indignation*'.

Moore made a speech of which Croker said he had a copy in which he asked 'death to arrest him ere he saw the day a Union takes place'. These were brave words, for which he might have been arrested; they were not calculated to forward his career in Dublin. For a boy of sixteen it was a very spirited performance. And it is interesting to note the reference to the threat of a Union in 1795, four years before the proposal was put before the House of Commons by Pitt.

In Trinity his friends included Robert Emmet, close in the counsels of the United Irishmen—of which his brother, Thomas Addis Emmet, was one of the leaders. They were actively conspiring to overthrow British rule in Ireland and were in correspondence with France. Moore was junior to Robert Emmet, whom he encountered in a small college debating society. He describes the young revolutionary in the *Memoirs*. As well as being 'the chief champion and ornament of the popular side in debates, Emmet had a brilliant scholastic career, and he was distinguished 'for the blamelessness of his life and the grave suavity of his manners'. Moore found the force of his eloquence on one occasion 'wonderful, and I feel at this moment as if his language was still sounding in my ears'. Later they were to meet in the college Historical Society, founded by Edmund Burke; political subjects were debarred from debate by the College authorities, but it was always possible by 'a side wind of digression and allusion' to get past this restriction.

Emmet was an adept at this; his speeches were so exciting and powerful and his opponents so little able to counteract their force that the Board sent 'a man of advanced standing in the University' to answer them. Moore expressed the mortification of himself and other friends and admirers of Emmet when he broke down. He faltered, repeated his words, and then ignominiously had to sit down.

The country at this time was rolling towards revolution; elements in the Government were using all the power of intimidation at their command to foment rebellion; it was a criminal but effective way to effect the union of the two countries; but, on the other side, conspiracy was far advanced. Emmet's elder brother Thomas Addis, Arthur O'Connor, and others in the United Irishmen set up their own newspaper, the *Press*, for propaganda purposes. Moore was not impressed by the literary content of the paper, but he was thrilled by its political complexion, and read every line to his parents at supper (he never lived in College). He aspired to write for the paper himself and only hesitated because of his 'poor mother's constant anxiety about me'. The dangers at this time were very real; treason was being smoked out with a vengeance. Mrs Moore's apprehensions were well-founded. Moore compromised by sending an anonymous letter addressed to the students of Trinity College and written in a 'turgid Johnsonian sort of style'. He found it difficult, as always, to conceal his emotion while he read it out to his parents, but he never betrayed himself. They were impressed by the letter but thought it 'very bold'. One of his friends, Edward Hudson, happened to drop in, and gave Moore away. He then had to promise his mother not to run such risks in future. 'Any wish of hers was to me a law, I readily pledged myself.'

A few days afterwards, walking in the country with Emmet, he confided that he had written the letter. So far from applauding his zeal, Emmet 'with that almost feminine gentleness of manner which he possessed'—often, as Moore remarked, a characteristic of the revolutionary—expressed regret. The effect of the letter was to draw attention to the politics of the University and to frustrate 'the good work (as we both considered it) which was going there so quietly'.

In the following year Moore published a piece in the Ossian manner, the sort of thing that fifty years later Oscar Wilde's mother, Speranza, produced by the yard. In doing this, Moore, let it be said to his credit, was breaking his promise to his mother.

Edward Hudson, who had given Moore away unwittingly, was one of the decisive influences on Moore's career. He was thick in the political conspiracy and was arrested at Oliver Bond's house in 1798. A handsome young man, he had made a collection of old Irish airs, taking them down from the harpers and playing them on the flute. As with his Latin teacher at school, Moore, spent a great deal of time with Hudson, sharing his principal enthusiasms—music and politics. Another of the charges made against Moore by his critics was that he stole the airs which he was later to write songs for from Edward Bunting; but Hudson was the first to open up this treasure-chest for him.

The truth of the story that Moore tells in his *Memoirs* of Emmet's interrupting him when he was playing *Let Erin Remember the Days of Old* and exclaiming passionately 'Oh, that I were at the head of twenty thousand men marching to that air', has been questioned by scholars of music. But Moore had a highly subjective recollection of things past. Some such incident took place and left a vivid impression. The details are irrelevant. The incident has the ring of truth; it was also one— perhaps the only—occasion when Emmet let his friend see into his mind. He never attempted to involve Moore in conspiracies, and left him at his mother's apron-strings, appreciating that he was not intended by nature to man the barricades.

Moore's tutor, one Burrowes, renowned for a celebrated song that he couldn't live down—*The Night before Larry was Stretched*—retired on a good living, 'the *euthanasia* of most of the monks of old Trinity', and in his place Moore was allotted to a lay fellow, Phipps. He was kinder and more concerned than his reverend predecessor; this led him to call on Moore's parents to warn them against Tom's being seen so much in the company of Robert Emmet. Soon after this an inquisition was held in Trinity, the Lord Chancellor himself coming down to interrogate the students. John Fitzgibbon (Lord Clare) was at this time the most active of the group which was determined to bring to an end the Irish Parliament. He was much hated, and the crowd threw dead cats at his coffin when he was buried in St Peter's Church close at hand to Moore's shop.

When the dreaded day came, Moore, who thought he knew about what was going on, was astonished to discover the extent of the revolutionary movement. He found it 'startling and awful' to hear the disclosures of every witness. A few, including Emmet, absented themselves. 'The dead silence that daily followed the calling out of their names, proclaimed how deep had been their involvement.'

Moore was made aware of the significance of his tutor's recent call on his parents when a friend of his, Dacre Hamilton, 'one of the most primitively innocent persons' of his acquaintance, because of his intimacy with Emmet—their bond being an interest in mathematics—was called upon to give evidence. He was, like Moore, quite outside any plots that were hatching. He refused to answer the questions put to him because—Moore was convinced—he was anxious not to incriminate his friends. His punishment would certainly be an end to his university career and exclusion from the learned professions.

If Hamilton took a noble line and Whitley Stokes a brave one (he insisted that all the conspiracies he was aware of were Orange ones) they were outnumbered by those who, to save themselves, came forward and gave evidence against their friends.

There was gloom at the Moores' when Tom came home. He was likely to be called up on the following day, and 'the deliberate conclusion to which my dear honest father and mother came was that if he were asked to incriminate his friends he must, as Dacre Hamilton had done, refuse'.

On the next morning he was summoned and stood before 'the terrific tribunal'. Here sat the formidable Fitzgibbon, whose name Moore had never heard mentioned but in connection with domineering insolence and cruelty; and by his side the Advocate General 'Paddy Duigenan—memorable, at least, to all who lived in those dark times for his eternal pamphlets sounding the tocsin of persecution against the Catholics'.

The oath was proffered to Moore. By his own account, and nobody has contradicted it, he refused to take it. Fitzgibbon then asked him his age. He was something past seventeen, but he looked younger. Scarcely five feet tall, he must have appeared as Puck or Ariel in those surroundings. The two inquisitors conferred together, then Fitzgibbon turned to him and said, 'We cannot allow any person to remain in our University, who would refuse to take this oath'. Moore then agreed to take it, but he reserved the right to refuse to answer questions that would incriminate others. Fitzgibbon—who was probably giving him more rope than he pretended—brought the argument rather sharply to a close.

Moore denied all guilty knowledge, and it must have been patently obvious that he was not made or ready for such dangerous adventures. When the questions had been put and answered, Fitzgibbon inquired why had he made such a fuss about taking the oath. 'I have already told you, my lord, my chief reasons; in addition to which, it was the first oath I ever took, and it was, I think, a very natural hesitation.' The impression he made was probably less solemn than he believed, as he discovered in his later meetings with the Chancellor.

Moore was ingenuously eager to discover how his performance had been received by the students. He was ever concerned about the impression he made—vanity, not conceit, predominated in his character. In his own mind he believed that he had acted 'with becoming firmness and honesty', but he could not feel quite assured on the subject till he had returned among his young friends and companions in the body of the hall, and 'seen what sort of verdict their looks and manner would pass on my conduct'.

He was instantly reassured; and hurried home to allay the fears for him there, and met with a reception that he forebore to describe. 'It was all that *such* a home could furnish.'

This was the whole of Moore's revolutionary experience. Someone who, he said, was later to hold a very high legal station approached Moore and asked him to join his lodge (the Masonic term used by the United Irishmen). Moore must have excused himself. Afterwards he sighed thinking of the danger avoided, 'how fatal might have proved the consequences of this short conversation both to myself and to all connected with me'. Moore's revolutionary ardour could not reconcile himself to 'such bad courses'. In his journal, he describes the rebellion of 1798, which led eventually to the loss of 30,000 lives and the suppression of the Irish colonial parliament, in a paragraph.

When he was comparing his early training with Walter Scott's and deprecating 'the sort of boudoir education' he had received, he added that 'the only thing, indeed, that conduced to brace and invigorate my mind was the strong political feelings that were stirring around me when I was a boy, and in which I took a most deep and ardent interest'.

He 'was also in another direction of feeling thrown in the way of impressions and temptations, to any which my time of life, vivacity of fancy and excitable temperament, rendered me peculiarly susceptible'.

Moore understood his own case very well. He wrote it down, and explained the use that he put his talents to and why he wrote the sort of poetry that won him an early reputation for licentiousness.

'My life from earliest childhood had passed, as has been said, in a round of gay society; and the notice which my songs and my manner of singing them had attracted led me still more into the same agreeable, but bewildering course. I was saved, however, from all that coarser dissipation into which the frequenting of men's society (particularly as *then* constituted) would have led me; and this I owed partly to my own disposition, which always induced me (especially in my younger days) to prefer women's society infinitely to men's, and partly to the lucky habit, which I early got into of never singing but to my own accompaniment at the pianoforte. I thus became altogether dependent on the instrument, even in my convivial songs; and except in a few rare cases, never sung a song at a dinner table in my life. At supper, indeed, and where there were ladies to listen and a pianoforte to run to many and many have been the songs I have sung, both gay and tender.'

The suppressed rebellion coincided with the completion of Moore's college course. He says he took his degree in either 1798 or 1799, a vagueness which would be suspicious if there were not sufficient evidence that he became absent-minded eventually to an absurd extent. There is no reason to believe—as some have said—that he never took his degree; but he was probably anxious to get away. London beckoned. He had refused to read an orthodox course, but his university career was not undistinguished. He had fared better than Swift or Goldsmith when they were undergraduates.

For all his affectionate subservience to his mother, he had exhibited unexpected independence. He was already feeling the stirrings of literary ambition 'accompanied by the sense of pride and pleasure which the first exercise of power of any kind is sure to afford: the delight with which my early attempt at composition were welcomed by her whom it was my delight to please'.

Although disqualified by religion for a scholarship, he sat for the examination. There he attracted Dr Kearney, who was impressed by his skill in Horace, and became another of Moore's good angels. Moore took 'a pretty high place' but was not allowed to collect the very useful sixty or seventy pounds a year attached to the scholarship. Kearney, however, took him up. He encouraged Moore to complete his Anacreon translations while relieving the Board from giving any form of official recognition to works so 'amatory and convivial'. Although he was sure, if brought out in book form, 'the young people will like it'.

Kearney invited Moore to his house, which was one of the most sociable in Dublin. He listed among the friends that he made before his twentieth year, Grierson, the King's printer, and Joe Atkinson, 'the lively and popular secretary of the Ordnance Board'. The Griersons had a house in Harcourt Street and a mansion in Rathfarnham.

In or about this time Moore met Sir George Shee, who held some official post in Dublin. The Shees were musical; Moore was alarmed when they invited him to dinner to meet the Chancellor Fitzgibbon. He was still a bogey man to Moore, who trembled when he went to take his degree for fear that Fitzgibbon would recognise him and refuse to grant it. When Moore appeared on that occasion, Fitzgibbon turned to the Provost and said 'Is that not—?'. But there was nothing unfriendly in the inquiry and, we may be sure, the Shees did not invite the Chancellor to dinner—a family party—without first telling him who the other guest would be.

Moore was tongue-tied at first, but Fitzgibbon (Lord Clare as he was then) 'with very marked kindness, asked me to drink a glass of wine with him'. Once afterwards, Moore met him in the street. Clare raised his hat, a circumstance which Moore in his occasional 'Diary of a Nobody' manner described as 'somewhat creditable, I think, to both parties'.

Moore suggests that he was so overawed at Shee's table that

he found it difficult to speak. This is probably an exaggeration. If he spoke up to the Chancellor in Trinity, he would not have been afraid to answer when he was spoken to by him at table. Fitzgibbon certainly received a favourable impression; Moore as certainly acquitted himself well, if not, as usual, giving a star performance.

Lady Morgan is one of the authorities for citing Mary Steele as Moore's first love. She was the same age as he and engaged to marry Sheares, one of the barrister brothers who were hanged for their complicity in the 1798 rebellion. There is no evidence of the length or nature of Moore's attachment—either he preceded Sheares in his courtship or it was a very brief one, because he left Dublin after the rebellion.

Moore was not cut out for tragedy. He could conjure up a Watteau impression of the annual crowning of the King of Dalkey, the Royal procession setting out by water from Dublin —crowds of boats 'vying with each other in gaiety of ornament and company', cannon planted along the shore to fire salute, and the whole length of the Dalkey road 'swarmed with vehicles all full of gay laughing people'.

The ceremonies (very unlike Barrington's sketches of such events) were conducted after precautions had been taken 'to keep the company on the island as select as possible'. There wasn't even rain to threaten the arrangements. Moore's poetical friend, Mrs Battier, the 'poetess laureate to the monarch of Dalkey' had on her appointment been created Countess of Laurel. Moore delivered a birthday ode to King Stephen, 'a very respectable pawnbroker of Dublin and a most charming singer'. There was a service and sermon enacted in the old ruined church by the archbishop ('a very comical fellow whose name I forget') and his clergy 'certainly carried the spirit of parody indecently far'.

Mrs Battier might have stepped out of *The Pickwick Papers*. She was 'an odd, acute, warm-hearted, and intrepid little woman', the widow of an army captain, who lived on very small means with two daughters, 'in lodgings, up two pairs of stairs in Fade Street'. She had acquired a reputation for satirical verse which, judging by this example, was not without tartness:

When Parsons drawls in one continuous hum,
Who would not wish all baronets were dumb.

Mrs Battier was much older than Moore's mother and, 'though with a lively expression of countenance by no means good-looking', he cited, as proof of the value he put upon female intellect, that he took 'great delight in her society and always very gladly accepted her invitations to tea'.

At one of these parties, the lion was a Mrs Jane Moore, who came from England 'upon the double speculation of publishing her poems, and promulgating a new plan for the dyeing of nankeens'. The young poet was gratified by the honour of an invitation to meet this celebrity, who had expressed a wish to read her own poems before a competent judge. Mrs Battier was reduced to a single room by the state of her circumstances, and tea was taken in the bed-room, Moore sitting on the bed. He listened while the poetess read aloud, 'making havoc with the v's and w's'.

'Another English impostor of the same kind' came to Ireland to give lectures on literature. A small but very select audience gathered to hear him. He had brought letters of introduction to some of the fellows of the college. Moore 'ventured to sidle up' to the group who were conversing with the speaker before the lecture. He began with a question.

'You know, of course, sir, Shenstone's *School Mistress*?'

'Yes, but haven't seen her for some time.'

This was part of Moore's preparation for the polite world. The time had come to attempt its conquest after 'such a combination of mental stimulants as few, I think, of the same period of life have ever been surrounded by; nor can I conceive a youth much more delightful and interesting to have ever fallen to any one's lot'.

3 LONDON CALLING

MOORE SAYS that he took his degree as Bachelor of Arts, but he was uncertain of the date. That it was presented by Lord Clare should have impressed the occasion on his mind. But he was disillusioned by Trinity and had no interest in his academic course. Like many distinguished Irish adventurers before him, his hopes lay in London.

Mrs Moore had 'long been hoarding up every penny she could scrape together'. She sewed this up in the waistband of Tom's pantaloons, concealed 'a small bit of cloth blessed by a priest' on some part of his person (until recent years most Catholic children wore scapulars) and then the young Whittington was ready to descend upon London. It had been decided that he should read for the bar, and he was entered for the Temple.

This had been arranged by the father of his old friend Beresford Burston. He, too, was destined for the bar, but Moore left Dublin before him and, as with many youthful friendships, the young men had now very little in common except 'the habit of early intimacy'.

Alarmed on the journey to London, he wrote gloomily from Chester: 'Alone and sooty as a sweep', he had 'wandered like a culprit through the streets'. To secure a seat in the coach he took the name of another passenger; a fellow traveller warned him that it was dangerous to take such risks 'in times like the present'. He wasn't able to sleep all night, but he put matters right in the morning.

Breakfasting at his inn, 'a frantic fellow came in who had just ridden post from Warrington'. After chasing the maids all about the house and beating them, he came into the dining-room and sat beside Moore. Moore's new acquaintance said that he had just escaped from a strait-waistcoat, boasted of killing a woman and child the night before in the theatre, and suggested, that as Moore had never been in Chester before, he would wait for him and they could make a tour of the city together. He took Moore over, insisted on finding him accommodation at the same inn, carried his portmanteau, ordered his room, gave instructions for a valet. He had no luggage of his own, and offered to share Moore's shirts. Moore succeeded in shaking him off.

On April 5th, 1799, Moore wrote from London to his mother to tell her that he was settled at 44 George Street, Portman Square, in a very comfortable little room on the second floor, at six shillings per week.

Irish friends were not wanting. Martin Archer Shee, who had come from Ireland and was to succeed Lawrence eventually as President of the Royal Academy, showed the young man kindness, and sometimes asked him to dinner, and Shee's less prosperous brother-in-law, Nugent, an engraver, offered tea and a chat about literature. A Dublin apothecary was also kind, and when Moore was in difficulties about his fees at the Middle Temple, his wife took Tom aside and offered to lend him the sum required. He refused the loan, but never forgot the offer.

He began to dine out regularly—'Lady Peshall's family have been very attentive to me, and so has Mrs La Touche; indeed if I had indulged in going out often (though here I cannot call it an indulgence) there is scarce a night that I should not be at some female gossip-party, to drink tea, play a little crambo and eat a sandwich'.

He had been 'dancing after' Joe Atkinson without success but had made a very pleasant acquaintance in a Dr Hume, a graduate of Trinity College, who set about finding him a publisher for *Anacreon*. Moore dined with a Captain Otway, who was extremely attentive, but he took no interest in either music or literature and 'My Lord This and My Lady That form the whole subject-matter of his conversation'.

This busy social life called for money. A man was hired to clean his shoes and brush his coat at two shillings a month.

In London Tom was going to be launched at a new level. His chief sponsor was Joseph Atkinson who had introduced him to Lord Moira, marking another milestone in his career.

Atkinson began life as a soldier, and was an early friend of the Prince of Wales. He gave up a military career and became an amateur of letters, writing poems and plays (Colman put one on at the Haymarket), but chiefly acting as a patron of young writers. He served in the American War with Lord Moira, and they were fast friends.

Moore had come to London to read for the bar, but in his luggage was a more exciting and immediate enterprise. He had shown his translations around. The Provost of Trinity had commended them. So had Atkinson. They were Moore's testimonial, and the introduction to Lord Moira was made with the object of collecting subscribers for a publication in book form. At once Moore started out upon a round of visits which, with necessary intervals, he was to continue to make for the next forty years.

Of his legal studies, no mention is ever made; they were probably nominal. He was working at his music, corresponding with William Warren, his sister's teacher in Dublin. By the end of the year songs of his were being performed. Johnstone of the Covent Garden Opera was reported to have sung them in company. Moore himself was beginning to perform in public. He began to study thorough bass with a Mrs Baron and became a nightly frequenter of the opera. Miss Biggs, the heroine at Drury Lane, met him and sent him an invitation for the following evening. He went, like the whole town, to see Sheridan's 'wonderful' *Pizarro*.

In July he returned to Dublin and stayed there until the autumn. It was probably during this holiday that he met John (later Sir John) Stevenson, who was to set Moore's songs to music. The meeting was momentous for both of them. Stevenson composed a series of glees from the Anacreon poems, and was knighted by the Viceroy, Lord Hardwicke, who dined with the Irish Harmonic Society in 1803 and heard one of them sung.

Many years later Lady Morgan was to write her memoirs and recall how she and her sister Olivia, 'two scrubby-headed and very ill-dressed girls', stood niched in a corner in the little crowded room over the grocery shop in Aungier Street close to the piano when Moore was singing *Friend of My Soul*. Little

Olivia wept with delight, and the poet perceiving the enthusiasm of the girls asked his mother to name them to him. Then
he bowed and sung *Will You Come to the Bower*—'a very improper
song by the by for the young ladies to hear'—and rushed away
to keep a supper engagement at Lady Antrim's.

Half a century had passed since then. She had not, she said,
heard of Moore until Sir John Stevenson delighted her with a
song:

> Friend of my soul, this goblet sip,
> 'Twill chase that pensive tear:
> 'Tis not so sweet as woman's lip,
> But oh, 'tis more sincere.

Stevenson (not Sir John then) was a friend of her father, the
actor Robert Owenson, and he had begun to put Moore's verse
to music. Moore, he said, was too great a man to be brought to
call, 'never was a man so run after in my day', but he would
take Sydney to a musical party at Mrs Moore's. And Olivia,
too—Sydney never forgot her sister.

Moore's sisters and his mother—'like Moore himself in
petticoats'—received the guests. The poet was not there. He
was dining in Trinity with the Provost, but he came in later with
Croker 'and some other pets of the Provost's lady, for she was
queen of the Blues in Dublin at that time'.

The little girls went home in such an ecstasy that they forgot
to undress before going to bed. When they woke up they began
to sing *Friend of My Soul,* and while Olivia was drawing Moore's
portrait, Sydney wrote a romantic description of him as a
minstrel at a lady's window.

Lady Morgan's picture was more accurate in outline than in
detail: this memorable evening might have been in 1806. It
could not have been before that. In 1806 Moore was twenty-
seven; and the writer was two years older than Moore. She
must have known all about him for years. But why spoil her
story?

Moore's letters home are strictly confined to his own affairs,
in particular his social engagements and the encouraging things
people say about him. But for this he submitted his own excuse
in a letter to his mother: 'Do not let any one read this letter but

yourselves; none but a father and a mother can bear such egotising vanity; but I know who I am writing to—that they are interested in what is said of me, and that they are too partial not to tolerate my speaking of myself.'

With any other correspondent of the same age an exclusive preoccupation with his career would not be surprising. Dick Whittington did not conquer London with such speed and ease. Moore literally strolled out of the top rooms in the little Dublin shop into the most exclusive drawing-rooms in England. Atkinson's introductions alone couldn't have achieved it. Everyone who met Moore was charmed by him. He was not self-assertive; he pleased. He displayed as much learning as made him interesting without ever becoming a bore. But his attraction must have lain in his manner and appearance. And when he was given an opportunity to sing, he completed his conquests.

But his patriotic ardour is difficult to chart. In his memoir of his early life, he gives this short account of the rebellion of 1798:

'It was while I was confined with this illness that the long and awfully expected explosion of the United Irish conspiracy took place: and I remember well on the night when the rebels were to have attacked Dublin (May, 1798), the feeling of awe produced through the city, by the going out of the lamps one after another towards midnight. The authorities had, in the course of the day, received information of this part of the plan, to which the lamp-lighters, of course, must have been parties; and I saw from my window a small body of yeomanry accompanying a lamp-lighter through the streets to see that he performed his duty properly. Notwithstanding this, however, through a great part of the city where there had not been time to take this precaution the lights towards midnight all went out.'

Nowhere does he say what the illness was, nor does it ever receive any other mention. But there is one piece of evidence to prove that he did not desert his friends or go into hiding. A casual footnote in his *Life* of Lord Edward Fitzgerald refers to a call he made on Edward Hudson (whom he doesn't mention by name) when the State prisoners were allowed to see their friends before they went into exile. Robert Emmet, who had taken refuge in France, and was to return to lead his own abortive rising in 1803, is not mentioned in Moore's letters, nor, when the time came, did Moore refer to his capture, trial or execution. But this may have been deliberate. Written evidence of concern could have been very dangerous, and this silence may well have been an arrangement, perfectly understood between son and mother.

We have the verses—*Oh, breathe not his name* and *When he who adores thee*; Moore introduced Emmet's story in an eastern setting in *Lalla Rookh*, but by then the rebellion was history. Robert's brother, Thomas Addis Emmet, who went to New York when he was released from prison, became Attorney General there and flourished at the American bar, referred in reminiscences to 'Thomas Moore, the faults of whose after life, manifested in his forgetfulness of the past, of the sorrow and suffering of his native land, and by his readiness to deny his birthplace with the object of winning position and the favour of his Tory friends in England, were atoned for in advance by his early poetry relating to Robert Emmet'.

This paragraph is distinguished by being untrue and misleading in every assertion it contains.

After Moore settled in England in the shelter of Lord Lansdowne's benevolence, when he was Lord John Russell's intimate friend, he wrote the *Life* of Lord Edward Fitzgerald, *Captain Rock*, and an Irish history. He also played with the idea of becoming a member of parliament. The verses on Robert Emmet and his one love, Sarah Curran, were published in 1808 and 1811 respectively in the *Irish Melodies*, the series which were for several years to provide Moore's chief means of living. None is revolutionary in sentiment; they are tender. *Oh! breathe not his name let it sleep in the shade* hardly makes a tocsin sound, and *She is far from the land where her young Hero sleeps* was not treasonable in its pathos. Moore in fact became much more openly pro-Irish and pro-Catholic in later years, when he was on close terms as an older man with Russell and Lansdowne and the Whig leaders—he never had anything to do with the Tories—than in the flower of his youth.

Thomas Emmet would have had a better case if he had

reproached Moore for his exclusive concentration on the further-
ance of his own career in these first years in London. It was for
the advancement of his career that he hung about Moira. And
if he found revolution romantic for the purposes of verse, he
did not approve the violent courses Robert Emmet followed.
And Emmet, as we saw, knew that Moore was not the man for
them, and did not like him less. But it is strange to find Moore
writing week after week to his mother and never once referring
to the news of the day, the progress of the Union debate,
Moira's inconsistent conduct—having voted by proxy against
the Union in the Irish House of Lords he withdrew his opposition
in England, and turned again when he joined the final protest
by the Irish peers against the measure—Moore makes no
reference to this or to any topic relating to Ireland at the most
critical moment in her history. When he returned to London
from Dublin his chief concern was to collect subscribers for the
publication of his Anacreon translations.

Hume consulted an eminent scholar, a friend of Burke—Dr
Lawrence—about the poems. Lawrence praised them highly
but touched in suitably circumlocutory terms on their occasional suggestiveness. This was all very heady, and Moore
hoped it would 'astonish the scoundrelly monks of Trinity'.
Only the Provost and his tutor had subscribed to the edition.

Moore (now twenty-one) was unusually belligerent about his
university. 'Tell Phipps', he wrote 'that I will not put F.T.C.D.
after his name, as I should be ashamed of the world observing
that but one of the fellows of the University where I graduated,
gave his tribute to a classical undertaking of this kind. They are
a cursed corporation of boobies, and if it were not for my
friend, their Provost, the public should know my opinion of
them . . . I was last night in company with Godwin.'

This is Tom intoxicated by success—but he is writing to his
mother. There was nothing to hold him in, and he was very
young. Very young to have Mrs Fitzherbert adding herself to
the growing list of subscribers; but if Mrs Fitzherbert, it was
but a step . . . On Saturday in April or May he wrote to say,
'I have got the Prince's name and his permission that I should
dedicate Anacreon to him. Hurra: hurra!' Moore had not as yet
met the Prince.

He was collaborating with Michael Kelly on a musical play, *The Gipsy Prince*—Kelly's brother Joe had brought them together after Stevenson, for some reason, declined to collaborate. Michael Kelly, seventeen years older than Moore, had risen fast to fame from his early beginnings as a boy singer and actor in Dublin. His mistress, the beautiful Mrs Crouch, acted with him, and their singing of duets was one of the sentimental treats of the day. The fact that he was prepared to collaborate with Moore shows that the young man had arrived in theatrical circles as well as in London society.

He was genuinely longing to come home. 'Good God! when do we *meet*, may it be in happiness! Write to me, dear father and mother; tell me you are in health and content, and I shall then be as happy as absence from you will allow me. Farewell. Forget me not.'

But he was held up, distributing the book, and waiting to be introduced to the Prince. He met the Duke of Clarence, another future king, and added him to his list of subscribers. A young girl at Lady Dering's party, where the meeting took place, told Moore that the Duke had been asking about his birth and parentage, 'with all the curiosity of the Royal Family'.

He sang on this occasion and was encored after each song. His career as an entertainer had begun, but he had not as yet turned it to business purposes, except insofar as he was using his gifts to forward his books and himself.

Among the people to whom he had been given introductions was Lord Lansdowne, known to history as Shelburne, who replied very civilly from Bath and invited Moore to come to see him. He had at once put himself down as a subscriber to *Anacreon* and straight away gave Moore introductions. Letters went regularly to Aungier Street to report a 'déjeuner' at Sir John Coghill's, where Tom sang duets with Lord Dudley and others, and further social triumphs.

Moore, it can be seen, had become a Whig property. It was inevitable, given his politics, but these Whig magnates were democratic only in their parliamentary opinions. Socially they were an exclusive caste. At the very beginning of his career Moore had joined a court which cut him off completely from the literary circles in which young men of talent without money

or connections make their way. Keats saw the dawn of fame
when he was taken up by Leigh Hunt. Hunt had gone to prison
for libelling the Prince Regent. A day would come when Moore
would make the Prince the object of his satire; but at the
moment he was proud to bask in the sunshine of the Royal
favour, as Sheridan had been before him. On August 3rd, 1800,
Moore was introduced to the Prince. 'When I was presented to
him, he said he was very happy to know a man of my abilities,
and when I thanked him for this honour he did me in permit-
ting the dedication of *Anacreon*, he stopped me and said the
honour was entirely his in being allowed to put his name to a
work of such merit. He then said that he hoped when he
returned to town in the winter, we should have many opportunities of enjoying each other's society; that he was passionately fond of music, and had long heard of my talents in that
way. Is not all this very kind? But, my dearest mother, it has
cost me a new coat . . .'

He was all the rage—at Donington Park in Derbyshire he
stays as the Moira's guest for as long as he pleases. His tall host
lights him to his bedroom, going ahead, holding up the candle
—as the Duke of Wellington for the young Queen Victoria
when she stayed at Stratfield Saye.

The Moiras press Moore to stay, to make use of the library,
to come whenever he pleases. After a three weeks' stay—
largely for the purposes of economy—he goes back to London.
Moira, when he arrives, calls on Moore and leaves a card.
There were rumours at this time that Moira might be taken
into the Government.

On Moira, Moore's hopes are set. His name appears regularly
in Moore's letters, but he had not read *Anacreon* until after the
Prince had agreed to accept the dedication. One suspects that
the amiable Joseph Atkinson was the moving spirit.

In his affectionate, triumphant letters home, Moore writes
of dinners with the Bishop of Meath, a party at Mrs Crewe's
the same evening—'there is not a night that I have not three
parties or a string, but I take Hammersley's advice and send a
shower of apologies'. His songs had 'taken such a rage'; even
surpassing what they did in Dublin. Lady Harrington sent her
servant after him to two or three places with a ticket for the

'Ancient Music', the King's concert, 'and which is so select that those who go to it ought to have been at Court before'. Lady Harrington got the ticket from one of the Princesses. At supper after the opera, he is introduced again to Mrs Fitzherbert, who was there with the Prince. He dines with the Moiras, and Lady Moira takes him to an assembly at the Countess of Cork's. At a fashionable ball the Prince calls out 'How do you do, Moore? I am glad to see you'.

The furore had nothing to do with the poems, which had not appeared as yet. 'Monk Lewis was in the greatest agonies the other night at Lady Donegal's, at having come in after my songs.'

Today Moore would have been snapped up by television producers. In society he did not get paid, but to some extent he sang for his supper. Given the *entrée*, so long as he remained a bachelor, he could depend, like Creevy, on being supported to a considerable extent by hospitality. The Moiras had set aside an apartment in their house for him. 'Dearest Mother'— he wrote from Donington Park on December 31st, 1800, at night—'dearest Mother! there is no fear of my not doing anything. Keep up your spirits, my little woman, and you'll find I'll make you as rich as a nabob.'

All this was expected to end in some lucrative employment. Moira was the source from which favour was to come. A careerist himself on a magnificent scale, there were smaller crowns for him to distribute. In Ireland, for example, Joe Atkinson was to be made Treasurer of the Ordnance. The Burke family in an earlier generation had gone the same road. Not only the great Edmund, but his unattractive relations, had lived on patronage and pickings.

What then could a patron do for Moore? Ireland had always been a place to find jobs and pensions for dependants. Burke's son had been placed there disastrously. When his hopes were highest Moore talked of an 'Irish Commissionership'. It was not forthcoming. Moira must have been puzzled how to help. Atkinson obviously exercised himself to suggest something. What Moore needed was to be

'Set upon a golden bough to sing
To Lords and Ladies of Byzantium.'

And this, as we shall see, was precisely what Moira, on Atkinson's suggestion, tried to bring about.

In later years Moore talked about these times with the Berry sisters, upon whom Horace Walpole doated (the 'Blackberry' and the 'Gooseberry'). They met at Bowood, Lord Lansdowne's seat, when Moore had been a long time in the near vicinity. Mary Berry had been present on that evening when he first sang in a London drawing-room. She described '(what I did not of course myself observe) the sort of contemptuous twitter with which the fine gentlemen and amateurs saw a little Irish lad led forth to exhibit after all the fine singing that had been going on—the change in their countenance when they saw the effect I produced . . .'.

'I didn't', Miss Berry said, 'like you so much in those days. I like you better since you have got these', and she pulled his grey hairs.

Women saw him very clearly and almost always sympathetically. Lady Morgan, who had had her own career to make, whom Atkinson had helped, and the Abercorns patronised, complained a little about him, but that was only the exasperation of a provincial hostess with an elusive addition to her parties. Women detected the unspoilt child in Moore. The letters of Lady Donegal and her sister, Mary Godfrey, show the affectionate concern of women for a young brother. And the writer who has best described the impression Moore made on people—most of the accounts in recollections are somehow overwritten—was Elizabeth Rennie. 'His warm and sunshiny nature soon made itself felt by those approaching him—you caught the all-pervading glow and radiance. He seemed so keenly and vividly to enjoy existence—making so light of its cares and burdens—on the other hand, so heightening and intensifying the pleasures, that his society exercised over you a species of happy spell, which you grieved to be divorced from and bereft of.'

The Anacreon translations appeared in July 1800. The *Morning Post* dubbed him 'Anacreon Moore', and the book received a wide and, on the whole, encouraging press. His second volume of poems was nearly ready. He was composing songs which Stevenson in Dublin put to music. His natural mode of composition was to fit a lyric to an air. For some reason he left his first publisher, Stockdale, and transferred his patronage to Carpenter of Old Bond Street with whom he remained until he divided his patronage between Murray and Longmans.

Carpenter took advantage of Moore when he was worried by a debt to Hume of £70 in connection with the publishing of *Anacreon*. Carpenter postponed publication of Moore's second volume and told him to draw on his account. Moore did so to pay off Hume and then faced with the debt to Carpenter was tempted into the bad bargain so often made by young writers, and was delighted to settle with the publishers for a cancellation of all debts (amounting to £60) in consideration of a transfer of the copyright in the new book by the anonymous 'Little'. The deal brought Carpenter £200 a year for several years.

Miss Godfrey, Lady Donegal's sister, wrote him a letter of disinterested advice. 'We lament and groan over your restless disposition. Your talents might fit you for everything, and your idleness unfits you for anything. You want to come to town, I know you do, merely to get away from those countrybred, sentimental ladies, the Muses, and I pray that you may have no other ladies in view to supply their place. You really might, if you pleased, study all the morning, and amuse yourself all the evening. I entreat you to make an effort and not to devote every hour and moment of your existence to pleasure.'

Moore was at Donington when the letter was written, where the Moiras were in residence and the guests included Lord Forbes, son of the Earl of Granard, who was married to Moira's sister. Moore made another conquest there. The Granards (who were to become bores) showered kindnesses on him and invited his sister, Kate, to go and stay with them at Castle Forbes in County Longford. Moore wrote home about this offering to help to buy her suitable clothes for the occasion. One suspects that the visit never took place.

At Donington, leading a country life, he was longing to come to London. It was not so much the pursuit of pleasure as an uncontrollable restlessness, and an itch to be involved in whatever was happening. He must for ever sacrifice whatever was going on for the sake of what was to follow, and no sooner arrived anywhere than he began to make excuses to get away. This was not because he had more ambitious quarry elsewhere —when he dined *en famille* with the Duke of Sussex, he was counting the moments until he could get away to call in at the opera.

Having anticipated the profits for his second book of poems and in debt to his friend Hume on the first, he was hard pressed for money. His tailor was a perpetual sore. He accepted a loan from his mother's brother. He was living on expectations. His memoirs and letters have gaps and there are inconsistencies, but the pattern of his life from when he first stayed with Lord Moira at the end of the year 1800 until he set out for Bermuda in August, 1803, seems to have been raids on London, endless entertainment, and then retreats to Donington where, certainly on one occasion, he was alone and time hung rather heavily on his hands. He went game-shooting because ennui made him slightly murderous. And he returned to Dublin for months at a time. There his life was probably more studious than in London, but he was now a lion. Success was not soured by envy in London, but in Dublin there were from the start, and there are still, those who grudged him his triumph, who listened for bad news. None of the warm and appreciative things Byron said about Moore are remembered by his countrymen, but if his name comes up there is always a savant present to tell the company that Byron said, 'Tommy loves a lord'.

At Donington he read in the library, in Dublin he wrote songs, which Carpenter began to publish, and discussed musical plans. He spent much of his time with Atkinson who, no doubt, kept him informed about Moira's plans.

Atkinson seems to have been more genial than sensible. He conceived the idea of an Irish Poet Laureateship, and suggested to Moira that he should propose the idea to Wickham, the Irish Chief Secretary, putting forward Moore's name for the post.

Before the Union, the idea might not have been quite so bizarre, but within three years of the suppression of Irish independence and the reduction of Dublin from a capital to a provincial city, it was a grotesque notion. Moore's father, who kept so studiously in the background, never appeared but to his advantage as, on this occasion, when he wrote to Tom and told him to refuse.

In Victorian editions of Moore's works some of the Anacreon verses were omitted, mild though they seem by contemporary standards. The 'Little' poems were a more daring venture. The adoption of a playful pseudonym was part of a charade. The true parent, one need not doubt, was known before the birth (in 1801) and was not kept secret. In the second edition he dedicated the volume to J.AT-NS-N, Esq. and put his own initials at the end, as also to the preface.

Except in those circles which took their tone from the Prince, Moore won a reputation for licentiousness which it took him years to live down. It is not easy to gauge the moral tone of the period. In later, Victorian years there was a blanket respectability over literature until Swinburne started the revolt. Moore performed this office, but in the mildest fashion, for his generation. In his *English Bards and Scotch Reviewers* Byron wrote of

> The young Catullus of his day
> As sweet, but as immoral his lay.

Lamb, the most companionable and sane of men, told Moore when he met him as late as 1823 that he had always held these poems against him, but he wouldn't, having met him, do so any more. Coleridge, writing in 1802 to a Miss Robinson, who had threatened to include his work in an anthology with one of Moore's, became hysterical. 'But, my dear Miss Robinson! (I pray you, do not be wounded—rather consider what I am about to say as a pledge of my esteem and confidence in your honour and prudence, a confidence beyond the dictates of worldly caution)—but I have a wife, I have sons, I have an infant Daughter—what excuse could I offer to my conscience if by suffering my own name to be connected with those of Mr Lewis or Mr Moore, I was the *occasion* of their reading the Monk or the wanton poems of Thomas Little Esqre?'

Fielding died in 1754 and Smollett in 1771; the new generation of novelists had given up their plain speaking; and even Sterne's suggestiveness had given place to the strict propriety of Jane Austen, Fanny Burney and Maria Edgeworth. Scott's lovers were cardboard figures.

It was several years before Byron was to keep his publisher in ceaseless agitation about the improprieties of *Don Juan*, and by then Moore was not infrequently advising against publication of the more daring stanzas. Even though the French Revolution had aroused fears of Jacobinism, the influence of the Regent, of Fox and his friends was still a force when Moore came into high society. He borrowed the plumes of a 'buck', but he was probably at his most daring with his pen. As Sheridan produced a politer form of Restoration drama, Moore did the same office for Rochester, Sedley, Suckling, and their kind. He never attempted the explicit eroticism of Donne. He could not have got away with that. He was only able to go a certain distance, and that meant the use of asterisks and cloying suggestiveness. The 'Little' poems had been in preparation for some years.

There was a certain cynicism:

> Our hearts have suffer'd little harm
> In this short fever of desire;
> You have not lost a single charm,
> Nor I one spark of feeling fire.

and a lightness:

> 'Good night! Good night!'—and is it so?
> And must I from my Rosa go?
> Oh, Rosa, say 'Good night' once more,
> And I'll repeat it o'er and o'er,
> Till the first glance of dawning light
> Shall find us saying, still 'Good night!'

And what would have shocked Coleridge:

> Still the question I must parry,
> Still a wayward truant prove:
> Where I love, I must not marry:
> Where I marry, cannot love.

And the little man of the world:

> Phillis, you little rosy rake,
> That heart of yours I long to rifle;

> Come, give it me, and do not make
> So much ado about a trifle.

And nothing with any depth of feeling.

What, one would like to know, would Jane Austen, then aged twenty-seven, have thought of this? It represents the Crawford influence which in *Mansfield Park* provides a worldly and dangerous contrast to the prevailing sobriety. What would Jane Austen have made of Tom Moore? But he would have been more concerned to know what Lord Moira was making of him. Some opportunity arose, but once again the prospect was paltry and Moore declined without offending his patron or Joe Atkinson.

And then came what Moore's hopeful fancy saw as a departure for Cythera, but what to a more sanguine spirit might have seemed like an attempt to get him out of the way. In August, Moore wrote to his mother to say that he had heard from Lord Moira that George Tierney, Treasurer of the Navy, had put the gift of a place at his disposal. It was somewhere far away—but he was prepared to put up with that if 'it promised me a permanent subsistence and the means of providing for those I love'. The journey was a 'new expense and perplexity' for him but he was very well able for it 'both in purse and spirits. God knows but it may be a "tide in my affairs" which will "lead to fortune".'

A month later he is packing to go; the place is Registrar of the Naval Prize Court in Bermuda. He confides in his Donington friend, the parson Dalby. He had every reason, he writes, to think the move will be advantageous, the climate is the 'sweetest in the world', and the registrarship lucrative during war.

The ordinary business of life perplexed Moore in the extreme; in old age he could not find his way to bed. On his first visit to Donington he had been bothered by his portmanteau which he found 'tormentingly troublesome'. He dreaded having to pack it again and had to *root* into it for everything he wanted. And his letter home carried a postscript of objects left behind.

There had always to be someone to wait on Moore. At Donington Dalby seems to have obliged without complaint.

Moore would not have gone on his adventures without the blessing of his family. This gave his father the occasion to write to him. It is one of the few occasions when anyone except his mother is seen directing him from home.

Aug. 16, 1803

'. . . Your uncle came here yesterday for the purpose of disclosing the whole secret to your mother, so that we only anticipated what you have done of yourself to-day. There could be no such deception carried on with her, where you or indeed any of her family, were concerned, for she seems to know everything respecting them by instinct. . . .

'Atkinson does not know of this business, nor do I think it right he should until it's all determined; for though he is, I believe, one of the best of men, he blabs a little too much. However you know when and how to let him know of it. . . For my particular part I think with you, that there is a singular chance, as well as a special interference of Providence, in your getting so honourable a situation at this very particular time. I am sure no one living can possibly feel more sensibly than your poor mother and me do at losing that comfort we so long enjoyed, of at least hearing from you every week of your life that you were absent from us; for surely no parents had ever such happiness in a child . . .'

That letter speaks for father, mother, sister and son; it speaks for itself. In only one matter is it manifestly misinformed. Providence, whatever else He may have been up to, was not specially interfering for anyone's benefit. The Bermuda journey was the first major miscalculation of Moore's life.

MOORE'S SHIP, the frigate *Phaeton*, set sail from Spithead on
September 25th, 1803, five days after the execution in Dublin
of Robert Emmet. A sailing ship was a new stamping-ground
for Moore. He had the necessary experience to cope with the
very English Merrys, who were going to Washington, the
husband having served as a diplomat in Paris. But sailors were
something else. One of the officers was afterwards to tell Moore,
'I thought you the first day you came aboard the damnedest
conceited little fellow I ever saw, with your glass cocked up to
your eye'.

But that impression was obliterated at once. Moore became
the life and soul of the company, and intimate with Cockburn,
the Captain ('a man of good fashion and rank'). At the end of
the voyage, Cockburn took a seal from his watch and begged
Moore to wear it in remembrance of him. 'Never was there a
better hearted set of fellows than the other officers of the ship.'

One of them in later years was to recall how Moore capti-
vated all hands.

The voyage was propitious, there was some rough weather,
and Moore was sick once. After six weeks at sea the ship put in
at Norfolk, Virginia. He dreaded meeting the British Consul
and was prepared for a 'consequential savage'. But his luck
held. Colonel Hamilton proved 'a plain and hospitable man,
and his wife full of homely, but comfortable and genuine
civility'. Moore tried a little tentative name-dropping. Moira's
worked like magic; but, to his disappointment, Joe Atkinson's
rang no bell. With the Merrys, Tom was taken into the Hamiltons' house and entertained for two days 'in a manner not very
elegant but hospitable and cordial'. A Miss Mathews played
and sang very tolerably, but talking about music to anyone
here was like 'whistling to a wilderness'. When Miss Mathews
played some of his sister Kate's lesson pieces, tears came into

Tom's eyes, but he was cheered to find some songs of his among the music books, and in a local periodical extracts from *Anacreon* and the poems of Thomas Little.

As to his prospects: from what he had heard since he 'came closer to the channels of correct information', he strongly suspected that it would not be long before he came home. He was beginning to look upon the Bermuda expedition as a test of his character, evidence of his resolution to make an effort. It might not be wise to absent himself long from his home opportunities of advancement. 'My foot is on the ladder pretty firmly, and that is the great point gained.'

Virginia had not impressed him so far. In Norfolk, nothing was to be seen in the streets but dogs and negroes, and 'the few ladies that *pass for white* are to be sure the most unlovely pieces of crockery I ever set my eyes upon'.

Certainly Moore at this date had shaken off rebel influences. He writes as one of the establishment. 'I have this instant received an invitation to dinner from one of the Yankees of this place: if the Ambassador and his lady go, of course I will. Oh! if you saw the vehicles the people drive about in here, white coaches with black servants, and horses of no colour at all; it really is a most comical place.'

Moore was waiting for a ship to touch Norfolk on her way from Halifax to Bermuda. One came at length, but the voyage was by no means pleasant; three days becalmed and then the worst gale for years. To eat it was necessary to be tied to the table. But Tom 'bore it all stoutly' and made the heartiest dinner of beefsteaks and onions that he had ever eaten in his life. And while the ship swayed and tossed he lay 'in his cot' writing ridiculous verses and laughing at them. The trip took seven days.

His spirits had been raised by the kindness shown him by the Hamiltons. His hostess cried at his departure and said she was never so sorry to see anyone go. Colonel Hamilton showered him with letters of introduction of a most flattering description. There followed Moore's first impression of what he did not hesitate to call a beautiful place; what strikes one at once is his comparative indifference to natural beauty. Tennyson scrupulously examining each wild flower is the very antithesis to

Moore who, when confronted with any wonder of nature, started at once to talk about something else.

He sent his mother an unflattering account of what he found, but he was not sorry that he had come; it was a 'valuable step towards preferment'; but that was all. So many prize courts were established that few cases were referred to Bermuda. Even a war with Spain would not bring in enough work to be worth his while waiting for; he had the experience of examining witnesses when two American ships came for trial. Meanwhile he had seen more of the world, learnt something of America and American affairs, 'become used to inconveniences and disappointments', and was never in better health. He was in perturbation at not hearing from home, and wrote affectionate, anxious letters. Complaint was not his way; if he was sometimes critical, here as elsewhere he found people far too pleasant to him to pine for long. 'There has been nothing but gaiety since I came, and there never was such a *furor* for dissipation known in the town of St George's before. The music parties did not long keep up, because they found they were obliged to trust to me for the whole orchestra; but the dances have been innumerable, and still continue with very great spirit indeed. The women dance in general extremely well, though, like Dogberry's writing and reading, it "comes by nature to them", for they never have any instruction, except when some flying dancing-master, by the kindness of fortune, happens to be wrecked and driven ashore on the island. Poor creatures! I feel real pity for them; many of them have hearts for a more favourable sphere; but they are thrown together in a secluded nook of the world, where they learn all the corruption of human nature, without any of its consolations or ornaments.'

Moore's sojourn in Bermuda had been recorded in several accounts of the island. He indulged in at least two flirtations which were serious enough to cause his poems to be refused entrance to one lady's house by her husband. Moore said the poems addressed to 'Nea', of which there were nine in his next volume, were inspired by a composite of two young women; the suspicious husband of one of them was William Tucker, and as he had only married his seventeen-year-old cousin, Hester Louise, 'an enchanting creature', six months previously, it was

understandable. How far the flirtations went nobody knows—
Mrs Tucker was pregnant at the time—but it is a reasonable
surmise that Moore tells something of his career in the poems.
He begins:

> Nay, tempt me not to love again,
> There was a time when love was sweet;
> Dear Nea! had I known thee then,
> Our souls had not been slow to meet!
> But oh! this weary heart hath run,
> So many times the rounds of pain,
> Not even for thee, thou lovely one!
> Would I endure such pangs again.

And in another mood:

> Oh! trust me, 'twas a place, an hour
> The worst that e'er temptation's power
> Could tangle me or you in!
> Sweet Nea! let us roam no more
> Along that wild and lonely shore,
> Such walks will be our ruin.

And there is something that recalls a type of letter many men
have written in the sober light of morning in

> Forget, forget that night's offence,
> Forgive it, if alas! you can;
> 'Twas love, 'twas passion, soul and sex—
> 'Twas all the best and worst of man!

Elsewhere he and Nea look at a 'curious gem' together.

> Come—closer bring that cheek to mine,
> And trace with me its beauties o'er.

And then

> Imagine, love, that I am he,
> And just as warm as he is chilling;
> Imagine, too, that thou art she,
> But quite as cold as she is willing;

So may we try the graceful way
In which their gentler arms are twined,
And thus, like her, my hand I lay
Upon thy wreathed hair behind:

And thus I feel thee breathing sweet,
And slow to mine thy head I move;
And thus our lips together meet,
And thus—I kiss thee—O my love!

According to the magazine, Dennie's *Port Folio*—the editor
became a friend of Moore and they corresponded—Moore
wrote a poem when on the island to celebrate an incident when
a young lady 'playfully proffered him a ring'. If she was
identifiable, a husband of a few months standing might well
have resented Moore's attentions to his seventeen-year-old wife.

While thus to mine thy bosom lies,
While thus our breaths commingly glow,
'Twere more than woman to be wise,
'Twere more than man to wish thee so.

Did we not love so true, so dear,
This lapse could never be forgiven . . .
But . . . hearts so fond! and lips so near!
Give me the ring, and now . . . O Heaven!

But there are two facts which combine to defuse the explosive
element on this occasion. In the volume in which it first appears
in 1806, this poem is dated 1801, two years before Moore came
to Bermuda. And as to later suppressions, in the edition of
Moore's collected poems dated 1883 the poem is as it was first
published and unabridged. The verses were cut out of a few
editions towards the end of Moore's life.

Moore remained a tradition in the Tucker family; two of the
great-grand daughters of Hester and her ruffled husband were
christened Nea. This could hardly have been the case if any
cloud hung over the association.

His parting gift to America appeared in Dennie's *Port Folio*,
verses addressed to Mrs Hamilton, the wife of the friendly

Consul at Norfolk. She had let her hair down for the poet, or so the last stanza suggests.

> But oh! 'twould ruin saints to see
> Those tresses thus, unbound and free,
> Adown your shoulders sweeping;
> They put *such thoughts* into one's head,
> Of deshabillé, and night and bed,
> And—any thing but sleeping!

The verses would have surprised Moore's mother—or would they? They were certainly in a different key to his letter home: 'Never did Heaven form a heart more kind than I have found in Mrs Hamilton of Norfolk, and she has caught the way to my heart by calling herself my *mother*. She sends a pair of ear-rings by me to Kate with the sincerest affection possible: she loves you all through me.'

Was this characteristic of Moore's approach at this time to older women—Cupid in person, as it were? If so, it may explain why he married late, and then a girl half his age.

Moore appointed a deputy before he left Bermuda, but nothing suggests that he had any hopes of much income; and it must have been because he did not want to annoy his patron that he did not—as he ought to have done—resigned. In 1809, five years later, when his friend and enemy, John Wilson Croker, was Secretary to the Admiralty, Moore wrote to see if he could get official approval of a deal with his deputy, whereby he would in effect sell him his interest. Apparently the first one had misbehaved, and Moore was in negotiation with a successor. The new man's name was Sheddon. Croker wrote Moore a letter which, when he fell out with him, he forgot, advising him to hold on. 'You do not tell me what the office now produces—I conclude next to nothing; but if is pays its own expenses you may look upon it as a lottery ticket in your drawer, which may turn up, one day or other, a £20,000 prize.' Croker added what was fatally misleading, but was most probably innocent: 'I doubt whether in want of any loss you could be held personally responsible.' He offered to recommend someone in the Naval department.

There was trouble later, and Croker, recalling the incident, affected to have been outraged by Moore's proposal to resign.

There was nothing left for Moore to do in Bermuda; he secured a passage in the frigate *Boston*, which sailed for New York on April 24th, 1804. Once again Moore made a devoted friend—Douglas, the Captain who admonished him when Moore adopted the critical manner of later travellers in America, Mrs Trollope and Dickens.

The *Boston* arrived in New York after a nine days passage from Bermuda. Thence it was going to Norfolk, where Moore would meet the Hamiltons again and, presumably, be stirred by Mrs Hamilton's hair. Waiting in New York he is diverted by a glimpse of Jerome Bonaparte, who had served in the French navy in the West Indies, and on a visit to America met and married Elizabeth Patterson of Baltimore. His brother the Emperor, who had taken upon himself papal powers, declared the marriage null. Moore was not impressed by New York:

'I go to the theatre this evening, and to a concert to-morrow evening. Such a place! such people! barren and secluded as poor Bermuda is, I think it is a paradise to any spot in America I have seen. If there is less barreness of *soil* here, there is more than enough of barreness in intellect, taste and all in which heart is concerned.'

Moore described New York in a letter to his mother. 'The environs are pretty, from the number of little fanciful wooden houses that are scattered to the distance of six to eight miles round the city; but when one reflects upon the cause of this, and that these houses are the retreats of terrified desponding inhabitants from the wilderness of death which every autumn produces in the city, there is very little pleasure in the prospect . . .'.

He planned to travel overland from Norfolk to Baltimore and Washington; if possible, Philadelphia and Boston, and thence to Halifax, where Captain Douglas would be waiting, and then to 'the dear old isles of the Old World again'. He requested his mother to say as little as possible about his return; he wanted to lie low and complete the work he had in hand. That should enable him to extricate himself from his financial difficulties. His uncle shall not want his money *one moment* after Tom's arrival.

He wrote again from Baltimore. From this point his strictures must be read in the context of the row which was then simmering in Washington. He had stayed there with the Merrys.

Relations between Britain and her former colony were uneasy to say the least. Within a few years that would boil over into a short and—for Britain—ignominious war.

Merry arrived in an unsuspecting temper. He did not realise that the United States government, pleased with having curbed Bonaparte, was 'preparing to chasten Spain and to discipline England'. Mrs Merry was appalled by living conditions in Washington. Henry Adams described the federal city as one that 'offered few conveniences, and was better suited for members of Congress, who lived without wives in boarding-houses, than for foreign ministers with complaining wives who were required to set up large establishments and to entertain on a European scale'. In order to satisfy her conception of what English prestige required, Mrs Merry took over two houses. Adams admits that if 'Washington was a pretty village . . . society was small'. Merry had not been prepared for President Jefferson's plans for reforming society. He laid it down that he was available at the White House to meet anyone who chose to call on him, eradicating the monarchical habits introduced by George Washington.

If Merry did not know what was in store for him, Jefferson did. Jefferson was determined to abolish diplomatic protocol. At dinner he took beside him the wife of one of his own Cabinet ministers and let the rest of the company find places for themselves—'The rule of pell mell'. Jefferson's philosophy persuaded him to appear to visitors to the White House dressed 'in an old brown coat, red waistcoat, old corduroy small-clothes (much soiled), woollen hose, and slippers without heels'.

This is the vision Merry saw when he arrived, fully dressed, in diplomatic rig. It made him feel foolish.

When Madison, the Secretary of State, gave a dinner, Merry was left to show his own wife to the table. When he complained that this was an insult to his country, he was told that wives of Cabinet ministers had precedence. After this the Spanish and British planned reprisals. They ignored American wives; they refused invitations. Merry accepted one, a tea-party, and failed to appear. The Merrys became the centre of every intrigue against the Government. The Federalist opposition took the Merrys into their plans which included the secession of New England from the Union. This was the state of affairs when Moore arrived on his way home. He at once associated himself with his friends and appeared in public under their auspices.

'The President had a habit of casting a cold first look at a stranger; and on this occasion, standing erect, six feet two inches and a half, he gazed for a moment silently down upon the perfumed five-foot poet . . .' So the incident was described in later years by a correspondent to *Harper's Magazine*.

It was only 'the precarious situation of Great Britain which could possibly induce us to overlook such indecent, though, at the same time, petty hostility', Moore writes to his mother.

The United States had not settled down comfortably as a sovereign power. Apart from the stresses of politics and the teething time which any country has to go through after a successful revolution, physical conditions were appalling. Lack of sanitation alone was the cause of widespread disease. Moore has been blamed for harping on all this; but American history confirms his unfavourable impressions. He became too much of a partisan because of Merry, and avenged himself meanly for Jefferson's frosty treatment:

> The weary statesman for repose hath fled
> From halls of Council to his negro's shed,
> Where blest he wooes some black Aspasia's grace,
> And dreams of freedom in his slave's embrace!

When Moore's *Irish Melodies* came out, Jefferson's granddaughter gave him a copy (sensitivity does not seem to have been a highly developed characteristic in that family). Jefferson, when he saw Moore's name said, 'Why this is the little man who satirised me so!' But he read the poems, and loved them. In the letter he wrote to his daughter when he was dying, he quoted several lines from Moore.

It was a great deal to forgive. Jefferson forgave. He was a big man.

G. P. R. James, the writer, who many years later succeeded

Hamilton as consul in Norfolk, according to *Harper's* anony
mous scribe, 'often wondered how Tom Moore, so good and
generous a fellow as he always seemed to be' could have done
it, and supplied the charitable answer: 'he was very young then,
only four or five and twenty'.

Very young, too susceptible to the prevailing tone in the
circles that approved him, too much impressed by his patrons
—but he had travelled very far, very fast, from his mother's
musical parties.

And he was encouraged by Mrs Merry, who is described by
this witness as 'one of those proud, conceited, censorious, and
generally disagreeable women who demand constant adoration
and obsequiousness, feel insulted by every apparent neglect to
honour their pretensions and see little to praise and much to
condemn in others. She flattered the vain young poet to his
heart's content'.

From the same source we learn about another of the girls to
whom Moore addressed poems. Mrs M—r, an elderly lady
then, living at Fredericksburg. She described Moore as she
remembered him: 'His eyes were dark and brilliant; his mouth
was delicately cut and full-lipped; his nose was slightly upturned, giving an expression of fun to his face; his complexion
was fair and somewhat ruddy; his hair was a rich dark brown,
and curled all over his head; his forehead was broad and
strongly marked; and his voice, not powerful, was exquisitely
sweet, especially when he was singing.'

What an impression he must have made upon 'a gay young
girl in her "teens" when, on a warm June evening, she met the
poet at the house of a friend, heard him sing, and received
from his hand a copy of the following sonnet . . .' The poem,
addressed to a firefly, had nothing whatever to do with her,
and had been composed during a night ride between Richmond
and Fredericksburg in a stage-coach with a Quaker and his
daughter.

Moore conquered Philadelphia: here there was an established society, one of the redoubts of the old régime, and it
took Moore to its hospitable bosom. He felt among friends, and
there are no people in the world who can inflate the ego better
than the Americans when they set about it. Moore wined and

dined and sang. Mr Hopkinson, author of *Hail Columbia*, was one of his delighted hosts. Mrs Hopkinson came in for Moore's special treatment. Moore described her to his mother as 'a very charming little woman'.

> Nor did she her enamouring magic deny,
> That magic his heart had relinquish's so long,
> Like eyes he had lov'd was *her* eloquent eye,
> Like them did it soften and weep at his song!

Dennie and Moore struck up an immediate friendship. Moore arranged for an introduction to the Merrys and wrote to Mrs Merry to recommend him; they made literary plans at once, and on leaving Philadelphia Moore enshrined his visit in a grateful poem.

Moore's fulsomeness was congenital; writing to his mother at this time he spoke of being soon 'in her arms'. An unusual expression surely. Moore was not so much a chartered libertine as Cupid with buttons on his arrows.

He was still young. His literary reputation, as ever in America, gave him too much licence. He needed a restraining hand, and there was none. His hosts encouraged him, glad to have the support of a visiting celebrity. Reproof came eventually from a wise friend, the kind Captain Douglas.

'Now, my good fellow, allow me to advise you not to be *too careless* about the *warm reception you received* at Philadelphia: in my opinion, these new acquaintances ought always to be treated with the greatest *respect* and *attention*. I wish you had come down yesterday, as I do think few of your friends would feel much more gratified by taking you by the hand than myself.'

In the preface to *Epistles, Odes, and Other Poems*, which was now in preparation and would be completed on his return, Moore questioned his own recent proceedings: 'How far I was right in thus assuming the tone of a satirist against a people whom I viewed but as a stranger and a visitor, is a doubt which my feelings did not leave me time to investigate. All I presume to answer for is the fidelity of the picture which I have given; and though prudence might have dictated gentler language, truth, I think, would have justified severer.' He had indulged in many of those illusive ideas in his native country where unfortunately 'discontent at home enhances every distant temptation'.

'The rude familiarity of the lower orders, and indeed the unpolished state of society in general' could be excused if they sprang from the simplicity of a new and inexperienced people. 'But when we find them arrived at maturity in most of the vices, and all the pride of civilisation while they are still as remote from its elegant characteristics, it is impossible not to feel that this youthful decay, this crude anticipation of the natural period of corruption, represses every hope of the future energy and greatness of America.'

In later years Moore was to repent sincerely. 'Ah those unfortunate letters of mine must have left a bad impression of me. Would to God I had never written them, that I had never so acted.' In a letter to John E. Hall, he declared 'there are few of my errors I regret more sincerely than the rashness I was guilty of in publishing these crude and boyish tirades against the Americans. My sentiments both with respect to their National and individual character are much changed since then, and I should blush as a lover of Liberty, if I allowed the hasty prejudices of my youth to blind me now to the bright promise which America affords of a better and happier order of things than the World has perhaps ever yet witnessed'. He calls Jefferson 'Washington'. This is the Moore who left everything behind him after a visit. And America was far behind him now.

Moore's journeyings, while Douglas waited to sail, included a visit to Niagara Falls. As later, when he was overcome by the splendour of the Alps, his mind was not engaged by the view; he made no effort, as Ruskin would, to find words to describe it; he was overcome by emotion and 'in that delicious absorption which pious enthusiasm alone can produce . . . My whole heart and soul ascended towards the Divinity in a swell of devout admiration which I never before experienced. Oh! bring the atheist here, and he cannot return an atheist.'

Risking Douglas' departure from Halifax without him, the restless Moore could not resist a boat journey up the St Lawrence to Montreal. In Canada he found that his fame had gone before him. At Niagara, a watchmaker had refused to charge for a repair; the Captain on the ship on the trip to Montreal insisted that Moore and friends should not contribute 'to what I know is always given'; the Governor of Lower Canada sent his aide-de-camp to the master of the vessel upon which Moore was returning to beg him to detain the boat's departure for a day to allow time for a party in Moore's honour; he was taken to the first examination at the new university at Windsor by the Governor of Nova Scotia. Every step of his was smoothed. 'This is the very nectar of life.'

He returned from America, he wrote to his mother, 'without a blemish either in heart or body'; but in spite of the raptures at the expectation of being united with his family, he stayed in London to finish his book.

SETTLED IN London, on a severe regimen—work all morning and a dinner now and then with Lady Donegal or Miss Tighe (then a fashionable poet)—Moore could not return to Dublin until his book was finished and his debts paid. That was understood. It was also understandable that he should not decline a small supper at Lord Harrington's to meet the Prince. 'I am very glad to see you here again, Moore. From the reports I had heard I was afraid we had lost you. I assure you (laying his hand on my shoulder at the same time) it was a subject of general concern.' Could anything be more flattering? Tommy asked his mother in a letter enclosing the invitation from Lord Petersham to excuse the break in his studious retirement.

He had consulted his landlady in Bury Street about tailors, being out of patience with his own, who was pressing him for a small balance owing. The landlady offered to put her savings at his disposal. He refused and 'went and thanked God on my knees for the many sweet things of this kind he so continually throws in my way'.

He was pressing on, and turned down an offer from George Thomson for songs for which Haydn was to provide the music; but he took time off for a dinner arranged by General Phipps to meet George Colman, and he went to Tonbridge to stay with Lady Donegal and Miss Godfrey. There was dancing at Tonbridge. Samuel Rogers, the banker poet, had taken him up. He called on Monk Lewis on several occasions and knocked without avail. Then he got ill.

There is some confusion about this illness in Moore's correspondence. From the date given by Russell, Moore would seem to have had a severe illness, which produced an abscess in his side, before he went to America. But in later years, he referred to this as having occurred in 1806, and he does not suggest that it was a recurrence of an old complaint. It must have been serious because he had to be operated on in April.

Pitt died in January 1806; the prospect of a change of government had Lord Moira in agitation again; and Moore's hopes and fears returned. He makes no other comment on the affairs of the day, and all he told his mother was that Moira, in April, had offered him something which he had written to thank him for but refused. 'Better to wait until something worthier both of his generosity and my ambition should occur.' But he had taken the opportunity to apply for some preferment for his father. This came off. Old Mr Moore was made a Barrack-master. The matter was put through by the faithful Joe Atkinson. He got a house as well, apparently, if a letter Tom wrote later bore fruit: 'The situation which your lordship's goodness has procured my dear father is now his only means of subsistence, as the attention which it requires renders it utterly impossible for him to undertake any other pursuit . . . A house is the great object to which he looks, and a few words from your lordship . . .'

In view of the charges which Moore was later to make against Lord Moira it is necessary—if painful—to consider the rest of this letter. It has not been quoted by Moore's biographers.

'And now, my Lord, for the last time to mention myself to your Lordship—I have begged of Dalby to procure me a little lodging in the village of Donnington, to which I shall retire as soon as my visit in Ireland is over, and what I have to entreat is that your Lordship will allow me (in case Dalby should feel any difficulty in procuring me a lodging) to go to the Park till I can settle myself in the Village—It would be worse than imprudent, it would be *dishonest* of me to return to the same mode of life which I have hitherto pursued in London, & my literary exertions will be completely adequate not only to my support in the country but to my releasement (I should hope) from all the difficulties I have involved myself in—Do not, my Lord, suppose that this is the language of despondency—Your Lordship has already by what you have done for my father, lightened my heart of its only burthen, and if you can but facilitate for him what I now request, you will leave me *nothing*

to feel towards you but the very fullness of gratitude & satisfaction, nor shall I ever again from this moment obtrude one
word about myself upon your attention.

'I have the honour to be your Lordship's very obliged &
devoted Servant.

Thomas Moore.'

Moira came again in June, this time to tell Moore he could
go to Ireland; he would not be forgotten. An Irish Commissionership was in the offing.

To Mary Godfrey, one of those who drew the best out of
Moore, he wrote at this time to reprove her for neglecting him,
'a poor forsaken *gander* whom you left *hissing hot* upon the
pavement of London, with a pain in his side and the wind-colic
in his heart, with the dust in his eyes and the devil in his purse
. . .'. He tells her that he is off to Ireland soon, that the Commissionership intended for him is to be in Ireland. 'London
shall never see me act the farce of gentlemanship in it any more,
and like a bright exhalation in the evening, I shall vanish and
be forgotten.'

What was holding Tom in London was anxiety to see what
the *Edinburgh Review* had to say about his new book *Epistles,
Odes and Other Poems*. The judgment, whatever it might be,
would have a significant effect on his reputation. This was his
third book. The first was remarkable for precocity; the second
had largely a *succès de scandale*, and it had been presented as
juvenilia; but, at twenty-seven Moore would not be let through
the critical net. The *Edinburgh* had been severe about the 'Little'
poems. 'A style so wantonly voluptuous is at once effeminate
and childish.' Moore had cause for fear.

The authority of the *Edinburgh* with the reading public was
unchallenged. Hazlitt described it as standing 'upon the
ground of opinion; it asserts the supremacy of intellect. The
pre-eminence it claims is from an acknowledged superiority of
talent and information, and literary attainment; and it does not
build one tittle of its influence on ignorance, or prejudice, or
authority, or personal malevolence'.

Jeffrey, the editor, Hazlitt wrote, 'is certainly a person in
advance of the age'. He acquitted him of any charge of bigotry,

enthusiasm or prejudice, and he was not 'the dupe of the prejudices of others'. It can be understood, then, that Moore was dazzled when in July 1806, he saw a long article devoted to his work.

But there was no comfort in it. Almost the entire space was given over to a steadily rising torrent of invective.

'He may be seen in every page running round the paltry circle of his seductions with incredible zeal and anxiety, and stimulating his jaded fancy for new images of impurity.' Comparing Moore to Rochester and Dryden, Jeffrey wrote: 'They indulge their own vein of gross riot and debauchery; but do not seek to corrupt the principles of their readers . . . The immorality of Mr Moore is infinitely more insidious and malignant. It seems to be his aim to impose corruption upon his readers, by concealing it under the mask of refinement . . . and to steal impurity into their hearts, by gently perverting the most simple and generous of their affections . . . He is at pains to let the world know that he is still fonder of roving than of loving, and that all the Caras and the Fannys, with whom he holds dalliance in these pages, have had each a long series of preceding lovers, as highly favoured as their present poetical paramour . . . To us, indeed, the perpetual kissing and turning and parting of these amorous persons is rather ludicrous than seductive. . . .'

To young men, because of the sort of talk they indulged in, there was not much danger. They would assess at their proper valuation 'a tissue of sickly and fantastical conceits, equally remote from truth and respectability'. What Jeffrey was principally concerned with, he said, was the effect the poems might have upon the other sex; it was on account of the 'insult to their delicacy' and the 'attack upon their purity' that he resented the publication.

Then followed a paragraph which is important because it was written by one fully qualified to assess the contemporary scene and whose attitudes were representative of educated opinion.

'We have been induced to enter this strong protest, and to express ourselves thus warmly against this and the former publications of this author, both from what we hear of the circulation which they have already obtained, and from our conviction that they are calculated, if not strongly denounced

to the public, to produce at this moment, peculiar and irred-
emable mischief. The style of composition, as we have already
hinted, is almost new in this country; it is less offensive than
the old fashion of obscenity; and for these reasons, perhaps, it
is less likely to excite the suspicion of the modest, or to become
the object of precaution to those who watch over the morals of
the young and inexperienced.'

And the reviewer also noticed with apprehension that 'many
of the pieces were dedicated to persons of the first consideration
in the country, both for rank and accomplishment, and the
author appears to consider the greater part of them as his
intimate friends, and undoubtedly patrons and admirers. Now,
this we will confess is to us a very alarming consideration. By
these channels the book will easily pass into circulation in those
classes of society, which it is of most importance to keep free of
contamination, and from which its reputation and its influence
will descend with the greater effect to the great body of the
community'.

As to the verses, he saw little to praise, and attributed its
popularity to the 'seduction of its subjects'.

There was—inevitably—a run on the book; and it was
notoriously popular among young women. No doubt the
eminence and respectability of the dedicatees gave them a
passport which they were glad to use. He dedicates poems to—
among others—Lady Donegal; Mrs Henry Tighe, author of
Psyche; several ladies of title; the Hon. William Spencer; and
the whole offending volume to the tantalising Lord Moira.

The fact that these people, including several respectable
women, did not object was a significant circumstance; and
Jeffrey must have been at a loss to explain to himself how they
had all allowed Moore to use them for his salacious campaign.
Jeffrey had observed Moore's tendency to combine tenderness
and exalted feeling with 'vile and vulgar sensuality'. The verses
were 'effeminate and childish'. This shaft went close home. The
answer to the question why the polite world was not outraged
by Moore was simply, that, unlike Jeffrey, it knew Moore. Very
soon, and in a dramatic fashion, he was to meet Moore. And
then he, too, would succumb to his fascination.

Before his review settled into its abusive stream, Jeffrey

acknowledged a 'singular sweetness and melody of versification
—smooth, copious and familiar diction—with some brilliancy
of fancy and some flow of classical erudition might have raised
Mr Moore to an innocent distinction among the song writers
and occasional poets of his day . . .'.

That was strict but fair. Moore was often emotionally out of
his depth. Whenever he attempts to portray passion he is
shallow. Sometimes he could strike a note of moving tenderness,
but when physical sexuality loomed up, it found Moore inade-
quate. With all his efforts not to offend against good taste,
he was cloying in his coyness.

In some of the poems he strikes the pose of the emotionally
exhausted rake begging the girl not to expect to find freshness
in a tired heart.

> Oh! thou has not my virgin vow;
> Though few the years that I have told,
> Canst thou believe I lived till now,
> With loveless heart or senses cold?
>
> No—many a throb of bliss and pain,
> For many a maid my soul hath proved;
> With some I wanton'd wild and vain,
> While some I truly loved.

Jeffrey found this 'more ludicrous than seductive', and so
should we. Moore was apt to make a sudden descent into
titillation and come close to bathos. He was posing as a libertine; he was also striking a rather pompous figure when he
addressed his young nobleman ('But, O my Forbes!'). He was
happiest when he deployed his 'singular sweetness and melody
of versification' as in the Canadian Boating Song (not to be
confused with Galt's), or when he was being witty.

He proved in these poems that he was a natural writer of
songs and composer of epigrams with a delicate ear. He was in
many respects an innovator, experimenting with verse forms;
anticipating Keats in one verse and Browning in another;
but the poet who was to come closest to Moore was Poe. It
could have been discerned that he was not intended for epic
adventures. Jeffrey saw all this, and if his long review is raked

over, most of what can legitimately be said against all Moore's work is there as well as an acknowledgment of its merits; but Jeffrey was carried away by his enthusiasm for the commonweal and said too much too warmly.

With his inevitable prefatory 'oh!' and the ubiquitous exclamation mark, Moore's success as a duodecimo Byron showed what an audience there was in waiting for Don Juan. Before Byron arrived on the scene, Moore had the success of a Tom the Baptist, but when Byron came Moore was to suffer. By then he had repented his youthful concupiscence. He turned to the East for inspiration and found Byron had got there before him.

In the light of Jeffrey's indictment it is amusing to recall Byron's letter to Moore, written fourteen years later. 'I have just been turning over Little, which I knew by heart in 1803, being then in my fifteenth summer. Heigho! I believe all the mischief I have ever done, or sung, has been owing to that confounded book of yours.'

Writing to George Thomson, who had been pressing for songs, Moore affected a lofty detachment. He thought Thomson might have sent him the copy of the peccant magazine. He had been 'agreeably disappointed' by the review of his poems. There was all the 'malignity which I expected but not half the *sting*, and I HOPE I SHALL ALWAYS be lucky enough to have such dull, prosing protagonists'. Does Mr Jeffrey live in Edinburgh? he wants to know. He thinks he may be there himself in the near future.

This is a hint at a project which was to cause Moore eventually more embarrassment than Jeffrey's review. He challenged the Scot to a duel.

MOORE USED different friends for different purposes. In this predicament he wrote to his doctor, who had attended him in his recent illness. He had employed him to witness his signature to an important contract with Longmans. He invested money for Moore, and looked after Moore's Bessy when she was ill. Woolrich advised caution. Moore then wrote to Hume, another foul-weather friend. Hume consented to act, and a challenge was sent to Jeffrey. Jeffrey appointed a friend named Horner as his second. Neither of the duellists had weapons. The deficiency was supplied by William Spencer, to whom one of Moore's recent poems had been addressed. Moore did not like pistols. In youth he had nearly blown off his thumb playing with one; but he went to an armourer's in Bond Street and bought enough ammunition to do for several duels.

He slept it out the next morning, and Hume had to wake him up, the chaise was ready; they drove to Chalk Farm, where a surgeon was in readiness, and Jeffrey and his party were waiting for them. Moore chose the word 'party' deliberately because, he generously admitted, 'two or three of his attached friends (and no man, I believe, could ever boast of a greater number) . . . in their anxiety for his safety, had accompanied him and were hovering about the spot'.

It was the first time the two men had ever met face to face. They took to each other at once.

The place selected was sheltered by trees. Horner, Jeffrey's second, thought he had seen some men suspiciously hovering about, but as they had evidently departed, the seconds retired behind the trees to load. It was just as well. Horner had to confess that he had no idea how to put bullets into a pistol. He asked Hume to load both weapons.

Meanwhile the antagonists were uneasily waiting. 'What a

beautiful morning it is,' said Jeffrey. 'Yes, a morning made for better purposes', Moore replied. Jeffrey assented with a sigh.

They found themselves walking up and down together, catching a glimpse of their seconds fumbling at their task.

The seconds appeared just then and placed the antagonists in position. They then retired; the pistols were raised; the order to fire awaited. But it never came; police officers rushed out from a hedge behind Jeffrey and struck up his weapon. Moore was also disarmed. The duellists were led to their carriage and ordered to drive to Bow Street.

There they had to stay until they could find bail. Moore sent for William Spencer who had supplied the pistols. While they awaited deliverance, the two prisoners fell into literary talk. Moore took 'only the brief and occasional share, beyond which, at that time of my life, I seldom ventured in general society'. But Jeffrey lay on his back on a form and poured 'volubly forth his fluent but most oddly pronounced diction . . . in every variety of array that an ever rich and ready wardrobe of phraseology could supply'. They were friends for life.

Spencer arrived with Rogers; having supplied the pistols, he may have considered that the banker poet should put up the money. Rogers obliged; but there were no pistols for Spencer. When Moore discovered the loss—Spencer had stressed the value of the brace of pistols—he had himself to return to Bow Street.

The little party had left the precincts of the court in good spirits, but when Moore returned he was given a nasty reception by the police officer. The magistrate had come to the conclusion foul play was intended. There was no bullet in Jeffrey's pistol. Hume had informed Moore on the drive back in the carriage that he had been in charge of the loading, and Hume had gone away. It was a dreadfully embarrassing situation. Moore hurried off to Horner's chambers, and found him at home. He 'in his honest and manly manner' put Moore at once at his ease. 'Don't mind what these fellows say. I myself saw your friend put a bullet into Jeffrey's pistol, and shall go with you instantly to the office to put it right.'

The magistrate was mollified, and the pistols with *one* bullet were handed back.

The report about the unloaded pistol reached Fleet Street, where an Irish journalist, to improve it, substituted 'pellet' for 'bullet'.

To avert the ridicule an official statement was required. The offending newspaper agreed to publish it. The magistrate and the two seconds had only to sign it. And then, what has never been explained, the impossible occurred—Hume refused to sign. He said that he didn't know who Jeffrey's second, Mr Horner, was.

Why did he fail Moore in such a crisis? He said that he did not want to 'expose his name'. But that in the circumstances was poltroonery. A possibility is that he was more devoted to Moore than he ever let be known and on an impulse removed the bullet that might have killed him. No explanation was ever given for its absence. Whatever the motive, he did his friend a disservice at the time. All Moore could do was to fall back on a letter of denial. In the circumstances, it carried, as he realised, no conviction.

J. W. Croker, when Moore was dead, wrote that his account of the duel was false; but, as least, we have his opponent's evidence, which leaves a pleasant impression. Writing afterwards to a friend, George Joseph Bell, Jeffrey described how they had 'breakfasted together very lovingly'. 'He has behaved with great spirit throughout this business. He really is not profligate, and is universally regarded, even by those who resent the style of his poetry, as an innocent, good-hearted, idle fellow.' In later years Moore named Jeffrey and Lord John Russell as the two men he cared for most. Moore was all ears for what the people who mattered to him had to say. It was encouraging of Lord Moira to write 'a very kind note', and Moore heard with satisfaction that Horner at Holland House had praised his feeling and fortitude. Kind Mary Godfrey wrote to say—exactly what Moore required to hear—that Rogers made him out 'a perfect hero of romance and your conduct quite admirable', and Lord Clifton was not less reassuring. Miss Godfrey had the diplomatic notion of sending a sympathetic account to Joe Atkinson, who could be trusted to spread it abroad. She was anxious that Rogers's account should be known and had persuaded her sister Polly to write to a friend 'in that line of life that the prejudice against your writings, and the envy of your talents are the strongest. The old ones have more morality, and the young ones more pretensions than one finds in the higher ranks of life'.

The Godfreys were the daughters of a learned Irish rector. Lady Donegal was the third wife of the Marquis, who died in 1799, before Moore met the sisters. They had contributed to his belief that 'after all it was in high life one met the best society', which, when he mentioned it to Rogers on one occasion, provoked violent opposition. But of all men, Moore assured him, none had in practice given greater proof of it, confining himself almost exclusively to that class of society.

To what extent did Moore live up to the character of his amorous verse? He said of himself that he was saved from the coarser dissipation of men's society by the nature of his talents which made him the frequenter of drawing-rooms; he preferred women's company to men's. To sisterly Lady Donegal and Mary Godfrey, he gave himself the character of a philanderer —flirt, they might have said. And this is the character he assumes in his letters to his mother—a comic opera gallant with an eye for every girl.

The Rev John Dalby, whom he met at Donington, and whose sister Mary was to be a lifelong friend of Moore and his future wife was unlikely to be chosen by a thorough rake as the recipient of his confidences; letters to him usually contained instructions to send on luggage left behind on visits to Donington or to look out for houses in his neighbourhood. When Moore was on his way to Bermuda he had implored Dalby to help.

'I have been a good deal puzzled about the moveables I left behind at Donington, but I know your usual goodness will assist me in this predicament . . . You will also find in the little trunk a little *steel bandage* which I generally wear when I take exercise from an apprehension which I have long had (I believe without any cause) of a Hernia in my right groin—cover it up securely at the bottom of the box.'

Dalby was one of those—James Power and Dr Hume were others—who served Moore and whom he exploited as only charmers can. (Byron exploited friends unmercifully.) In the same vein as when he is writing to Mary Godfrey, Moore asks Dalby to 'offer up a few prayers for me as I shudder at the grip of Demon Dissipation . . . Cleanthea and Lamia have gone to sleep, *together*, since I came to town, but as soon as I am settled in my lodgings I shall waken them *rousingly*—I know you doubt this—but you shall see.' Moore invoked a stoic philosopher and a witty courtesan when he was writing to his kind friend the clergyman; there is a more sophisticated note in a letter written about this time to Lord Strangford.

Percy Clinton Sydney Smythe was the 6th Earl. His father had retired from the army to become Rector of Kilbrew in County Meath. Strangford took his degree in Trinity College in 1800. Disraeli described him as 'an aristocratic Tom Moore'.

Strangford was translating poems by the Portuguese writer Camoens, which when they were published Byron satirised as plagiarisms of Moore. But Moore, at twenty-three, is quite happy to act as an oracle to the nobleman, one year his junior, parading his authorities impressively, and in the same letter, with the air of an old campaigner, gives his friend the benefit of what he described as his 'morale de galanterie'.

'Between ourselves, my dear Percy, and in the beaten way of friendship, I *must* condemn your levity about Mrs Walpole— it was unworthy of you—you make a discovery almost inevitable, and you *must* know too that this is not Diplomatique, for whatever a man may think of a woman, he should *seem* to respect her for indulging him, or he will hardly be indulged by any other—no, no, I agree with my friend Tom Brown that

> Of all the crimes on this side Hell
> The blackest sure's to—and tell.

And you are quite right in saying "le jeu ne vaut pas la chandelle" for such games should be kept quite *in the dark* . . .'

Many years later Moore is shocked, not by Byron's Venetian amours, but by his parade of them. Whatever course his life took when he first came to London, Strangford was one who travelled it with him. He was one of the people to whom Moore wrote on the eve of his duel with Jeffrey in 1806: 'The cloth has been but just taken from the table, and though to-morrow may be my last view of the bright sun, I shall (as soon as I have finished this letter), drink to the health of my Strangford with as an unaffected a warmth as ever I felt in the wildest days of our fellowship. My dear friend, if they want a biographer when I am gone, I think in your hands I should meet with most kind embalment . . .'

Strangford's rather chequered career took a Tory course,

and Moore made his friends in the opposite camp; but when Moore was in financial trouble over his Bermuda business, Strangford wrote offering to help. 'My dear friend', Moore replied, 'how delightful to have the companion of one's young days taking the part you have done in the moment of need, and showing that, even scapegraces as we were, there was stuff in us for better things'. Strangford's son, immortalised by Disraeli as Coningsby, was dissipated, but his father did not have that reputation. Moore was written of at this period of his career as if his verses made him the Rochester of his day; they were very mild by that comparison, and his libertinage milder still. Atkinson's phrase 'an infant sporting on the bosom of Venus' persists; it explains and is consistent with Moore's marriage. A Miss Rennie has given a picture of Moore after marriage. She may be called in here, although the Moore she knew was an older and more celebrated man.

"He said nearly all the heroines of his lays and melodies were flesh and blood, repeating several of their names, and where they lived, many of them merged into honoured wives and mothers. Though it would be doing him gross injustice to assert that he boasted of his successes with women, still he was very content you should guess and divine he was the admired of many. I believe that was quite the truth. He told us of one young lady who laid regular siege to him; not content with meeting him in society at the house of friends, whom they mutually visited, she used to wait for him in a carriage, accompanied by a female companion, in sight of the house where he was lodging in Bury Street, St James, watching his return from his evening round of parties, frequently till two or three o'clock in the morning, and then pounce on him.

I naturally enquired

"And what then? Surely, if, as you say, she is a girl of character and in a good position, she does not enter your apartment, even with a friend, at that unseemly hour?"

"Oh dear, no," he plaintively and naïvely answered, "she makes me get into the carriage with her".

"And what then?"

"Why she tells me—but I must not repeat it—how much she admires my writings."

"And yourself also, I presume?"

"Indeed, I am afraid so."

"And do you not reprove her, and point out how wrong all this is, as you are a married man?"

"Indeed I do and implore her not to come again; but she begins to cry, and what can a man say or do then? Of course, I was silent; what argument can you oppose to woman's invincible weapon—tears? The other night" continued Moore, "she cried so dreadfully, I was afraid she was going to have hysterics, and that I should have to go into my room for Eau de Cologne. I was quite in agony".'

'She was a very pretty girl,' Miss Rennie added (Moore must have given her name), and, considering how much distressed and annoyed he had expressed himself at her nocturnal visitations to Bury Street, he certainly lavished on her no small share of gentle and assiduous attention.'

A half-letter in the National Library in Dublin to Crofton Croker, written from the house of Moore's friend Hume, two years after his death, is the most explicit attack on Moore's moral character. The writer was incensed by the report of the duel in the *Memoirs* which alleged that Moore spent the night before in Hume's rooms, having brought his own linen as Hume kept a slovenly house. 'The ungentlemanly and false accusations about the sheets. Hume's house not in use by him and his beautiful young wife (Hume not quite tired of her in a year as another Tom was*) . . . Wife young and beautiful, naturally a coquette—and Moore's habits the most loose and disreputable.' Hume had taken her out of Moore's reach. The letter goes on to say that Moore had picked his own wife from the lowest walk of life. It is, whoever wrote it, clearly the production of a prejudiced witness. Perhaps Leigh Hunt, in his verse on Moore's marriage, put Moore as an amorist in the truest light:

> There are very few poets, whose caps or whose curls
> Have obtained such a laurel by hunting the girls.
> So it gives me, dear Tom, a delight beyond measure
> To find how you've mended your notions of pleasure.

---

* A snide reference to Moore.

The more detailed impressions of Moore in public describe him at a later period, and on his entry to society we know from his diaries that he was diffident. Leigh Hunt met him in the years when the *Melodies* were coming out, and Hunt's description may be taken as reasonably accurate and impartial because he could not bring himself to mention Moore's name after he learned that Moore had advised Byron against joining with the Hunts in producing a magazine.

'I thought Thomas Moore, when I first knew him, as delightful a person as one could imagine. He could not help being an interesting one; and his sort of talent had this advantage in it, that being of a description intelligible to all, the possessor is equally sure of present and future fame. I never received a visit from him but I felt as if I had been talking with Prior or Sir Charles Sedley. His acquaintance with Lord Byron began by talking of a duel. With me it commenced in as gallant a way, though of a different sort. I had cut up an Opera of his (*The Blue Stocking*), as unworthy of so great a wit. He came to see me, saying I was very much in the right, and an intercourse took place, which I might have enjoyed to this day had he valued his real fame as much as I did.

'Mr Moore was lively, polite, bustling, full of amenities and acquiescences, into which he contrived to throw a sort of roughening of cordiality, like the crust of old port. It seemed a happiness to him to say "yes". There was just enough of the Irishman in him to flavour his speech and manner. He was a little particular, perhaps, in his orthoepy, but not more so than became a poet; and he appeared to me the last man in the world to cut his country, even for the sake of high life. As to his person, all the world knows that he was little of stature, as he is great in wit.'

Hunt reminds us that Moore always got on well with every kind of man. There was nothing effeminate about him. 'Horseback, and a little Irish fighting, would have seen fair play with his good living, and kept his looks as juvenile as his spirit. His forehead is long and full of character, with "bumps" of wit, large and radiant, enough to transport a phrenologist. His eyes are dark and fine, as you would wish to see under a set of vineleaves: his mouth generous and good-humoured with dimples;

his nose sensual, prominent, and at the same time the reverse of aquiline. There is a very peculiar expression in it, as if it were looking forward, and scenting a feast or an orchard.

'His voice, which is a little hoarse in speaking (at least, I used to think so) softens into a breath like that of the flute, when he is singing. In speaking he is emphatic in rolling the letter R, perhaps out of a despair of being able to get rid of the national peculiarity.'

Sydney Smith, that great rollicking wit, the funniest parson that ever stood in a pulpit, not given by nature to soft speeches, confirmed Hunt's impression, boisterously.

'By the Beard of the prelate of Canterbury, by the Cassock of the prelate of York, by the breakfasts of Rogers, by Luttrell's love of side dishes, I swear that I would rather hear you sing than any person, male or female. For what is your singing but beautiful poetry floating in fine music and guided by exquisite feeling?'

A Journal entry for May 20 1833 records that Moore had not laughed so much for a long time as that evening, when Bowles came to dinner. 'He was very amusing about my theology and Miss Martineau'.

The latter a formidable person, tells in her autobiography how she refused to be introduced when Moore came up with Rogers at a party. She had heard he was the author of a lampoon at her expense in *The Times*.

Afterwards Moore sang several songs at the piano. 'Then, he screened his little person behind a lady's harp; and all the time she was playing, he was studying me through his eye-glass.'

BACK IN Dublin in September 1806, Moore affected contempt for the local scene. The tone of his letters to Mary Godfrey and Lady Donegal was sometimes insufferable. 'You cannot imagine how desperately vulgar and dreary this place is. I have not even Mrs Tighe to comfort me, but I expect she will be in town in a week or two. I regret very much to find that she is becoming so "furieusement litteraire"; one used hardly to get a peep at her blue stockings, but now I am afraid she shows them up to the knee . . .'

Lady Donegal was informed that 'Dublin had at length become gay; but it is a kind of *conscript* gaiety, in which the people all assemble with the ill-grace of French *volontaires forces*. My heart is sick of them all . . . Any little hopes I have of advancement are gone. Among the great, both in England and Ireland, there is nothing left now but pride, self-interest, and, I think, a fatal insufficiency . . .'

It does not make pretty reading.

But his letters, even now, show him as in at least two respects immature. He knows he can be confident of affectionate eyes and need not guard himself, but, still, even on the unfailing Joe Atkinson, a man of the world, it must have grated a little to read 'Next week I go for two or three days to Brocket Hall, Lord Melbourne's, the most recherché house in all the fashionable world, and the most difficult of access'. Apart from any other consideration that was a clumsily patronising tone to take, as if Atkinson, who had launched him in London, did not know who Melbourne was, as if Atkinson was the dimmest of country cousins.

The other tiresome facet of his character—but she did nothing to discourage it—was disclosed in his letters to Mary Godfrey when he is assuring her that he is working hard in Dublin; he has to add, that he has failed to write as soon as he intended because 'once I get into that bewildering *seraglio*, what with making real love to one, flirting with some, and merely throwing my eye upon others, the whole day has passed in dalliance . . . I have now, however, bade adieu to this harem'. He refers to a rumour of his engagement to an apothecary's daughter. He is pleased that Jeffrey took a great fancy to him. He has written nothing since he came to Dublin but one song which everyone tells him is the best thing he has ever done.

In a week he will be returning to Donington. Donington! Seat of his illusions. Moira was satisfied to let him stay in that enormous house whenever he wished. He had his house in London, and in Dublin a beautiful residence on the Liffey which, stripped of a storey, became in later years the Mendicity Institute. A silent comment on Moore's relations with its owner. Neither of the Godfrey sisters seem, in all the wise counsel they gave him, to have tried to shake him in this faith. Nor did he despair when Moira was taken into the Cabinet and still failed to place him.

In Dublin, Moore must have gone through some sort of self-appraisal; if nothing else he prescribed for himself the soul-restoring benefits of study and retreat, first in Dublin, then at Donington if Lord Moira would agree to his settling in the village. The discipline was soon to bear fruit; his next song, as he told Mary Godfrey, was considered by his Dublin friends to be his best. Whatever he was suffering of remorse about Robert Emmet—and he probably shied away from the subject in conversation, as he did about his own troubles—it was working upon his imagination. Yeats, after the 1916 Rising in Dublin, went into a similar retreat and pondered the fate of the rebels and his own responsibility for having helped to fan the flames in which he was not to burn. Nothing so magnificent as the poem to which Yeats's introspection eventually gave rise was ever to issue from Moore; but a new note was struck when he began, as he did now, systematically, to base his songs on traditional airs.

It brought him as close as he was ever to get to the elementary source, to which his Scottish contemporary, Burns, had uninhibited access—in France Beranger had ploughed the same ground. Moore was beginning to write the *Irish Melodies* that won him a deserved popularity with the general public, and in Ireland, from the second half of the century on, his place as the National Bard. To the present writer they are associated inextricably with the pure tenor voice of John McCormack. Moore can be quoted against himself in every context except this. He never lost faith in the *Melodies*. But he interrupted the flow of the new inspiration to write two tedious satires in the Dryden manner; they were published anonymously by Carpenter in London and fell flat. The only interest of these pieces now is the insight they give to what Moore was thinking when they appeared in 1808. *Corruption and Intolerance* the volume containing them was called; there must have been some sale, because a second edition was published. Here is the first glimpse of Moore with his concern for his country renewed. He had still to find a form more suitable to his temperament in which to express it.

Another anonymous poem—*The Sceptic*—made no stir; and again its interest now is the light it throws on Moore's mind. Nowhere else does he discuss his beliefs. His thought never goes so deep or winds so intricately that there is any breathlessness in following him; he ends in his little boat rocking on the wavelets close to a sunny shore.

> Hail, modest Ignorance, thou goal and prize,
> Thou last, best knowledge of the simple wise!

Moore's *Letter to the Roman Catholics of Dublin*, his first serious and considerable writing in prose, published in 1810, was the fruit of the reflections of this time. It is proof of a new and genuine seriousness, a maturing. He recalled the independence of the Irish Church in the time of the Irish Kings, when such matters as the fixing of Easter and monks' tonsures were contested with Rome. That anti-canonical boldness was justified retrospectively by canonisation. 'It was not till the Reformation added religious schism to the differences already existing between these countries that Ireland was effectually thrown into the arms of Rome. I ask whether you can think without shame and indignation that for a long period you have been the only people in Europe (with the exception of a few petty States in the neighbourhood of the Pope) who have sunk so low in ecclesiastical vasselage, as to place their whole hierarchy at the disposal of the Roman Court?'

But his most telling argument was the undeniable fact that in 1799 when the Union with Britain was in preparation ten Irish bishops were willing to concede the power of veto to the Crown in return for emancipation. When O'Connell—nine years later—said it would be the death-warrant of the Faith, the bishops decided that it was 'inexpedient at the moment'. Later they were to say that only the Pope could legislate in the matter.

Moore was beginning to find his way. Mercifully, he abandoned weighty satire for persiflage, for which he had a talent far beyond all his contemporaries, Byron excepted; and the *Melodies* which alone of his work have survived in popular memory were published in this decade.

The story of the *Melodies* began in 1800, when Moore was approached by Thomson to put words to Haydn's music. (With his offer, he enclosed the *Edinburgh Review* which led to the duel with Jeffrey.) Moore did not resume negotiations with Thomson. But he was approached in Dublin by two young music sellers, William and James Power—William acted as spokesman. He suggested that Stevenson should write the music for lyrics to be collected from Irish poets. Moore was enthusiastic.

He wrote to Stevenson:

'I feel very anxious that a Work of this Kind should be undertaken. We have too long neglected the only Talent for which our English neighbours ever deigned to allow us any Credit. Our National Music has never been properly collected; and while the Composers of the Continent have enriched their Operas and Sonatas with Melodies borrowed from Ireland, very often without even the Honesty of Acknowledgement, we have left these Treasures in a great degree unclaimed and fugitive. Thus our Airs like too many of our Countrymen, for want of Protection at home, have passed into the Service of Foreigners . . .

'The task which you propose to me, of adapting words to these airs, is by no means easy. The poet, who would follow the various sentiments which they express, must feel and understand that rapid fluctation of spirits, that unaccountable mixture of gloom and levity, which composes the character of my countrymen, and has deeply tinged their music. Even in their liveliest strains we find some melancholy note intrude—some minor third or flat seventh—which throws its shade as it passes and makes even mirth interesting. If Burns had been an Irishman (and I would willingly give up all our claims on Ossian for him) his heart would have been proud of such music, and his genius would have made it immortal.'

James Power went to London; William remained in Dublin; as a result Moore had all his future dealings with James, although William had been the first brother to approach him. This was to have significance when the brothers quarrelled, as they did eventually. By that time James was—under stress—complaining of Moore's use of him as an agent and banker. But that was far in the future. Before the talks began, Moore had written *O Breathe not his Name*, which was his first public tribute to Emmet. James in London and William in Dublin published the first number of the *Melodies* in April, 1808.

Their success was immediate. There was no further mention of 'other' poets. The arrangement made with Moore was that he should go into society in London and popularise the songs. As a retainer he was to receive £500 a year. This continued for twenty-seven years, and was his only regular source of income.

Already, writing from his Dublin lodgings at 22 Molesworth Street, Dublin, Moore after a few months is drawing on James Power. He offers to pay back the first advance 'partly or entirely' in songs as James pleases. While not asking James to keep this dark, he says he would prefer to tell William about it himself. 'He would have a right to think me very extravagant of late, knowing how much he has accommodated me in; but the truth is a very expensive honour has been conferred upon me, in the shape of admission to our leading club here . . .' The club was probably Daly's in College Green, of which the Kildare Street Club was an off-shoot.

At the same time Moore is writing to Carpenter in London, who has the less enviable task of selling his anonymous satires, to ask for aid. Money was a great question with him just then. '*Money I must* have, if the Muses were to die for it', he wrote to Lady Donegal, to whom the *Irish Melodies* were dedicated. He enquires about her own finances, but in a sympathetic spirit, not with any predatory designs. That was not Moore's way. A Mrs Ready pressed money on him. He refused to take it.

He complains of Carpenter's nearness. He had refused to finance a journey to London; and William Power would have been surprised at the tone of a letter to Moore's mother. 'I quite threw away the *Melodies*; they will make that little smooth fellow's fortune.'

Notoriety, certainly, and fame of a sort, Moore had enjoyed since a very early age—as is not seldom the case with the musically gifted. That art is the most innate. But now he was to find his true medium. Verse and music came to him together; they came to him as he walked up and down in the fresh air. He could not divorce them.

He did not write verse with the facility its manner suggests. If he questioned, he envied Byron the speed with which he composed; and the further his verse was from song the more he had to labour at it. *Lalla Rookh* took him five years to write. Composing to an air lent him wings. It purged his verses of their principal faults and their adolescent sensuality. And always he was aware of the needs of the singer's contribution.

Moore's shortcomings as well as his gifts contributed to his success as a song-maker. Hazlitt, who has to be heard when it comes to any final assessment of Moore as a poet, is the most powerful voice against even the *Melodies*. Listen to him.

'If these national airs do indeed express the soul of impassioned feeling in his countrymen, the case of Ireland is hopeless. If these prettinesses pass for patriotism, if a country can hear from its heart's core only these vapid, varnished sentiments, lip-deep, and let its tears of blood evaporate in an empty conceit, let it be governed as it has been. There are here no tones to waken Liberty, to console Humanity. Mr Moore converts the wild harp of Erin into a musical snuff-box.'

The case could not be more forcibly made. After that there is no need to call upon any further witnesses for the prosecution. Hazlitt was prepared only to praise Moore as a satirist. His own gift was for prose, and a prose that was always at its best in denunciation. Moore backed his claim to remembrance on the *Melodies* and, in the event, he was right. Hazlitt has been proved wrong by the suffrage of time. Who reads or knows or remembers Moore's satires? Who has not got the first lines, at least, of half a dozen of his *Melodies* by heart? How many poets have written better *first* lines?

It is not a critical test; it will not pass in the academies, but who, given the choice, would rather have an existence in the foot-notes of scholars than in the hearts of living men?

Leonard Strong, in his sympathetic study of Moore, insisted on the point that the poet never intended that the words should be printed without the accompanying music. On their own they suffered as songs must from the imperative necessity of simplicity. Subtleties are not only wasted; they are disastrous; the effect of singing is immediate.

James Joyce, in his passionate concern for his awkward children, intent on promoting Georgio as a singer, advised him to study Moore. A few days later (18th February 1935) Joyce writes to Georgio and his wife Helen. 'Buy Moore's Irish Melodies and learn the following

a) Fly Not Yet
b) O, ye dead
c) Quick We have but a second (this needs a lot of breath)
d) The Time I lost in wooing
e) Silent, O Moyle (This is a lovely air but G. should study the legend of Lir's daughters).'

The second verse of 'O, Ye Dead', he adds in a postscript, should be sung almost in a whisper.

'The lovely arias for deep voices among Thomas Moore's *Irish Melodies* are "O Ye Dead" (sung by Plunket Greene), "Silent, O Moyle" with harp accompaniment, "The Time I've lost in Wooing" (for an encore) . . . Moyle is that part of the Irish Sea which is now called St George's Channel. The three daughters of Lir (the Celtic Neptune and the original of Shakespeare's King Lear) were changed into swans and must fly over those leaden waters for centuries until the sound of the first Christian bell in Ireland breaks the spell.'

And he came back to the songs in a subsequent letter. They must have often heard him singing 'Silent, O Moyle'. The best setting was by Sir Henry Bishop. Joyce knew the *Melodies* thoroughly.

According to Stanislaus Joyce, *Oh, ye Dead* gave his brother the theme of the story in *Dubliners*. It is very Joycean in feeling. The first stanza is as exquisite as anything Moore ever wrote.

> Oh, ye Dead! oh, ye Dead! whom we know by the
>   light you give
> From your cold gleaming eyes, though you move like
>   men who live,
> Why leave you thus your graves,
> In far-off fields and waves,
> Where the worm and the sea-bird only know your bed,
>   To haunt this spot where all
>   Those eyes that wept your fall,
> And the hearts that wail'd you, like your own, lie dead?

Joyce's enthusiasm for Moore is known only to those who have delved into three formidable volumes of the collected letters. For the general reader Moore is known as one of the targets of his derision. He used the same expression to damn Moore that Yeats employed—they lent it to each other, perhaps—calling him a Firbolg, one of the small dark Celts who were in Ireland when the Gaels arrived.

Yeats and Joyce agreed about Moore the man—how much did they know about him?—but Yeats did not share Joyce's admiration for his work. When Leonard Strong asked permission to dedicate his book on Moore to Yeats, the great man assented and—making presumably his best effort in the circumstances—admitted to liking *two* of Moore's lyrics.

Yeats was not more exigeant than Joyce, nor had he a better ear; why this very different assessment of Moore? It derives, I believe, from the circumstance that Joyce was a singer with an ear for music; Yeats was tone deaf, and could not recognise the tune of the National Anthem. Moore, had he known the two men, would not have been surprised by this disparity.

On May 4th, 1828, Moore breakfasting with two friends: 'Some discussion with respect to Byron's *chanting* method of repeating poetry, which I professed my strong dislike of. Observe, in general, that it is the men who have the worst ears for music that *sing* out poetry in this manner, giving no nice

perception of the difference there ought to be between animated
reading and *chant*.'

This, Russell observed in an editorial note, was very much
the style of reciting of the admirers of Pope in the eighteenth
century. It was also very much the style of Yeats; and Moore
would not have liked it. Yeats intoned.

Hector Berlioz, when he was being embraced by Mlle Patti,
gave Moore credit for the expression of a feeling which had
escaped the attention of Shakespeare and Balzac, when he
wrote

'Believe me, if all these endearing young charms
Which I gaze on so fondly to-day,
Were to change by to-morrow, and fleet in my arms,
Like fairy-gifts fading away,
Thou wouldst still be adored, as this moment thou art,
Let thy loveliness fade as it will
And round the dear ruin each wish of my heart
Would entwine itself verdantly still.

'It is not while beauty and youth are thine own,
And thy cheeks unprofaned by a tear,
That the fervour and faith of a soul can be known,
To which time will but make thee more dear:
No, the heart that has truly loved never forgets,
But as truly loves on to the close,
As the sun-flower turns on her god when he sets,
The same look which she turn'd when he rose.'

Hazlitt would have had Moore compose something as stirring
as the *Marseillaise*. But he was not intent on raising street
barricades; his purpose was other; he sought to charm. The
tocsin does not sound in *The Minstrel Boy*, or if it does, not so
loud as to shake the teacups; but it was a considerable achieve-
ment to have brought Ireland's story into those London lives.
Again we are at sea as to the impression made by the words
unless we can imagine Moore singing them.

Songs about Brian Boru and Tara's halls were not calculated
to lead to bloodshed, whatever the audience. A threnody
that is expressly addressed to one whose memory could arouse

contemporary feeling is not identified by Moore in the notes with which he afterwards illuminated his text. Put beside one he wrote when he heard that his recently married uncle had died at Madeira—

> It is not the tear at this moment shed,
> When the cold turf has just been laid o'er him,
> That can tell how beloved was the friend that's fled,
> Or how deep in our hearts we deplore him.

Moore's lament for Emmet is in the same strain of gentle melancholy, and not less discreet.

> Oh! breathe not his name, let it sleep in the shade,
> Where cold and unhonour'd his relics are laid;
> Sad, silent and dark be the tears that we shed,
> As the night-dew that falls on the grass o'er his head.
>
> But the night-dew that falls, though in silence it weeps,
> Shall brighten with verdure the grass where he sleeps;
> And the tear that we shed, though in secret it rolls,
> Shall long keep his memory green in our souls.

The melody that has a truly martial air, the one that, according to Moore, made Emmet wish he were at the head of twenty thousand marching men, is *Let Erin Remember*. The late Professor W. F. Trench tried to persuade the Irish Government to substitute this for the second-rate National Anthem that was adopted at the setting up of the Irish Free State, but without success.

The Last Rose of Summer, *Oft in the Stilly Night* and *Believe me if all those Endearing young Charms* are almost embarrassingly sentimental; but they are irresistible. Sometimes Moore let humour in, as in *The Young May Moon*.

> The young May moon is beaming, love,
> The glow-worm's lamp is gleaming, love,
> How sweet to rove
> Through Morna's grove,
> When the drowsy world is dreaming, love!

Then awake! the heavens look bright, my dear,
'Tis never too late for delight, my dear,
And the best of all ways
To lengthen our days
Is to steal a few hours from the night, my dear.

Now all the world is sleeping, love,
And the Sage, his star-watch keeping, love
    And I whose star,
      More glorious far,
Is the eye from that casement peeping, love.
Then awake! till rise of sun, my dear,
The Sage's glass, we'll shun, my dear,
Or, in watching the flight
Of bodies of light,
He might happen to take thee for one, my dear.

The most subtly exquisite of the *Melodies* is *At the Mid Hour
of Night*:

At the mid hour of night, when stars are weeping,
    I fly
To the lone vale we loved, when life shone warm in
    thine eye;
And I think oft, if spirits can steal from the regions
    of air,
To revisit past scenes of delight, thou wilt come to
    me there,
And tell me our love is remember'd, even in the sky,
Then I will sing the wild song 'twas once such pleasure
    to hear,
When our voices, commingling, breathed, like one,
    on the ear;
And, as Echo far off through the vale my sad orison
    rolls,
I think, oh my love! 'tis thy voice, from the Kingdom
    of Souls,
Faintly answering still the notes that once were so dear.

Tennyson, the most fastidious of metrists, might not have
been expected to enthuse over Moore's lyrics, and he would

probably have not taken into account the fact that they had to be supplemented by music and the human voice. But, even he, approved *Oft in the Stilly Night*, muttering 'O si sic omnia'.

There has been from the beginning controversy about Moore's use of Irish traditional airs, and at times he has been accused of mutilating them for his own purposes. The marvellous fraud of Ossian deceived the western world; it was an aspect of the Celtic revival which itself was a romantic reaction against classical restraint. In Ireland there was a new enthusiasm among scholars to research in the Celtic past. The harp became a symbol for it because the traditional harper was becoming an extinct species, and he was the last living link with the pre-Norman society of the tribes.

Bunting noted down and published Irish airs in 1796 and 1809. Smollet Holding published another selection in 1806. Bunting growled, resenting Moore's popularity; but there was never any question of Moore's stealing from other men. The charge of distortion was made, and most authoritatively by Charles Villiers Stanford as late as 1895. 'There is scarcely a melody which Moore left unaltered and unspoilt', he wrote in a book the title of which proclaimed a pedant on the pounce—*The Irish Melodies of Thomas Moore. The Original Airs Restored.* One of the tunes which Stanford accuses Moore of having taken from Bunting and altering was procured by the latter from George Petrie in 1839 and published in 1840. Moore learnt it from Holden in 1806. This sort of controversy inevitably breaks out when workers in any field find others engaged in competition. The instinct of monopoly is universal. Dogs mark out their territories in their own way; they do it themselves. Scholars are apt to perform that office for others. Moore's reputation has been rescued by other scholars, who have justified alterations and discovered some in Bunting's work. To enable music composed for harp strings to be sung by the human voice inevitably involved adaptation.

The attack of the musicians was predictably reinforced by pure Gaels who resented the cut of Moore's coat. Some of them accused him of vulgarising the Irish originals; but he must be acquitted on this charge and disqualified from praise because he had no knowledge of Irish and could not read a word of it.

He had ears only for the music. Moore anticipated some of the later criticism. He praised the work of his 'ingenious co-adjutator', Sir John Stevenson, who had from the first been blamed for having spoiled the simplicity of the original airs. He maintained that Stevenson would be upheld by 'those who study the delicate artifices of composition'.

The happy arrangement by which the Powers provided Moore with an unusual income and he repaid them with songs led not only to trouble between composer and publisher; the Powers fell out among themselves. Moore did his best to keep out of the fratricidal struggle. If William was the first Power he met, James in London had become, to all intents, his agent.

A sale of James Power's correspondence with Moore, after the publisher's death, gave an opportunity to Thomas Crofton Croker, who had a crow to pluck with Moore (who was dead by then) to expose the poet as an exploiter of his good-natured publisher.

Moore came to London to see Power and question his account, to appear at a St Patrick's dinner, and to look into a projected nomination as Parliamentary candidate for Limerick as a supporter of Daniel O'Connell.

According to Power, whenever he tried to get Moore to talk about business he was 'always in a flutter about lords and ladies and lobsters'. Moore, after fourteen years, woke up to the fact that Power was deducting from the £500 a year he paid Moore a contribution towards Stevenson's charges for setting the *Melodies* to music. Because he was so much overdrawn Moore had never looked at the accounts before he lighted accidentally upon this information.

There is nothing to learn from the recital of grievances. Moore's easy-going ways, and his chronic failure to follow Mr Micawber's advice, was at the root of the trouble. What Croker failed to point out was that Power owed the success of his business to Moore. And Moore's exploitation of the relationship—the making use of Power as a general factotum—was something that grew up and was, no doubt, encouraged because Moore was more important to Power than Power was to Moore, who made his best contracts with Murray and Longmans.

The letters show a most amiable relationship existing before the rift. Moore invites the Powers to come to Sloperton for a change of air, but he certainly made use of their house in London as a convenience, and, no doubt, with their delighted acquiescence, when it suited him. As well he was forever giving Power commissions.

The letters to Power are of particular interest because Moore treats him like an old family retainer in whom he can confide, certain of loyalty. Power was his best man and in the secret of his wedding. He tells Power of his successes as a child might regale his former nurse with news of her charge's progress. He assumes that Power is always at his service, and addresses him formally in letters. Precedence was rigidly observed at the time. Moira addressed Moore as if he were a total stranger. Moore's form of address to Lansdowne was always formal. But Power kept a shop; so did John Murray, and this made all the difference. Even though Moore's father had been a grocer, he was himself independent and—by definition—a gentleman. Publishers, keepers of book shops, were not on his level. They would not expect to be invited to great houses. Talent could gain the entry here. But it was better to be in parliament. A statesman had the entrée. Another of Moore's letters to Power, written many years later, makes the position quite clear.

Sloperton,
October 27 1830

'My dear Sir—I send you some more of the *Summer Fête*, which will still spread out to two or three hundred lines more—all good for your letter-press book. I inclose also Lady Headfort's letter which you will return to me some time or other. You had already seen the mention of poor Stevenson's paralytic attack in the newspapers.

'It will not be necessary for you to make provision for the Bill which (having found your stray letter) I see will come due the 26th of November—as I had already apprized the Longmans of my intention to renew it—but I shall perhaps have to ask you to let me *increase* the sum, as my resources are at present in a most deplorable state.

'I have been passing three days with the Duchess of Kent

and our little future Queen at Erle-State Park and we had a great deal of music. The Duchess sang some of my Melodies with me better than I ever heard them performed—I promised to send her some of the songs of mine she most liked, and I should be glad if you would get them bound together (not *too* expensively) for me to present to her . . .

'She had promised me copies of some very pretty German things she sang.'

Yours very truly,
Thomas Moore'

'I should be glad to have my hamper of wine down as soon as you conveniently can send it.

'Bessy will be obliged to you to buy her a slop-bason, and another bason a size smaller, of the same pattern as the egg-cup inclosed—and they can come with some things which are to be sent to your house for me.'

THOMAS CROFTON CROKER said that Moore was always acting. He was certainly one of those people who dress for the part
and perform. Even in his college days, after taking a stand on
principle, his first concern was to find out what impression he
had made. One of his first ambitions was to play Harlequin.
His singing performances gave his exhibitionist tendencies their
most appropriate outlet; nevertheless he kept up a flirtation
with the stage until he married an actress.

It seems appropriate to set that, the wisest action of his life,
in the context of Moore's work in the theatre. The ubiquitous
Joe Atkinson, who himself had aspirations as a dramatist, was
Moore's mentor in this as in much else. When the young poet
first came to London he had introductions to the theatre world
as well as to the drawing-rooms. Private theatricals were an
obvious way of entertaining people with too much time on their
hands. There was a craze for them at this period, and we know
from *Mansfield Park* that it was not approved by the godly and
serious. Moore joined a group in London which performed in
January 1807 for the benefit of the Royal Hospital.

There was at this time a flourishing theatre festival in
Kilkenny. A theatre had been built there by Robert Owenson
(Lady Morgan's father) in 1794, and the project had failed; but,
in 1802, Richard Power of Kilfane, a local magnate with a
passion for theatricals, formed a group to put on a season of
plays for charity. The actors were to be amateurs, the actresses
engaged in Dublin. As Joe Atkinson was involved, it is not
surprising to find that Moore was introduced to the group.
He made his first appearance in October 1808 as David in *The
Rivals* and Mungo in *The Padlock*. He played Trudge in *Inkele
and Yarico*. As well he was heard during the month singing his
Melodies, not only in the theatre, for while the festival was in
progress, there was an endless round of entertainment—dances,

shoots, balls. The hotels gave public dances; there were *déjeuners* at the Castle, where the Countess of Ormonde was in residence. Lord Mountjoy's costume in one performance was reckoned to be worth eight thousand pounds.

Reports of the proceedings were published in the London papers; it was a great social event, and Moore had a triumph. As David in *The Rivals* 'he kept the audience in a roar by his Yorkshire dialect and rustic simplicity'. 'The delight and darling of the Kilkenny audiences appear to be *Anacreon Moore . . .* who speaks and moves in a way that indicates genius in every turn.' So spake *The Leinster Journalist*.

Moore returned in the following season and was again the principal attraction. In the curtain-raiser of the first night Moore played Peeping Tom, and Lady Godiva was Miss E. Dyke. This is the first time the poet's name appears in conjunction with his wife-to-be.

There was something characteristically Moorelike in the circumstances. In the previous year Miss A. Dyke had acted with the company. This season she was joined by her sisters, Mary and Elizabeth, but she was called on all occasions Bessy or Betsy. As Bessy, Moore immortalised her.

The Dublin Satirist, intent only on distraction, and not having to mind its manners when referring to hired play-actresses, described the sisters as 'frivolous'. But they were 'certainly pretty and possess an unconquerable propensity to coquetry'.

In the following season Tom was back with four extra parts—old favourites were revived at the Festival. Two Miss Dykes acted with the company, but not Miss E. A benefit performance had been organised for the sisters in Dublin in the meanwhile, when a Miss Smith recited Moore's *Melologue on National Music*, a composition which he had recited himself at the Festival in 1810. Then it received the adulation to which he had grown accustomed.

'We hardly ever heard a more beautiful composition, and never, perhaps, a more delightful piece of recitation. Mr Moore's voice is to a degree musical, his accent pure, his elocution articulate, and his manner simple, spirited, and feeling.'

The Festival ran for three weeks and concluded with a banquet when 'the sweetest of the poets was among them'.

These theatrical ventures of Moore are never referred to in his surviving correspondence except in letters to James Corry, one of the founders, with whom Moore planned to write a history of the Kilkenny entertainments. It came to nothing. In 1811 Moore acted in one play only and recited his *Melologue*. Miss E. Dyke was back with the company.

After the season closed, Moore went to London, returned to Dublin, went back to London, took lodgings in Bury Street. On the 25th March 1811, in St Martin's Church, Moore and Elizabeth Dyke were married. Their witnesses were James Power and Anne Jane Dyke. The bride was aged sixteen; the groom almost exactly twice her age.

The information available about Moore's Bessy is meagre. We only know from his diaries, the evidence of anyone who met her, and her behaviour in every crisis, that she was at least as good as he maintained on every occasion that he referred to her. For an actress, she was remarkable in her dislike of the lime-light. It was as much by her choice as his that she stayed in the country and left him alone to make his way in society.

Portraits of Moore are plentiful; a miniature of Bessy was exhibited in Dublin in 1879; in the 'Moore Centenary Scrap-book', T. M. Ray made the following note: 'Very light brown hair in profuse broad curls at both sides of face—very hand-some face—fine full blue eyes—nose longish, slight bend towards aquiline—mouth rather broad—lips handsome—neck bare—face oval but inclined to roundness.' Two unnamed chalk drawings in the front of Bessy Moore's Album, until recently preserved at Bowood, answer this bald description so faithfully that they must be portraits.

Of the wooing Moore left no particulars, and he kept the wedding a secret from his family for several months. In his diaries there is one retrospective reference. Twenty years later, when Bessy came over to Ireland with Moore, they stopped at Kilkenny. He noted in his diary. 'In looking along the walk by the river, under the Castle, my sweet Bess and I recollected the time we used, in our love-making days, to stroll for hours there together. We did not love half so really then as we do now.'

There is no explanation of Bessy's absence from the Festival in the 1810 season. A cryptic letter to Lady Donegal—in which

Moore confided even his misdemeanours—hardly hinted at a romance.

'So much for the main subject of my epistle; and now, having made such a bad hand of what I have not done, I wish I could give you even a tolerable account of what I *have* done; but, I don't know how it is, both my mind and heart appear to have lain for some time completely *fallow*, and even the usual crop of *wild oats* have not been forthcoming. What is the reason for this? I believe there is in every man's life (at least in every man who has lived as if he knew how to live) one blank interval, which takes place at that period when the gay desires of youth are just gone off, and he has not yet made up his mind as to the feelings or pursuits that succeed them—when the last blossom has fallen away, and yet the fruit continues to look harsh and unpromising—a kind of *interregnum*: which takes place upon the demise of *love*, before ambition and worldliness have seated themselves on the vacant throne.'

This evidence could be used to support an unfavourable version of Moore's love affair. One came, inevitably, from the Crokers. When John Wilson Croker wrote to *The Times* in 1853 to protest against references to himself in Russell's *Memoirs* of Moore, his namesake, Thomas Crofton Croker, supplied him with information about Bessy. She was born, according to him, on board ship in Plymouth Harbour on November 15, 1793, but a baptismal record in the Stoke Damerel Parish Church says, 'January 9, 1795, Elizabeth, daughter of Thomas and Joanna Dikes'. Crofton Croker sketched in her family background for his angry friend:

'[The] father, old Dyke, gave me a few lessons in a Street off Patrick Street in Cork, after I left *my Bishops* dancing School in George's Street, conducted by Fountaine. He (Dyke) wandered about to teach dancing at the Schools at Fermoy . . . and Middleton School, and became a great favourite by making puppet Shews for the boys. I think I have some of the scenery of one painted by him . . . and it really is a very clever scene painting . . . But I well remember he was a drunken fellow, who generally brought home with him a black eye or two from his weekly visits to Fermoy and Middleton, and I think my lessons in that or in any piece of tuition under his instruction did not exceed half a dozen in consequence of some desperate affray in which a poker was used to the disadvantage of a very dirty wife who was cooking his dinner. It is quite clear to my mind that . all the three Miss Dykes were dancers originally however after- wards they may have been promoted . . .'

Croker was anxious to disparage; to suggest that the girls were originally dancers was a side-swipe at their morals.

John Wilson Croker had another correspondent as a result of his correspondence in *The Times*. Thomas Mulock* wrote to him, March 14th, 1854, 'By the way I knew Bessy (Dyke) before Moore was acquainted with her—and my clear opinion was that Moore wished to have her on other than conjugal terms—which however her sharp English mother prevented by forbidding his further visits until a formal proposal was made— this fell within my own knowledge'.

In another letter to J. W. Croker, Crofton recalled dancing with the youngest Miss Dyke 'in a wretched ruinous house'. She blacked the eye of one Spencer Vassall and kicked him downstairs. This was Anne, Bessy's sister and, if the story is true, Croker was eight, Vassall ten, and Miss Dyke eleven or twelve years of age on the riotous occasion.

Very probably Dyke père was incorrigible, gifted and improvident. If he were prosperous the girls would not have had to earn their livings as children. But they would not have been invited regularly to Kilkenny if their mother had not kept them in good order. Croker's insinuation about Moore's intentions is, at any rate, a credit to their mother's care, and only malice called that sharpness. Moreover, all three girls turned out well. When Mary married John R. Duff of the Dublin Theatre in 1810 she had already made a name for herself in Shakespearean rôles. She went to America, where she won a reputation on the stage, and her career has been recorded in the *Dictionary of American Biography* and in a book *Mrs Duff*, by Joseph N. Ireland. Anne married William H. Murray of the Theatre Royal, Edinburgh, in 1819. She also made stage appearances in Shakespeare plays, and her husband was eminent in the theatrical profession. The Dykes were obviously exceptional girls, and it is more than likely if they inherited

* See Crabb Robinson's *Diaries* for an account of this saturnine man.

talent from their sire, their mother supplied what had been deficient in his character.

In Ireland's biography of Mary Duff, he asserts that Moore 'found himself passionately in love with her'. It was only when she rejected his offers of marriage that Moore turned his attention to her younger sister. He quoted in support of this a poem which began:

> Mary, I believe thee true,
> And I was blessed in this believing;
> And now I mourn that e'er I knew
> A girl so fair and so deceiving—
> Fare thee well! Fare thee well!

As evidence it is unsatisfactory because, like other poems which have been used to compromise Moore, it was published in *The Poems of Thomas Little* many years before Moore met the Dyke girls or trod the boards in Kilkenny.

Julian Charles Young, a clergyman, in his *Journal* cited an unnamed authority for a rather melodramatic account of Bessy's hurling herself from a window when Moore approached her too amorously. The Moore family doctor, Philip Crampton, was summoned at 2 a.m. when Bessy, bruised and unconscious, was picked up off the pavement. The story is as tall as the hour seems incompatible; but the determination of the action is certainly in character. It fits in with Moore's cryptic references to his courtship.

There is still extant an attempt in Bessy's handwriting to reply to her lover in verse. It tells us why she did not feel happy at grand parties; it is the inarticulateness of a simple, honest, loving heart.

> 'I'll fly from the world dearest man with thee
> Without thee there's no pleasure in it',

it begins; and after a short struggle with spelling and syntax, she assures him

> 'that when Life's Glass is quite run we will each other
>   embrace
> And thy kiss sign Bessy's Passport to Heaven.'

Whatever determined Moore to marry, it was not prudent counsel. His finances were in a parlous state. He regretted his too hasty sale of copyright in the *Melodies* to the 'smooth little fellow' William Power; he writes to James Carpenter who had taken advantage of his inexperience at the beginning of their connection and asks permission to 'make use of your name' to help him through 'a little hobble'. A few weeks previously he had asked Carpenter to advance him his fare to London to see a publication through the press. It was probably *A Letter to the Roman Catholics of Ireland*. In requesting this he seems to have forgotten his complaints, two years previously, when Carpenter refused to advance his fare, thinking, no doubt, that Moore in Dublin doing nothing would spend less than Moore in London on business.

In a letter to Lady Donegal he confesses 'I am not doing much; indeed the downright necessity which I feel of doing something is the great reason why I do almost nothing. These things should come of their own accord, and I hate to make a *conscript* of my Muse; but I cannot carry on the war without her, so to it she must go. London is out of the question for me, till I have got ammunition in my pocket, and I hope by April to have some combustibles ready . . .' Not long after this he writes to James Power to regret the necessity for 'drawing upon you very soon'.

In later years Rogers was to bewail Moore's extravagance. While Bessy kept their home running on a guinea a week, Moore on his trips to London let money fly through his fingers, on cabs, gloves, and all the exigent demands of a fashionable appearance. His efforts to establish himself in a serious political figure had failed. His *Letter to the Roman Catholics* was masterly, but he was too well known in his character as an entertainer to attract support in any other. Writing in April 1808 to Lady Donegal, Moore told her to deny a rumour that her sister had heard that he was in love. 'I have not felt one flutter these three years.'

In the very long letter to Lady Donegal, written two years later, from which I have already quoted, he does not sound like a man in love or in any certainty about anything. He is still hoping that the Whigs may come in to office, to his advantage.

'When I mention my hopes from the Whigs, I found them chiefly upon the impression which my last pamphlet has made among them.' He had had letters 'of the most kind' from Grattan, Lord Lansdowne, Lord Morris, the Duke of Bedford, etc. From Stockholm a letter came to inform him that he had been elected a Knight of St Joachim, an honour conferred upon Nelson. He declined the honour. The *Melodies* had now reached their fourth number, but Moore always anticipated his earnings on these.

In December he writes from Birmingham to inform Lady Donegal and her sister that he is on his way. There is not a word about Bessy or even a hint. He expects reproaches for his failure to come up to the hopes of his friends. 'All I entreat of you is that, for a little while at least, you will neither ask me what I *have* done, or even what I *mean* to do, but draw upon your *first* good opinion of me (if that fund be not entirely exhausted) to enable you *still* to look forward with a hope of something good and respectable from me.'

By January (1811) he is again in Dublin, writing lyrically to Lady Donegal with young rose trees under his window and impudent birds peeping out as if it were May-day; 'on my right is the "hanging wood" of Kilmainham, and from my left I catch the oderiferous breezes of a farmyard.' He intends to return to London in a fortnight but his stay will be short. In Dublin he is staying a good deal at home with his father and mother, eating boiled veal and Irish stew. In a P.S. he adds 'I have kept Cupid too long for my drawing-boy, and as he is quite as blind as Fortune, it is no wonder that nothing capital has come forth, but I have dismissed him this good while'.

Back in London, Moore met his old friend Douglas, whom he hadn't seen or heard from since he came back on his ship from America. After an hour's conversation, Douglas said: 'Now, my dear little fellow, you know I'm grown rich. There is at present seven hundred pounds of mine in Coutts bank; here is a blank cheque which you may fill up while I am away, for as much of that as you may want.'

He could not have made that generous offer at a more crucial time; but Moore refused the loan. It was, as he said, 'an unexampled instance of a man bringing back the warmth of friendship so unchilled, after an absence of five years'.

Why was Moore so very secretive about his marriage? By inviting James Power to act as witness he made it clear that no glory was attached to the office. Power, as he was later to complain, was put to every possible use by Moore, including that of his 'boot-black'. Their friendship was that of business associates, and when business prospers few are closer. Power did not mix with or meet any of Moore's friends in London society. And as Moore, given his nature, would have had to confide in someone, Power was very suitable. How long it was before he told his closer friends is a matter of conjecture. Because of Russell's careless editing of the letters, particularly in the matter of dates, this has been confused. According to Russell, Moore wrote to tell the news to his parents in May, two months after the marriage, and this has been accepted by subsequent biographers; but the authoritative Dowden edition of the correspondence corrects this. Mary Godfrey, who seems in her letters to be more sisterly than any of his other correspondents, wrote to him on September 22, 'Be sure, my dear Moore, that if you have got an amiable, sensible wife, extremely attached to you, as I am certain you have, it is only in the long run of life that you can know the full value of the treasure you possess'.

Writing to her sister, Lady Donegal, on October 28, about his opera, Moore concludes, 'I have nothing more to say now, but that I am as tranquil and happy as my heart could wish, and that I most anxiously long for the opportunity of presenting *somebody* to you. If you do not make haste, I shall have *two somebodies* to present to you'.

In a letter written within a few days of his marriage Moore deliberately deceived his mother by saying, 'I have at last got a little bedroom about two miles out of town, where I shall fly now and then for a morning's work'. He did not mention that a wife was in it; and the time of day was misleading.

From this it would seem that Moore could not pluck up the courage all summer to break the news to his closest friends; but some years later when Moore introduced Joe Atkinson to Bessy she burst into tears at the recollection of advice Joe had given Moore against his marrying her.

Moore's relationship with Atkinson was a very old one, how close only letters could show, and these are not available. On more than one occasion, writing to his mother, Tom warns her against Joe's incontinent, good-natured tongue. But yet he let him into the secret of Bessy; or was it that Moore boasted of her as a conquest—a matter which Atkinson as a friend and a man of the world would exercise discretion about—and then found himself in a situation in which marriage was the only manner in which he could enjoy Bessy's favours? Her virtue, rather than her mother's superintendence—both perhaps—holding her firm against surrender. Having gone far in confidence, Moore was obliged to go further. But when he did marry, he cannot have told Atkinson. And Joe may well have been priding himself that he had saved his friend from his folly. In a letter written some years after this to James Corry, Moore says he sent two letters a week to Atkinson 'for my mother, and she answers them punctually'.

As for his telling his family—the date is uncertain, but it was not until November at the earliest, because of the reference to parties in Bessy's honour. This is the November letter which Russell erroneously put back to May:

'My dearest Mother,
  'I have just seen Lady Donegal, as kind and delightful as ever. Her praises of *you*, too, were not the *worst* recommendations she returned with. I breakfast with her on Monday and dine to meet her at Rogers's on Tuesday; and there is a person to be of both parties whom you little dream of, but whom I shall introduce to your notice next week. God bless you, my own darling mother,
                                            Ever your own,
                                            Tom.'

In a subsequent letter (in which he refers to the fact that he always wrote home twice a week) he mentions a letter from his father, who was evidently despondent and spoke of letting the house. 'If I thought, for an instant, that this resolution arose in any degree from any feeling of *hopelessness* or disappointment at my marriage, it would make me truly miserable; but I hope, and, indeed, am confident, dearest mother, that you do me the justice to be *quite* sure that this event has only drawn closer every dear tie by which I was bound to you; and that, while my readiness to do everything towards your comfort remains the same, my power of doing so will be, please God! much increased by the regularity and economy of the life I am entering upon.'

He is more garrulous than usual, discusses the wisdom of letting the house, promises to continue to lend support and ends on two characteristic notes. 'If my father wants some money now, let him only apprise me, and draw on Power for it without hesitation. I have not a minute to write more: my next letter shall go through Lord Byron.'

Moore's marriage was improvident; it was so completely at variance with his predilection for fashionable society that it embarrassed him to try to explain it to his parents. Was he, in fact, forced into the marriage by the watchful Mrs Dyke? Why did he not seek a bride who might have improved his fortunes?

To answer the last question first: society was so constituted in Moore's day that he could only marry into an aristocratic family if he could persuade a light-headed girl to run away with him. No family would have consented to the marriage. Rogers stated the case, and in doing so explained the manner in which Moore conducted his married life:

'Indeed, society is so constituted in England that it is useless for celebrated artists to think of bringing their families into the highest circles, where themselves are admitted only on account of their genius. Their wives and daughters must be content to remain at home.'

At Kilkenny Moore was the lion in a very fashionable gathering, by Irish standards. If his charm had conquered in every other circle, in Bermuda and Philadelphia, as well as in London, a small-part actress, aged fourteen (or sixteen, as Bessy believed) was likely to be overcome if he paid her conspicuous attention. No doubt, he had slipped out of many similar situations. If Bessy had been what 'a dancer' was supposed to be, he would probably have taken advantage of her. But as she was, as Curran said, 'an excellent creature', he was as much trapped when he discovered that as he would have been by any police-work by her mother.

In the ordinary course he might never have married so long as his mother was alive, and his own attitude to society would have helped to keep him a bachelor. Whoever it was, he would have had an inhibition about telling his mother; even at thirty-two a mother's darling does not feel sure that he can marry without permission. His mother is being displaced by a rival.

Moore mentions in his Journal how he found himself staying in a house where there was a governess with whom he had had a romantic interlude many years before. He is persuaded to see her, and regretted it afterwards. It spoiled a dream. In that incident he seemed to sketch what these encounters were like: an hour or two of sentiment one night, a brief tearful farewell next morning; and an addition to the store of nostalgic impressions for future retrospection. He might have hesitated to attempt them with great ladies; his correspondence with them is confined to older women, surrogate mothers.

The pattern was set from the start. Only Tom went into society. But Samuel Rogers, as a rich bachelor, could make his own laws. He was at this time Moore's closest literary friend. He was charmed by Bessy, and she was happier in his house than at the Moira's palatial residence when they, too, made her acquaintance. Not that Rogers's was by any means a humble home. After his death his pictures were sold for £50,000. To breakfast with him was to have arrived in literary London.

The months after marriage in 1811 were spent in waiting for the Prince. When he met Moore, he was his usual affable self. Meanwhile Moore had written a comic opera. He read it to Arnold, the manager of the Lyceum Theatre, who agreed to produce it in September.

No writer can succeed in a medium he despises; and to write down for the theatre is always fatal. Moore's description of his opera—'Writing bad jokes for the gallery of the Lyceum' —in a letter to Leigh Hunt did not suggest a prosperous outcome.

M.P. or the Blue Stocking was produced on the ninth of September. Nobody else but Moore would have written to the newspapers calling the piece a bagatelle and denying that it had political implications. Arnold, the manager, was forced to reply. He described the piece as a 'brilliant and unqualified success'. Only *The Times* was critical; the opera had a run of eleven performances, and was revived on several occasions.

It seems to have been a characteristic of Moore to agree straight off to any business proposition, and then resent it when he discovered he had made a bad bargain. He would not himself be tempted to unprincely behaviour, and he didn't expect it from others. But he was dealing with business men. On this occasion he was worried because he feared that he had forfeited any claim for royalties by accepting an advance.

If the order in which he introduced topics in his letters are an indication of his priorities, a letter Moore wrote to his mother towards the close of the year is instructive.

'My dearest Mother,

'I find the Master of the Rolls is in town and, if possible, I shall go in to meet him. There is so much call for the opera, that I have *made* a *present* of it to little Power to publish; that is, *nominally* I have made a present of it to him, but I am to have the greater part of the profits notwithstanding. I do it in this way, however, for two reasons—*one*, that it looks more dignified, particularly after having made so light of the piece myself; and the *second*, that I do not mean to give any more to Carpenter, but do not think it worth breaking with him till I have something of consequence to give to Longmans. Little Power is of wonderful use to me, and, indeed, I may say, is the first Liberal man I have ever had to deal with. I hope both for his own sake and mine, that his business will prosper with him.

Ever your own,
Tom.'

The Master of the Rolls, it should be said, was John Philpot Curran, the most celebrated Irish wit, already an acquaintance. Moore had spent a journey to London laughing hilariously at his conversation. Byron said of Curran, 'I never met his equal'. So that Moore's anxiety to see him was not mere deference to office. On this occasion, according to Byron, Curran said to Moore, 'So, I hear, you have married a pretty woman, and a

very good creature too—an excellent creature—pray—um—
how do you pass your evenings?'

There was a fashion for long poems before the novel became
family reading; and Moore was following the practice of most
poets who took themselves seriously when he sat down to 'do
something, I hope, that will place me above the vulgar herd
both of wordlings and critics; but you shall hear from me again
when I get among the maids of Cashmere, the sparking springs
of Rochabad, and the fragrant banquets of the Peria. How
much sweeter employment these than the vile joke-making I
have been at these two months past'!

He was writing to Mary Godfrey. The poem was *Lalla
Rookh*, for which Longmans agreed to give him £3,000. This
was a splendid sum, and Moore had done good business. But
he was not a quick writer; he was not writing out of experience,
but from an idea of the Orient delved out of books (fatal to the
poem's vitality). He began composition—the first draft shows
—on November 11th, 1811.

He had had a wholly unexpected success in March 1813
with the *Twopenny Post-bag*. He gave it to Carpenter to publish
under the pseudonym 'Thomas Brown, the Younger', and as
he had not had any success with his anonymous contributions
to the Catholic controversy he had no great hopes. This was a
selection of his newspaper squibs with some additions. On this
occasion his timing was exactly right and the satire ran through
fourteen editions. He had made a palpable hit. The basis of the
joke was that a packet of letters, dropped by the postman, were
picked up by a representative of the Society for the Suppression
of Vice. The letters, according to the preface, disclosed pro-
fligacy 'in those upper regions of society which their well-bred
regulations forbid them to molest or meddle with'. The pseudonym 'Thomas Brown, the Younger' did not deceive anybody.
In the preface to the last edition Moore described the author as
an Irishman from a Roman Catholic family. He added: 'But
from all this it does not necessarily follow that Mr Brown is a
Papist; and, indeed, I have the strongest reasons for suspecting
that they who say so are totally mistaken. Not that I presume
to have ascertained his opinion upon such subjects; all I know
of his orthodoxy is, that he has a Protestant wife and two or

three little Protestant children, and that he has been seen at church for a whole year together, listening to the sermons of his truly reverend and amiable friend Dr —, and behaving there as well and orderly as most people.'

MOORE PLANNED to settle near Donington for many years, and removed from London to a house John Dalby found him at Kegworth in May 1812, determined to live by his pen, although even now he was still nursing the chimera of some change in his fortunes if Lord Moira was given a political opportunity. Bessy was now brought out as if from a conjurer's hat, three months after the birth of her child, Anne Jane Barbara, on 4th February. 'If we had staid much longer in town the curiosity to see "Moore's wife", combining with the kindness of my friends, would have ruined us', he wrote to James Corry, whose franks, as a Member of Parliament, he sometimes made use of—they could post letters free of charge to the recipient. Moore was for ever looking for this convenience. Byron was one of the many who obliged him. Bessy, he tells Corry, was invited to 'the three most splendid assemblies in London'. Evidently she did not accept the invitations. 'Lady Lansdowne's disappointment at her not going to hers was quite diverting.'

Moore did not tell Croker about his marriage until he had transplanted to Kegworth. Then he did so at once.

'I dare say you have heard of my having appeared suddenly to my friends in the new character of a husband and a father. If I were quite sure that you feel interested enough about an old friend to wish to know the particulars of my marriage, you should know them. At all events, I hope it will give you pleasure to learn that, though I thought it necessary to conceal the business so long (from everyone but my friend Rogers and the Dowager Lady Donegal) yet the moment the revelation took place, all my friends took the excellent creature I had married most cordially by the hand, and Lady Lansdowne and Lady Charlotte Rawdon were amongst the first to visit her. They knew the story, and could not but respect her.'

What did Moore mean? He would hardly have admitted that he had attempted to seduce Bessy or had taken her on the rebound from her sister or had been out-manoeuvred by her mother. Could the clergyman's story have been true? Did Bessy take fright unnecessarily at an innocent display of ardour? If her mother decided Moore had compromised her he might have been forced to propose before he was financially in a position to marry anyone. Mrs Dyke is not mentioned. There was no sign of her at the marriage or at the birth. This seems the most likely and more in keeping with the characters of the parties than the other suppositions.

Moore uses similar obscure phraseology in a letter to Edward Dalton, a Dublin friend, married to a daughter of Sir John Stevenson, thanking him rather too effusively for his congratulations, as if they were a concession. 'It has been a happy marriage indeed, my dear Dalton, and I doubt whether I could have arrived at a wife by any other process that would have made me equally sure of her attachment, purity, and disinterestedness'. He invites Dalton to come and settle close by— they could make music together, use the library, and live cheap while Moore gradually liquidated his debts 'of all kinds'.

In August 1812 he writes to Leigh Hunt to announce the birth of his daughter. He had played with the idea of letting Hunt into the secret of his marriage at the time. 'I rather think too that if you were acquainted with the story of my marriage, it would not tend to *lower* me from that place which I am proud to believe I hold in your esteem.'

He tells Hunt that he and his wife have recently been on a visit 'to our noble neighbour, who is at length preparing for an old age of *independence* by a manly and summary system of entrenchment. He has dismissed nearly all his servants and is retiring to a small house in Sussex leaving his fine Park and Library here to *Solitude and me*. How I have mourned over his recent negotiation! A sword looks crooked in water, and the weak medicine of Carleton House has given an appearance of obliquity even to Lord Moira, but both Sword and he may be depended upon still—at least I think so'.

When Moira drove him to Holland House to dine, from the way in which the other politicians present treated him, Moore was convinced that they saw him as very close to the centre of influence. It is a pointer to the vividness of his hopes that he chooses this time to write disingenuously to his parson friend, Dalby, asking him to find him a house near Donington 'from the convenience of the library and from the advantage of having a friend like you so near me'.

In June Moira was authorised by the Regent to discuss the formation of a Government with Lords Grey and Grenville. In the negotiations Moira was so staunch to the Regent that he annoyed the Whigs, and the upshot was Lord Liverpool's appointment, and a renewed lease of life for the Tories. Moira dined with Moore and hinted that there was still a chance of his going to Ireland. The stumbling-block was the Lord Chancellor, Eldon, who stood firm against relief to the Catholics, to which Moira was pledged.

Moore dined again with Moira on August 12th to celebrate the Prince's birthday—'a sudden summons to the Park'. Pineapples and other presents came to the cottage from the big house. Moira was so kind as to enquire, in his own delicate manner, about Moore's finances. 'There will soon be a change which will set us all on our legs', he said. He was being abused in the *Edinburgh Review* for having sold himself to the Prince and betraying his colleagues. Moore confided to his mother that Moira had 'ruined his reputation as a statesman' by his recent conduct. His only hope now was to be sent to Ireland.

Less than a month after that Moore is writing to Lord Moira to congratulate him on his appointment as Commander in Chief in India and Governor of Bengal. He was to sail in January; and as he had not received any communication, Moore told Mary Godfrey, he assumed that Moira had no intention of taking him with him. Nor was it likely (owing to 'the hungry pack of followers who surround him') that he would get Moore anything at home worth his acceptance. 'I doubt whether I would accept it. Poor Lord Moira! his good qualities have been the ruin of him.'

Moore at this time was writing to James Power in Dublin for 'three or four pounds by return of Post'.

Power shared with Moore's mother the privilege of an unobstructed view of the mercurial workings of his mind. He had

received a letter from Moira with—Moore confides in Power—
'not a single word in it about me . . . All this elaborate explanation shows not only his own sensibility upon the subject, but
certainly proved very flattering by the anxiety he felt with
respect to my opinion of his conduct. I cannot, however, but
think it very singular that, after the renewed pledges and promises he made me so late as the last time he was here, he should
not give the remotest hint of either an intention or even a wish,
to do anything for me. I shall be exceedingly mortified, if he
should go away without giving me an opportunity of at least
refusing something . . .'

The Observer of Sunday 15th November 1812 told its readers
that Moore was going to India as Moira's secretary at three or
four thousand pounds a year.

For days Moore had been waiting for him to come to Donington, where he was expected. Then he would know his plans.
Moira came and did not send for Moore. When they met
accidentally, Moira was out shooting. 'You see a schoolboy
taking his holiday', was all he had to say—a hint, surely, that
he did not want to discuss jobs.

Moore wrote to Lady Donegal a few days later to say that
he had had his interview at last. Moira assured Moore that he
had not been 'oblivious' of him. 'All the patronage he could
exercise *here* was exhausted; but if when he got to India . . .' In
the meantime he hoped that Ministers would serve his friends
here as he had served their friends in India. He would see what
he could do about that. Moore firmly refused this. 'From *his*
hands he would always accept anything, but . . .'

Moore was not mollified. He resented the word 'oblivious'.
Having launched himself on his career as a satirist, it would not
suit him now to have his hands tied by small favours from those
he had planned to pillory. 'He has certainly not done his duty
by me; his *manner*, since his appointment, has been even worse
than his deficiencies of *matter* . . .'

Any deficiency in Moira's manner could be explained. It is
very difficult to look pleasant when dashing hopes one has
helped to raise. As soon as the deed was done, the Moiras
resumed their former ways. They called with presents of fruit,
cases of wine, a book Moore had been looking for. Their

cousin, Sir Charles Hastings, invited the Moores to stay on a long visit.

To no avail. 'His kindnesses to me', Moore wrote to Leigh Hunt in prison, 'of course, I can never forget—but they are remembered, as one remembers the kindnesses of a faithful mistress, and that esteem, that reverence, which is the soul of all is fled'.

Power was allowed once again to see in what manner Moore's mind was working.

'Between ourselves, my dear friend, I have not so much merit in these refusals as I appear to have, for I could see very plainly through how Moira's manner that there was very little chance of his making any proper exertion for me whatever, and putting conscience out of the question, policy itself suggested to me that I might as well have the merit of declining what it was quite improbable would ever have been done for me.'

Rogers cheered him up by reporting that Moira was in low spirits and conscious of failure. Rogers was hearing nothing but praise of Moore's conduct.

'Dalby went up to London yesterday', Tom told his mother, 'to take leave of the Moiras: I believe, only for Bessy's state, I should have paid them the same mark of respect myself.' Bessy's condition rarely held Moore back from anything he wanted to do, and then never for long.

A laconic reference to Moira in a letter to his mother in March, and after that little is heard of him in Moore's correspondence.

Moore's relationships with people elude definition. When Rogers made a reference to the portraits of his patrons which he hung in the dining-room, Moore took the observation amiss. 'A good-natured man would have said *friends*.' Was Moira's face on exhibition in that gallery?

In later years Moore was taken aback when Lord Holland asked him if he had shown Lord Moira his parody on the Regent's letter to the Duke of York explaining why he was retaining his father's Government instead of putting in the expectant Whigs. That had been much appreciated by the Holland circle—for whom it was written in February 1812.

Why, Moore asked himself, was Lord Holland asking that question in 1821? And, four years later, when Holland read aloud passages from his own *Memoirs* in which he described Moore's parody as showing more of Irish humour than wordly prudence, Moore exclaims (but to himself) 'This is too bad'. He had preened himself on the praise his satires had received in Holland House, but as the watchful Croker was later to point out, Moira was much more a friend of the Regent than a favourite with his party. He, Sheridan and Fox were the Royal cronies, and when Fox died, Moore's chance of preferment effectively died with him. The Whigs, as such, had no influence with the Prince. It is curious that Moira never remonstrated with Moore. Croker said he did; but gave a date that impugns his accuracy.

Corry, with whom Tom was supposed to be collaborating on some sort of memoir of the Kilkenny festival, invited him over to Dublin in December, 1812 for an 'author's night' in the theatre. *The Blue Stocking* had been performed in Dublin without success. Moore refused to go. 'Alas! to lay myself under an obligation to—and to have tickets ostensibly for my benefit, circulating among the low, illiberal, puddle-headed, and gross-hearted herd of Dublin (that "palavering, slanderous set" as Curran once so well described them to me)—this, my dear Corry, would never do.'

When Anastasia was born at Kegworth on March 16th, 1813, Moore wrote to James Power to ask if his wife would act as godmother. He had, he wrote, intended to invite them both to sponsor the child 'as it would create a *kind* of relationship between us, and draw closer (if they require it) those ties which I trust will long keep us together. But I am obliged to confine my request to *Mrs* Power, and leave *you* for some future and (I hope) very-far-off little child; for our rector, Doctor Parkinson, very kindly *offered*, of himself to be godfather, and it is such a very flattering tribute of his good opinion to us, that I could not hesitate in accepting it'.

When he was brooding over the prospects of Lord Lansdowne as godfather to the next, the promise to James was forgotten. Lord John Russell and Byron were future godfathers; but with them Moore stood on an easier footing than with Lansdowne, whom he invested with the patron's rôle; it was a relationship that something in Moore's nature seemed to need. Was it a consequence of his upbringing as a Catholic in a country of Protestant Ascendancy?

With the collapse of all hope of patronage, Moore is discussing a move to London in the beginning of the New Year. His parents gave an example, letting Kilmainham Lodge, where they had gone after leaving Aungier Street, and moving into Abbey Street, where the rest of their lives would be spent.

Rogers had gone on a walking tour with Moore in the previous autumn; his rather captious criticism (as Moore saw it) had been a damper on the progress of the great poem; but Scott's *Rokeby* renewed his courage. It was such a poor thing.

Writing to James Power, Moore was more likely to disclose his plans than to a social acquaintance—Moore represented Power's principal source of income. Power was trying to persuade Moore to come to London. Moore wrote that there was nothing he would personally prefer to do, but he had to 'sacrifice his wishes to prudence'. He wished to impress upon Power how much 'I *begin* to set *business* and the interests of our *concern*, above every other consideration, either of pleasure or convenience'.

Only two months were left of the Kegworth lease, and he wanted in that time to find something cheaper and pleasanter elsewhere. 'I have sucked pretty well out of the library, and shall I think be able to wean myself of it without injury; indeed, I have got quite sufficient material out of it for my poem, and as to my musical works, it has nothing to assist me there, so that I now consider myself free to choose where I can live cheapest and most retired during the remainder of my rural exile. We are too much in the midst of my fine acquaintances here, and are obliged to keep up an appearance which might be dispensed with in a more retired situation . . . I am at my wit's end for *the supplies* . . . the sale of my *immoveables* here will pay all bills, and get me up to town; but your brother's bill, my aunt's, my father's! Do not be alarmed; I am safe from all these but your brother's; but I want (if I can) to take from the shoulders they are on to my own.'

Moore went in search of a new house—Donington had lost its attractions—and while the search was on an aptly named friend, Mrs Ready, offered him and Bessy a suite of rooms for as long as they pleased at Oakhanger Hall. Even the death of the host on the day before the Moores arrived was not allowed to depress them. A 'gay barouche and two smiling servants' was a pleasant introduction to their temporary home. 'If there was not such a thing as a *corpse* still in the house, you would scarcely suppose that Death had ever showed his ugly face within the walls . . . Mrs Ready takes most violently to Bessy', Moore wrote to his mother.

The two years at Kegworth, however uncomfortable the little house, were those in which Moore produced his best lyrics, his most loved, on Sarah Curran: *She is far from the land where her young hero sleeps*, *'Tis the last Rose of Summer*, *By that lake whose gloomy shore*, admired by Poe.

Would that he had been satisfied with the steady output of the *Melodies* and the *Sacred Songs* which he began to compose and produced in 1816. He was endlessly worrying about money. He had tried to persuade James Power to take him into partnership; he thought of compiling a dictionary of music, of lecturing. All the while he was reading in the library at Donington for the sustenance of *Lalla Rookh*, whose parturition was elephantine.

The hunt began. In Wales first of all; the scenery was splendid but Moore found he was deceived when he was told it was cheap. The hunt ended near Ashbourne in Derbyshire in June 1813. Mayfield, the cottage, was pretty; the rent, twenty pounds a year. No sooner had they settled in than Whitbread wrote inviting Moore to write for Drury Lane. He declined to until his poem was finished. He was flattered to hear that Madame de Staël, recently arrived in London, had 'a passion' for his poetry. He pursues the subject in a letter to Mary Godfrey. He was curious about Madame de Staël and would have liked to see her; but 'young Marlow was not more afraid of a *modest* woman than I am of a learned one'.

Mrs Ready, who so obligingly refused to allow the presence of her husband's corpse to dampen the spirits of the Moores on arrival at her house, persisted in her kindness—'She is a good-natured woman, with all her nonsense, for she has taken great offence with me because I will not let her lend me two or three hundred pounds.'

Moore described his condition to Mary Godfrey: 'I am leading a life which but for these anxieties of fame, and a few ghosts of debt that sometimes haunt me, is as rationally happy as any man can ask for . . . As for Bessy, she is the same affectionate, sensible and unaffected creature as a mother that she is as a wife, and devotes every thought and moment to them and to me. I pass my days at present going through Miss Edgeworth's works, and then after tea I go to my study again. We are not without distractions of society, for this is a very gay place, and *some* of the distractions I could dispense with; but being far out of the regular road, I am so little interrupted as I could possibly expect in so very thick a neighbourhood. Thus I have a little panorama of me and mine, and I hope you will like it.'

The rural bliss, broken by occasional flights to town, in these first years of marriage, made these among Moore's happiest days. Arriving too early for a dinner party, the Moores set to practising country dances, in the middle of a retired green lane, till the time had expired. 'Beautiful, beautiful' was echoed on all sides when Bessy attended a ball. She wore a turban to please her husband; he thought it suited her better than anything else and brought out a resemblance to the famous dancer Catalini, 'and a turban is the thing for that kind of character'.

Children came—Barbara Anne and Anastasia were followed by Olivia Byron on August 18th, 1814, then Tom, October 24th, 1818. John Russell in 1823 was the last. They were all in turn and in different ways to bring sorrow to their parents, and precipitate Moore's eventual decline; but rolling in the hay in Derbyshire with little Barbara Anne, Moore knew only that his cup of happiness was full. He had chosen the right wife. His poem was proceeding. In London he had the most exciting friend he was ever to make. Byron had come into his life.

BYRON DID not fail to notice the duel in that August of 1806. More than a year was to pass and Moore seemed to have lived it successfully down when Byron, aged nineteen, read the critique of his *Hours of Idleness* in the *Edinburgh Review*. It was not calculated to relieve an author's anxiety or nourish dreams of fame. Hobhouse, who knew Byron so well, said that he was 'very nearly destroying himself'. Byron's most complete biographer has described it as 'provocative and meanly personal'. The critic, Leslie Marchand points out, laid bare the very vanities Byron thought he had concealed in the preface. To Godwin, another friend, Byron confessed that he was 'in such a rage as I never have been in since'.

His revenge was one that only a poet who was a lord could have, at his age, attempted. He published his satire *English Bards and Scottish Reviewers*. He had no animus against Moore, who had excited his adolescent fantasies with his Boucher images; but, with the harshness of the young, he was indifferent to Moore's feelings when he found he fitted into his plan for hitting back at the author of the *Edinburgh Review*. The lines (which in his days of friendship with Moore he altered) read:

> Can none remember that eventful day,
> That ever glorious, almost fatal fray,
> When Little's leadless pistol met his eye,
> And Bow-street myrmidons stood laughing by?

In order to ensure that the blow went home, Byron added a note to inform the reader that 'In 1805 Jeffrey and Moore met at Chalk Farm. The duel was prevented by the interference of the Magistracy; and, on examination, the balls of the pistols, like the courage of the combatants, were found to have evaporated. This incident gave rise to much waggery in the daily press.'

This appeared when Moore had hoped after a tactful retreat to Dublin and a course of conduct calculated to show that he was a serious force in politics to live down the humiliation. And it must have been painful to discover that the story was not only still alive but put now into fresh circulation.

The first edition of Byron's poem appeared in March, another came out in October. On the first day of the following year Moore wrote from 22 Molesworth Street, Dublin.

My Lord,

'Having just seen the name of 'Lord Byron' prefixed to a work entitled *English Bards and Scotch Reviewers*, in which, as it appears to me, the *lie is given* to a public statement of mine respecting an affair with Mr Jeffrey some years since, I beg you will have the goodness to inform me whether I may consider your Lordship as the author of this publication.

'I shall not, I fear, be able to return to London for a week or two; but, in the mean time, I trust your Lordship will not deny me the satisfaction of knowing whether you avow the insult contained in the passage alluded to.

'It is needless to suggest to your Lordship the propriety of keeping our correspondence secret.'

I have the honour to be
Your Lordship's very humble servant,
Thomas Moore.'

Byron's version of the duel had it that neither pistol was loaded; the story at the time was that it was Jeffrey's pistol which was empty; but in either event, Moore had publicly stated that both were loaded. Byron had given the lie to that. Is it possible that Moore had only heard of the reference to himself nine months after the poem appeared? Or, was this another carefully calculated challenge? Mary Godfrey had advised him never to take up a pistol again. He had made himself ridiculous on the last occasion. And yet, here he was, not only trying to bring on a duel, but in doing so resurrecting again the whole absurd story of the non-duel with Jeffrey.

The most likely explanation of his conduct is that in the top layer of his mind was the idea that if he showed courage on this occasion he could blot out the farcical impression left over by

the other encounter. His temper was not blazing hot; when
Byron left the letter unanswered, Moore let the matter drop as
if it had been an invitation to dinner that had gone astray. He
knew Byron had gone abroad.

On October 22nd 1811, Moore wrote again. In the meantime
he had married. The letter begins:

27 Bury Street,
St James's

My Lord,
   'As understood, soon after your Lordship's return to
England that a melancholy event had occurred in your family,
which must have very painfully occupied all your thoughts, I
forbore from troubling you with the subject upon which I
now have the honour of addressing you; and, indeed, if in
what I have to say at present there were anything of hostility
or unkindness towards you, I should think it too soon even
now to disturb you unpleasantly from your retirement. But I
trust you will find that, notwithstanding the injury of which
I complain, the spirit in which I address you is neither
revengeful nor ungenerous.'

Byron's mother had died; there was no insincerity in Moore's
sympathetic concern; never was letter about a duel couched in
such disarming phrases. Then Moore got down to business, and
in doing so revealed another of his characteristics. Referring
to the still unanswered challenge, he describes it as having been
posted *three years* before. Half that time, as it was in fact, was
long enough, but it is the measure of Moore's habitual vagueness that he should have got the time so ludicrously wrong.
Moore was in Dublin, he explains, when he wrote the letter, and
as Byron went abroad so soon afterwards it might not have
reached him.

   'It is useless now to speak of the step, with which I intended
to follow up that letter. The time, that has elapsed since then,
though it has done away neither the injury nor the feeling of it,
has so very materially altered my relative situation in life—
has laid me under so many obligations to friends, and fettered
me with so many serious responsibilities, that I should consider
myself, at present, not only selfish but unprincipled, were I to

consult any punctilious feeling of my own, at the risk of leaving undischarged the many duties which I owe to others. The only object, therefore, which I have now in writing to your Lordship is merely to preserve some consistency with the letter which you may have formerly received from me, and to prove to you that the injured feeling still remains, however circumstances, at present, may compel me to be deaf to its dictates.'

In short, Moore was now a married man.

'When I say "injured feelings", I must again assure your Lordship that there is not one vindictive feeling in my heart towards you—I mean merely to express that *uncomfortableness* under a charge of falsehood, which must haunt a man of any feeling to his grave, unless the insult be retracted or atoned for, and which if I were not sensibly alive to, I should indeed deserve much worse than ever your Lordship's satire could inflict upon me. So *very* far am I, however, from treasuring any ungenerous revenge, that it would give me at this moment the most heart-felt pleasure if I by any kind, candid and satisfactory explanation, you would enable me to ask for the honour of your intimacy, and let me try to convince you that I am *not exactly* the kind of person, who would set his name to a mean and cowardly falsehood.

'I have never mentioned *to any one* my former letter to your Lordship, nor ever hinted at the feeling which your work excited in me, except to one person, who is, I believe, an intimate friend of your Lordship's. If, however, you should feel inclined to meet my sincere wishes for reconcilement, I shall mention the subject to my best and most valued friend Mr Rogers (whose worth and talent your Lordship seems justly to appreciate) and I have no doubt that he will be most happy to become a mediator between us.'

That tone would make an unpleasant impression today. It is interesting to see how it affected Byron. And, again, we must remember that he, a literary novice, was being courted by one of the leading poets of the time, and an established favourite in society. Byron, too, was concerned for his honour. Implicit in the strange correspondence was a determination to prove that he had not avoided a challenge.

He replied: 'Your former letter I never had the honour to

receive;—be assured in whatever part of the world it had found me, I should have deemed it my duty to return and answer you in person.

'The advertisement you mention I know nothing of . . . With regard to the passage in question *you* were certainly *not* the person towards whom I felt personally hostile. On the contrary, my whole thoughts were engrossed by one, whom I had reason to consider as my worst literary enemy . . . I can neither retract nor apologise for a charge of falsehood which I never advanced. Your friend Mr Rogers, or any other gentleman delegated by you, will find me most ready to accept any conciliatory proposition which shall not compromise my own honour, or, failing in that, to make the statement you deem it necessary to require.'

In what followed Byron was punctilious about his own honour and insistent that Moore should see that the original letter was still in the possession of Mr Hodgson, who had never sent it on to Byron when he went abroad. Then he suggested that it be returned to Moore to examine. In the letter proposing this, Byron added: 'A few words more and I shall not trouble you further. I felt, and still feel, very much flattered by those parts of your correspondence, which held out the prospect of our becoming acquainted. You have *now* declared yourself *satisfied*, and on that point we are no longer at issue. If, therefore, you still retain any wish to do me the honour you hinted at, I shall be most happy to meet you, when, where, and how you please, and I presume you will not attribute my saying thus to any unworthy motive.'

It could not be more clear that so far from being put off by Moore's convolutions, Byron was pleased. To Hobhouse, his most familiar friend, he wrote at the time to describe his correspondence with 'Anacreon Moore'. Reconciliation had been effected under the auspices of Scrope Davies, who would have acted as Byron's second had there been a duel, and 'on Monday next we are to meet at the house of "Pleasures of Memory" Rogers, who is Moore's friend and has behaved very well in ye business.—So as dinners are preferable to duels, and nothing has been conceded on my part . . . and as the Bard has been graciously pleased to talk about his "sincere respect for my talents" and "good will" &c, why—I shall be glad to know what you think of the matter.—You will remember that the first hint towards acquaintance came from Moore, and coldly enough I met it, as I fairly told him till the principal point was discussed between us, I could not reply to the other part of his letter, but now that is settled. Mr Rogers (whom I never saw) has sent me an invitation to meet the Irish Melodist on Monday. However you shall see all the letters and copies of mine when we come together.'

Byron's tone is hardly less consequential than Moore's. They were dealing with a most delicate matter; it takes an effort after it has dropped out of the current vocabulary to realise how precious honour was.

After Byron met Moore, he returned to the subject with Hobhouse.

'Moore and I are on the best of terms, I answered his letters in an explanatory way, but of course conceded nothing in the shape of an apology, indeed his own letters were an odd mixture of complaint, and a desire of amiable discussion—Rogers said his behaviour was rather Irish, and that mine was candid and manly, I hope it was at *least* the latter . . . Rogers is a most excellent and unassuming Soul, as Moore an Epitome of all that is delightful.'

Even after this we find him writing anxiously to Hodgson to recover the fateful letter. He is still concerned that Moore should see it, but, by then, they were boon companions.

In accepting Moore's suggestion that they should meet at Rogers's house, Byron wrote to Moore: 'should my approaching interview with him and his friend lead to any degree of intimacy with both or either, I shall regard our past correspondence as one of the happiest events of my life.'

The evening at Rogers's house has been often described. For his dinner on November 4th, the banker-poet had planned only to have Moore and Byron; but Thomas Campbell happened to call in the morning and was invited to join the party. Byron, knocking on the door of literary London, was meeting three lions on the same evening. The host was forty-nine, Campbell thirty-four, Moore thirty-two; and Byron at twenty-four, much the youngest of the party. All of them, it may be said, were much admired by the young lord. He was conservative, not to say, restricted, in his literary tastes, firm in his worship of Pope, contemptuous of the revolution against the claims of rhymed couplets. (Byron was as hostile to Keats as any of the reviewers who have been accused of killing him.) Rogers, after Pope, was Byron's favourite poet at this time. It seems incredible but, then, in what admiration Coleridge held Bowles! Poets are as fallible as anyone else when judging their contemporaries.

Rogers had planned the evening carefully. Moore and Campbell were not to be present when Byron arrived. Then the guests, who had stayed in another room, came in and were introduced. He, too, had carefully staged his own entrance. He wore mourning black. Young Hamlet!

Rogers was a legendary host, and the dinner was all that it should have been for the occasion; but, to his chagrin, there was nothing Byron wanted to eat. Offered soup, he said he never eat it, fish, he never eat either, nor mutton. Wine? No. He never tasted wine.

The host gave up. What would Lord Byron eat? Nothing but hard biscuits and soda water. Rogers had overlooked both of these in his preparations, so Byron had to resort to 'potatoes bruised down on his plate and drenched with vinegar'. Rogers recalled the evening in an old age, and his meeting some days afterwards with Hobhouse, the man who knew Byron best. At that time he was in Ireland with his regiment. How long, Rogers wanted to know, will Lord Byron persevere in his present diet? Hobhouse replied, 'Just as long as you continue to notice it.' Rogers was subsequently to discover that at the end of the evening, Byron went to a club in St James's Street and ate a hearty meat supper.

Once the food embarrassment was disposed of, the dinner was a triumph. There was no talk of duels, but the merits of Walter Scott and Joanna Baillie were discussed. Byron, encouraged by the older men, whom he fascinated, became animated and forgot his melancholy pose. He could in this mood charm anyone. Moore, recalling this evening, wrote 'From the time of our first meeting there seldom elapsed a day that Lord Byron and I did not see each other, and our acquaintance ripened into intimacy and friendship with a rapidity of which I have seldom seen an example'.

1 Anastasia Moore and John Moore, the poet's parents. Attributed to Martin Cregan

2a Tom Moore when young, from an engraving by H. H. Meyer after an unknown artist

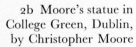

2b Moore's statue in College Green, Dublin, by Christopher Moore

3a Moore by John
Jackson, painted in
Rome, 1818

3b Bessy Moore,
sketch for a portrait
by Gilbert S. Newton

4a Francis Rawdon,
First Marquis of
Hastings and second
Earl of Moira,
Sir Martin Archer
Shee P.R.A.

4b Henry Petty-
FitzMaurice, third
Marquess of
Lansdowne, by
H. Walter

5a John Wilson
Croker, by W. Owen

5b Samuel Rogers,
by T. Phillips

6a Moore, by
William Essex
after Lawrence.
Miniature on
enamel

6b Hon. Caroline
Norton, by John Hayter.
Chalk and pencil
drawing

7a Lord Edward
Fitzgerald, by
Hugh Douglas
Hamilton

7b John Cam
Hobhouse, engraved
by James Hopwood
from a drawing by
Abraham Wivell

8a Moore, by George Richmond. Chalk sketch
(1843)

8b 'O' Connell and his Contemporaries: The Clare Election, 1828,
by Joseph Patrick Haverty

It was true; nor did Moore ever have to make the running again. Byron in his letters, while he remained in London, mentions Moore regularly, and usually with some expression of approval. If Moore was proud of the acquaintance, so was Byron. It is surely a tribute to Moore that with all the evidence he has left in letters and diaries of recognition, it always came as a surprise to find himself being lionised by people whom he describes with such guileless pride to his mother. Byron invites Hodgson to dinner to meet Rogers, Campbell and Moore. He is as proud of his new acquaintances as Moore was of the high society he met in London when he was even younger than Byron, not a lord but a grocer's son from Dublin. Rogers invites Byron to hear Coleridge ('who is a kind of rage at present') lecture: Campbell confides that he is terrified by criticism: his bookseller sends him a manuscript for approval. Moore's friendship is a great part of this sudden success. He and Rogers are 'truly men of taste'; and Moore 'the Epitome of all that is exquisite in poetical or personal accomplishments'. A month after their first meeting, Byron in a letter begs Moore to agree to drop 'our formal monosyllables'. He had proposed Moore for the Alfred Club and invites him to come and stay at Newstead. When guests fall out of Byron's parties, it matters not at all so long as Moore be there. He 'supplied all other vacancies most delectably'. He thinks the critical Hobhouse will like Moore and plans to bring them together.

By January they have become such friends that Byron is found writing

'My dear Moore,

'I wish very much I could have seen you; I am in a state of ludicrous tribulation * * * Why do you say I dislike your poesy? I have expressed no such opinion, either in *print* or elsewhere. In scribbling myself, it was necessary for me to find fault, and I fixed upon the trite charge of immorality, because I could discover no other, and was so perfectly qualified in my innocence of heart to "pluck that mote from my neighbour's eye".

'I feel very, very much obliged by your approbation but at *this moment*, praise, even *your* praise, passes by me like "the idle wind". I meant and mean to send you a copy the moment of publication; but now, I can think of nothing but damned, deceitful,—delightful woman, as Mr Liston says in the Knight of Snowdon.

Believe me, my dear Moore, ever yours and affectionately
Byron.'

The asterisks are the result of Moore's bowdlerization. Byron was having trouble over Susan Vaughan, a pretty Welsh servant; she had deceived him, as other members of the staff were not slow to inform him, and her own letters betrayed the extent of the kitchen gossip. Byron, already with a reputation as a rake, was inviting his friends to console him to his heart-broken condition. How could 'such a thing as I am ever be beloved?' His thoughts turned back to Edleston, the romantic choir-boy, and he dismissed his 'Seraglio'.

He was less mature than Moore had been at the same age, for all his parade of cynicism. But their respective places in the literary hierarchy—Moore close to Scott at the top, Byron on the first step of the ladder—changed dramatically when *Childe Harold* appeared in March. None of the older men thought his autobiographical poem would succeed. Moore gave as his tactful reason that it was 'too good for the age'. In the event it made Byron famous in a day. The publisher—Murray—could not cope with the rush for copies. If Moore felt a twinge of jealousy, he never exhibited it. It was not one of his failings. 'My friend Lord Byron's poem is doing wonders, and there is nothing talked of but him everywhere . . .' Moore wrote to his mother. Byron had asked Moore to act as his second in a duel (it didn't come off); and invited him to meet his new flame, Caroline Lamb. (Moore 'is in great distress about us'.) And Byron had met Bessy at last. The poets had been friends six months before this was brought about. Byron reported to Caroline Lamb that 'she is beautiful, with the darkest eyes, they have left town'.

Murray's offer of an editorship came through Lord Byron; it was for a new review to rival the *Edinburgh* and *Quarterly*. After an unkind reference to Madame de Staël, Byron continued, Murray 'has a design upon you in the paper line. He wants you to become the staple and stipendiary Editor of a periodical work. What say you? Will you be bound like "Kit Smart" to write for ninety-nine years in the *Universal Visitor*? Seriously, he talks of hundreds a year and—though I hate prating of the beggarly elements—his proposals may be to your honour and profit, and I am very sure, will be to your pleasure.

'I don't know what to say about "friendship". I never was in friendship but once, in my nineteenth year, and then it gave me as much trouble as love. I am afraid, as Whitbread's sire said to the king, when he wanted to knight him, that I am "too old": but, nevertheless, no one wishes you more friends, fame and felicity than

Yours etc.'

Moore must have used the word friendship with his own connotation which carried in his heterosexual mind no passionate undertones. It was not so for Byron, whose nature had bisexual elements. He was always chary of the word, and in a letter to Shelley's widow said that the only *male* human being for whom he felt friendship deserving the name was Lord Clare, son of John Fitzgibbon, the Irish Chancellor, who had played such a significant part in Moore's days in Trinity College. But it was certainly to Edleston, the choir boy, who was drowned, that Byron referred in his letter to Moore.

In despite of what looks like a rejection of a naïve overture, Byron was the more attached of the two friends and the one whose nature needed affection more, because his disposition was self-hating, and he had never known the security of love which Moore had enjoyed since the beginning of his existence without intermission. If he asked Byron for a declaration of friendship such as he obtained so readily from uncomplicated men, including Walter Scott, the motive was vanity.

The success of Byron's *Giaour* was certain to produce imitators on Eastern themes. As a result the poem was coming between Moore and his sleep. In a letter to James Power he admits that he would ask for a few months leave from his engagement to produce songs so that the poem might get finished but 'I dread your brother'. When the poem was finished he would be 'yours till death' and his very first production would be an operatic drama.

He makes no secret of his depression after Byron's invasion of his territory. At the same time he rejoices in Byron's success. He saw himself relegated to the position of a follower of Byron. Moore was wounded 'in a very vital part', but he could not abandon his own coral island method of composition.

Within a year Byron had out-distanced his mentor. He was the rising sun. But his affection for Moore grew. With Moore, as with Scott, he showed himself at his best; and besides they had what makes friendship delightful, they amused each other. They laughed at the same absurdities. They raised each other's spirits and dissipated melancholy humours. Byron needed this restorative more than Moore, who was a happy man.

Byron was forever writing to Moore; and the other, as with all his correspondents, was tardy in replying.

Glancing through the letters with which Byron regaled Moore, at a period when the young poet's amorous life was in legendary disarray, affection and esteem can be seen to grow. Familiarity inevitably dulls the glamour of such exhilarating relationships; however versatile the friend, a time comes when dominating traits begin to pall, and the wind of affection shifts temporarily to the east. Byron complained about Moore very occasionally; his 'Tommy loves a lord' is the hardest saying on record. Byron would not have given up his own title unless it was to change it for a kingship. Moore watched the mail for letters from the young lord in London. Byron reminds him of an evening with Rogers when Byron read aloud a poem by Thurlow, the Chancellor, when all three had broken down with laughter.

He drew a pyramid in his journal: Scott was at the apex, Rogers underneath him, by himself; then Moore and Campbell together. Below them, as a trio: Southey, Wordsworth, Coleridge. And after that 'the many'. He confessed that he had marked the names on the triangle more upon what he believed as popular opinion than his own. 'For, to me, some of Moore's last *Erin* sparks—"As a beam o'er the face of the waters"—"When he who adores thee"—"Oh blame not"—and "Oh breathe not his name"—are worth all the epics ever composed.'

That was Byron talking to himself, he found his friend too diffident. 'My dear Moore, you strangely underrate yourself. I should conceive it an affectation in any other; but I think I know you well enough to believe that you don't know your own value.' Describing the affect of his singing on the wife of a friend—it made her cry—he tells Moore in another letter of this time that nobody is his equal in writing songs or in satire. He wants a longer work from Moore. Fatal advice. And he says of his own *Bride of Abydos*, 'Mine is the work of a week, written, *why* I have partly told you, and partly I cannot tell you by letter—some day I will'.

To his journal he confides that 'Moore has a peculiarity of talent, or rather talents—poetry, music, voice, all his own; and an expression in each, which never was, nor will be, possessed by another. But he is capable of still higher flights in poetry. By the by, what humour, what—everything, in the *Post-Bag*! There is nothing Moore may not do, if he will but seriously set about it. In society he is gentlemanly, gentle, and altogether more pleasing than any individual with whom I am acquainted. For his honour, principle and independence, his conduct to— speaks "trumpet-tongued". He has but one fault—and that I daily regret—he is not *here*'.

And in a fit of *ennui* in December, when he is playing with the idea of shooting himself to annoy his half-sister Augusta, he notes in the next paragraph of his journal that he had 'the kindest letter from Moore. I *do* think that man is the best-hearted, the only hearted being I ever encountered; and, then, his talents are equal to his feelings'.

Byron dedicates 'The Corsair' to Moore at some length, and in doing so referred to Moore's forthcoming Eastern poem. *The Corsair*, published on February 18th, 1814, sold 10,000 copies that day. Seven years later Byron wrote in his journal how he remembered going with Moore ('the poet *par excellence*, as he deserves it') to dine with Lord Grey. They looked at a gazette from Java that Murray had posted to Byron. It contained a discussion on the relative merits of Moore and Byron. There, he decided, 'was *fame* for you at six and twenty'. And he added, 'It was a great fame to be named with Moore; greater to be compared with him; greater—*pleasure*, at least—to be *with* him . . .'

Byron expressed a wish in his journal that he had a talent for the drama. He would have liked to have written a tragedy. 'Moore should try. He has wonderful powers, and much variety; besides he has lived and felt.'

The following year was the prelude to Byron's career as a damned soul. He had begun his half-hearted courtship of Annabella Milbanke, and in September his tentative proposal was accepted. How much did Moore know about Byron's involvement with his half-sister, Augusta? In all his writings about Byron he only once referred to her. Byron consulted him about Lady Adelaide Forbes; Moore had praised her. She was Lord Moira's niece. 'Is she *clever*, or sensible, or good-tempered?' the ardent suitor inquired. 'My circumstances are mending, and were not my other prospects blackening, I would take a wife, and that should be the woman, had I a chance.'

The English—Byron had the make-up of an Englishman of his class—are sometimes puzzled by what they see as touchiness in the Irish. Sensitivity, the Irish would call it; and the lack of an excess of this, in all classes, helped England to make an empire. Byron ran into this complication with Moore who, on the evidence of vast correspondence, was not a difficult man. He took criticism in good part, and he was signally lacking in conceit, a fertile source of prickliness.

'Your letter set me at ease'; Byron wrote, 'for I really thought (as I hear of your susceptibility) that I had said—I know not what—but something I should have been very sorry for, had it, or I, offended you;—though I don't see how a man with a beautiful wife—his *own* children—quiet, fame, competency and friends (I will vouch for a thousand, which is more than I will for a unit in my own behalf), can be offended with anything'.

We have seen how Moore from his very earliest days was over-anxious to see what effect he had created and seemed extravagantly to need the support of general opinion. Where his valued friends were concerned he was almost pathetically exercised if letters of approval did not arrive when he published a book.

The affectionate tone of Byron's letters was as reassuring as the most anxious friend could expect. That they should fall off in quantity during the first year of Byron's marriage was natural enough. But the letters give no indication of any impending tragedy. He refers frequently to Lady Byron's pregnancy, and gossips agreeably. To his credit, he asks Moore to give Coleridge a boost in the *Edinburgh*. How much did Byron confide in Moore? Hobhouse, a friend from Cambridge days, resented Moore's pretensions; the notes he wrote on his copy of Moore's biography of the poet suggest that Hobhouse knew a great deal to his friend's moral discredit of which Moore was unaware. This must have included Byron's homosexual excursions which would almost certainly have alienated Moore. But there is no doubt that Byron found in Moore a complete man of the world. They could not have arrived at such a degree of intimacy if Byron had had to censor his own conversations. But he respected Moore and accepted him in the character of a devoted husband. There is no evidence of his trying to shock him as Byron was all too apt to do—women particularly —hinting at fearful crimes. He knew and liked him too well; he did not have to act for Moore's benefit.

Like Scott, Moore attributed much of Byron's alleged wickedness to his desire to cause a sensation. What is one to make of an enquiry in Moore's letter to Byron, written in the beginning of 1816, within a few weeks of the birth of Allegra, and after wife and child had left Byron's house?

'There is *one* circumstance of your late life which I am *sure* I have guessed rightly—no I sincerely hope it is not as bad as sometimes horrible imaginings would make it—you need not recur to it till we meet, nor even *then*, if you don't like it—but at least with me you are safe—the same *malgré-tout*—I could love the Devil himself, if he were but such a *bon diable* as you are— and after all this is the true kind of affection—Your love that *picks* its *steps* was never worth a rush—'

A few days before this Moore had been asking Rogers for information about rumours that all was not well with Byron's marriage. Moore must have heard that Lady Byron and the child had left Byron's house soon after this; Moore wrote to him twice in March. In the first letter he says he doesn't know how to write about the things Byron has told him; they must wait until they meet in May but, he added, 'The world, in their generous ardour to take what they call the weaker side, soon contrive to make it most formidably the strongest.' He had not defended Byron to anyone except himself, 'considering the little I know upon the subject'. And he ends 'After all, your *choice* was the misfortune'.

In the next letter he says he had no right to say anything about the unluckiness of Byron's choice, but was glad that he did so as it had drawn from him a tribute 'highly honourable to both parties'.

After Byron's defence of his wife, Moore had to back-track, which he proceeded to do with some unction. 'I only feared that she might have been too perfect—too *precisely* excellent—too matter-of-fact a paragon for you to coalesce with comfortably; and that a person whose perfection hung in more easy folds about her, whose brightness was softened down by some of "those fair defects which best conciliate love" would, by appealing more definitely to your protection, have stood a much better chance with your good nature. All these suppositions, however, I have been led into by my intense anxiety to acquit you of anything like a capricious abandonment of such a woman.'

So that was what Moore must have been alluding to when he spoke of 'horrible misgivings'. If Moore appeared to be satisfied, he was not. He wrote to Mary Godfrey: 'In a letter I had recently from Lord Byron he says "There is not existing a brighter, or more amiable creature than Lady Byron". Is not this odd? What can be the reason of the separation?' Of Leigh Hunt he enquired whether it was true that 'Lord B. has taken to the beautiful marmosa, Mrs Mardyn, who after this will call him a searcher of dark bosoms. Not a word to *him*, however, about this question of mine'.

The lurid account of Byron's marriage that some of his biographers tell is almost impossible to reconcile with the tone of his letters to Moore while the marriage lasted. He urges his friend to write for the theatre, tells of a party Sheridan got hopelessly drunk at and a story of how, when asked his name by a night watchman, who picked him out of the gutter, he said 'Wilberforce'. Each letter ends with a reference to Lady Byron's forthcoming child. And his promptness, even after the marriage broke down, to defend his wife to Moore, suggests that, had she been willing, the marriage could have continued. 'I still, however, think that if I had had a fair chance of being placed in even a tolerable situation, I might have gone on fairly.'

Looking among the many avowals of Byron's affection for Moore none reads more convincingly than a phrase in a letter he wrote to the Irishman when his daughter, Barbara, died. 'Throughout life, your loss must be my loss, and your gain my gain; and though my heart may ebb, there will always be a drop for you among the dregs.'

When Byron left England, Hobhouse (who was so jealous of Moore's friendship with the poet and irritated by Moore's parade of it) was on the pier to see him off. Byron, on the deck of the reeling vessel, raised his cap and waved at his friend, who watched until he could see him no more. 'God bless him for a gallant spirit and a kind one,' said Hobhouse.

But when Byron took up a pen it was to write:

> My boat is on the shore,
> And my bark is on the sea;
> But, before I go, Tom Moore,
> Here's a double health to thee!

LALLA ROOKH remained Moore's principal object; nothing could induce him to hurry or scamp his work, but every now and then he fretted to get away from the monotony of country life.

Frequently the idea of Paris tempted him. Napoleon was his hero; during the lull when the Emperor was at Elba and, again, after Waterloo he was tempted to go over and see what it was like in Paris. Chronically in debt, he tried to keep away from the expenses of London; and he was giving—with Bessy's blessing—some assistance to his parents in Dublin. A letter to Lord Morpeth procured a pension for his father, who had been retired from the job acquired through the Moira influence.

When the Duke of Devonshire invited him to Chatsworth, he did not forget to mention the matter to various correspondents. To Rogers, he is the man of the world: 'I took the Derby Races and Ball in my way hither (he had gone to Donington to use the library), and met a very tolerable cluster of London stars there: your old friend Miss Fawkener in the character of Mrs Henry Cavendish; which connection I was so totally ignorant of, that I told her I was quite surprised to meet her in Derbyshire.' He had been invited for a week's stay 'to meet the Harringtons'. He decided at last to refuse. He had no servant to take with him; his hat was shabby; the seams of his best coat were beginning to look white. At a dinner or a ball, he could have held his own but 'a whole week in a man's house detects the poverty of a man's ammunition deplorably'. The invitation was later renewed and Bessy was invited as well. Moore went alone. 'I could have wished Bessy were here, but that I know she would not have been comfortable in it. She does not like any strangers and least of all would have liked such grand and mighty strangers as are assembled here.'

He had some trouble in rigging himself out. The coat sent

down by his London tailor didn't fit him, he had been obliged to engage an 'Ashbourne bungler'.

There were three children now, girls; the last, Olivia, had Byron as a second name. Correctly anticipating the verdict of history, Moore told his friend that he and Napoleon were the world's great men. Bessy, we may be sure, made little of the rigours of child-bearing, although Moore frequently refers to her run-down condition. Two days after Olivia's arrival he went off to Donington. Perhaps Bessy liked to have him out of the way.

After the offer of an advance of £1,000 from Longmans for *Lalla Rookh*, he spoke of a move to London.

'This is a pleasant prospect', he wrote to Rogers, 'and what chiefly determines me in the step, for there are many considerations against it, of sober and shadowy hue, economy, prudence, etc. etc., all of which are best consulted in the country; but then I flatter myself I am become steady enough (with Bessy's aid, who is a very Minerva of economy) to resist all Town's temptations to expense; and then the times are getting cheaper, and I shall, I hope, be getting richer, and to crown all, I shall see you and the Donegals—shall hear music—go laugh at Liston—go walk in Hyde Park, and a thousand other intellectual amusements. Here, I really am in a desert; if I go to a dinner, the dullness of the good people is like suffocation,—I can hardly draw my breath under it. I have hopes, too, that the change of scene may do poor Bessy service, who has fallen off in everything but her sweetness of heart, most sadly . . .'

Within a few days he is off to business in London, and on his return writes to Rogers again. 'I feel so happy and quiet once more with my cottage, and my Bessy, and my books, and my Barbara . . .'.

Lady Donegal 'had the courage' to ask Princess Elizabeth for a ticket for Moore to see the Royal Wedding. Up he came to London.

'The Princess Charlotte stopped, as she passed, to shake hands with Lady Donegal, by whose side I stood so that I had an admirable view of her. I am about tired of the bustle of this place already, and even after a short week begin to sigh for my little cottage and Bessy again.'

And to his mother he wrote to say that although he was 'in *terrible* request, never half so much so before, and that, flattering as it is all, I am delighted at the idea of being off on Friday next (as I expect) to the cottage. This, I know, will give you more pleasure than anything else, as it proves I am happy at home, which is the source of every comfort and virtue in this life. I only wish you were there to make it still happier to me. God bless my darling mother'.

Olivia Byron Moore lived only for ten months. Bessy was overcome at her death, and Moore decided to take her to Dublin. Sea-water had been prescribed; and he decided to introduce her to bathing at Sandymount, the seaside resort of his youth.

The Moores arrived in Dublin on 26th May, 1815. Richard Power, the patron of the Kilkenny Theatre, lent them his well-appointed house, 7, Kildare Street. 'Every body in hysterics of joy to see us. All Dublin is at our doors, in carriages, cars, tilburies and jingles, from morning till night', he wrote to Rogers. His parents were overjoyed and delighted in their two grand-children; there was the happiest birthday for Tom with the family; the young Moores were going to pay visits in the country, among others to Lord Granard. But Moore is looking forward with feelings 'ungratefully impatient' to his 'return to the dear cottage at the end of August'. What he meant, perhaps, was that he fretted at the thought of *Lalla Rookh* abandoned for so long.

He refused to allow a public dinner to be given in his honour. 'I found', he wrote to Lady Donegal, 'there were too many of your favourites, the Catholic orators at the bottom of the design . . .'. Lamenting the state in which he found the country, he wished the Catholics in 'their own Purgatory' if it were not for their adversaries, whom 'one wishes still further'. He wrote as one belonging elsewhere; his roots were now transplanted.

As well as visits to the Duke of Leinster, Lord Granard, Richard Power at Kilfane, the Moores spent three weeks with his sister Kate, now Mrs Scully, in County Tipperary.

He described 'groups of ragged Shanavests (as they are called) going about in noonday, armed and painted over like Catabaw Indians, to murder tithe-proctors, land-valuers etc.

You have the most stimulant specimen of the sublime that Tipperary affords. The country indeed is in a frightful state: and rational remedies have been delayed so long, that nothing but the sword will answer now. We lost a visit to the Grattans by this barbarous trip . . .'.

Kate had a miscarriage when the Moores were on their visit; so that it was possibly a less than hilarious occasion.

Even now, with his marriage so well established, he must be for ever weighing and measuring it. Poor Bessy was often sick. 'I never love her so well as when she is ill, which is the best proof how *really* I love her', he wrote to Rogers, and he can still tell his mother that Mary Dalby says 'I do not think in the world you could have found another creature so suited to you as that' (in the context the tribute sounds as if Tom thought that his mother had not seen Bessy to her best advantage away from home), and Lady Donegal is told that Bessy was 'delighted with the confidential frankness of your letter to her, and felt something far beyond the mere *honour* that it did her, though that was felt too, as it ought to be'.

He was obviously uneasy—as Croker saw—about the way the world (and his mother) regarded the step he had taken and anxious for their good opinion of Bessy. He kept her out of Byron's way and seldom referred to her. But to Dalton, an old Dublin friend—and with these he was more spontaneous than with some of his later and more exalted correspondents—he wrote what Bessy would have recognised as the truth about his feelings. Olivia Byron Moore had been given the same first name as Dalton's wife. Apologising, as usual, for Bessy's inability to accompany him to London to meet Mrs Dalton again, Moore proceeds. He had, he said, been recently telling Tom Sheridan that 'he was one of the very few fellows in this world who, I thought, might compare with me in the article of *wives*, and *you*, my dear Dalton, are another of this very few; for to have a wife *pretty* as well as *everything* else she *ought to be* is a thing us men ought, morn and night, to bless God for'.

The cynical Rogers was always Bessy's champion; Moore writes to tell him that 'yesterday evening which was a very beautiful one while Bessy on her donkey and I with a child in each hand were taking our after-dinner ramble, she said "how

I should like Mr Rogers to meet us all this way unexpectedly" '.
In this letter he entreats Rogers to read *Emma*. 'It is the very
perfection of novel-writing . . . so much effect with so little
effort!'

When the subject of Paris was raised again, Bessy removed
her objections when she heard that living was cheap. The money
from advances on *Lalla Rookh* made up Moore's mind. He was
going to leave Mayfield. Once again he took refuge in a friend's
house before embarking on a move. The wealthy Strutts in
Derbyshire put the Moores up for two months, and would have
kept them for ever. Mr Strutt could never see him without
giving him something. One of his presents was a very snug and
handsome easy chair for Moore's study.

Douglas, the sea captain, who had laid his purse open to
Moore, now a Rear-Admiral, had been appointed Governor of
Jamaica; he offered Moore the post of secretary. But Moore
had had enough of the Pacific. Life in the Caribbean would
have been exactly of that idyllic kind he honoured only in
verse. He refused. Can he be blamed for occasional fits of
complacency when people were for ever trying to attach him to
themselves?

In January 1816 he told James Power that he would not
'encounter another winter in this coldest house of a most cold
country, and I dare say it is somewhere near town our next
move will be to'. Power offered him a present of a new piano.
And Moore had declined it while he was in his vagabond state.
To Mary Godfrey, reporting on the family ills, he told the truth.
He was waiting on for the completion of his long poem, on this
all his hopes rested, then he would shift his quarters nearer to
her for good and all, 'indeed *here* it is impossible to stay for
another winter; so I have said for these two winters past, and,
then, like the returning smiles of a mistress, the sweet summer
looks of the little place made me fall in love with it again'. But
now he was determined to avoid a repetition of these horrors.

Sheridan died on the 7th of July. In a recent letter to Rogers
there was no sign of heartbreak in his enquiry after 'poor
Sheridan' whom he had seen 'is nearly gone and that his
numerous friends are so anxious in their enquiries that the
knocker and bell are obliged to be taken off'! He leaves the

subject to make references to a solicitor and some joke that Rogers made about a subscription to a monument. There is nothing to suggest that the circumstances of Sheridan's death would fire him to an indignant outburst nor did he know that soon he would be collecting material for Sheridan's biography.

Moore does not refer in this letter to the occasion in the previous month when he was with Rogers and a note arrived from Sheridan, asking Rogers for £150. 'I am absolutely un-done and broken-hearted', Sheridan had written. 'I shall negotiate for the Plays successfully in the course of the week, when all shall be returned. I have desired Fairbrother to get back the Guarantee for thirty. They are going to put the carpets out of window, and break into Mrs S's room, and *take me*—for God's sake let me see you. R.B.S.'

Rogers and Moore—it was after midnight—walked down to Savile Row together to assure themselves that the threatened arrest had not yet been put in execution. A servant spoke to them out of the area and said it was intended to paste bills over the front of the house next day.

Rogers, the unfailing, sent Moore with the money on the following morning. Sheridan was as 'good-natured and cordial as ever . . . His voice had not lost its fullness of strength, nor was that lustre, for which his eyes were so remarkable, dimi-nished'. Within a month, Sheridan was dead, but not before the sheriff's officer had arrested him in bed and was about to carry him off to a spunging house when the doctor interfered.

The verses which Moore then sent anonymously to the news-paper could not have been inspired by sudden grief or indigna-tion; the opportunity to vent his spleen against the Prince was irresistible. In later years he did not regret his indignation: the Prince was linked in his mind with Lord Moira and his own bitter recollections of patronage run to seed. He wrote of Sheridan:

Whose humour, as gay as the fire-fly's light,
Play'd round every subject, and shone, as it play'd;
Whose wit, in the combat as gentle as bright,
N'er carried a heart-stain away on its blade;

and of the Prince:

> And thou, too, whose life, a sick epicure's dream
> Incoherent and gross, even grosser had passed,
> Were it not for that cordial and soul-giving beam
> Which his friendship and wit o'er thy nothingness cast.

It would not have been difficult to trace the writer, but Moore was not threatened; this was not due to the Prince's indifference. When the *Life* of Sheridan appeared, he called in John Wilson Croker and gave him a long, carefully prepared and plausible account of his transactions with Sheridan.

In Derbyshire Moore served notice of his intention to quit on his landlord, but when autumn came he lingered, unable to make the break—Bessy was worried about the expenses. Christmas came and found him still at the cottage. 'Bessy', he wrote to his mother, 'is continuously making projects for our all living together . . . I am not without hope that some of her visions may yet be realised.'

The key to this indecision was still *Lalla Rookh*; when in March 1817, he went up to London to deliver the manuscript to the printers he settled on a cottage at Hornsey at the foot of Muswell Hill. Longmans had advanced a thousand pounds. The other two thousand he was going to invest for his father to draw the interest. If Bessy ached a little at this—outwardly she probably accepted it cheerfully—she gave no sign.

Before moving into the London cottage, the Moores stayed with Mrs Branigan, 'an excellent person'. One night they went to Drury Lane; the next to the Opera. 'Bessy has just gone out with Lady Donegal in her carriage to look for a new bonnet.' *Lalla Rookh*, so long awaited, looked like Aladdin's cave.

In a cheerful mood he wrote to the obliging Mr Strutt, his October host in Derbyshire, praising his new abode, cheerfully announcing the presence of rats, and with his genius for giving friends commissions, asking for the tailor's bill. 'He at present being the only person in Derbyshire to whom I owe money.'

Lalla Rookh saw the light of day on 27th May 1817, within a few days a second edition was in preparation, a third was issued in July, and in March of the following year Moore wrote that the seventh edition was printing. An East Indian ship was called after the poem; on a state visit to the court at Berlin, the

Grand Duke Nicholas (afterwards Czar) and his wife took part in an elaborate stage adaptation of it which, to Moore's satisfaction, was made the subject of a volume illustrated with plates. Moore was now the most popular poet in the world, according to Edgar Allan Poe.

Reviews were glowing. He had hit exactly the taste of his time, and Byron's pioneering had, if anything, the effect of creating an expectant audience. The general tone of the reviewers was not much short of rapturous, and this included the criticisms in the more distinguished journals. *Blackwoods*, for instance, called him the 'most ingenious, brilliant and fanciful Poet of the present age'; the *Edinburgh Review* on this occasion found 'the very genius of poetry' in the work while finding faults of style. 'The Rising of a sun which will never set' was but one of many laudatory expressions, and the most touching tribute of all was a present of three pounds from an unknown girl, her only way to express the delight she had experienced. But Moore's active service for the Whigs and his satires had to be paid for; an enemy had written a book with the consequences that usually follow. When friends such as Leigh Hunt (there had been no quarrel yet) and Byron disliked the poem, it was not difficult for a jaundiced eye to see plenty to pillory. It was inevitable that he should be accused of imitating Byron and carped at for going to the East instead of writing about English themes. It remained for the *British Lady's Magazine* to find underneath the gorgeous draperies 'immorality, impiety and voluptuous vice'.

Was it translated into Persian, as rumour spread abroad? Did witty Luttrell think so, when he wrote:

> I'm told, dear Moore, your lays are sung.
> (Can it be true, you lucky man?)
> By moonlight in the Persian tongue,
> Along the streets of Ispahan.

Some of the critical notices seem nowadays to be far closer to the mark than the volleys of praise. *Lalla Rookh* is now almost unreadable. Those months in the library at Donington were wasted. That is not the way to furnish the imagination. Moore's slow progress was not altogether perfectionism at work. He lacked inspiration. The poem achieved exactly what he intended. He was now consecrated. The ghost of Little was finally laid. He had, in modern jargon, become an unassailable figure of the establishment. He noted Croker's attentions at a Trinity College dinner in London. 'I could not have had a better proof of the station which I hold in the public eye than that Croker should claim friendship with me before such men as Peel, the Duke of Cumberland, etc etc.' Lady Bessborough sent for the Moores to go to her box. And Lord Lansdowne, a quiet and gentle but enormously influential Whig nobleman, 'said he should feel delighted if I would fix my residence near his house in the country, and that my best way would be to take Bessy there on a visit to him and Lady Lansdowne this summer'. More was to come of that.

Meanwhile Moore never lost his head. He was too much on the look-out for the effect he was making to get carried away for long; and his self-appraisal was always cool and well-judged. At this time a row between the Power brothers over Moore's copyrights was at its height. Moore was chafing over the delay in putting *Oft in the Stilly Night* to music.

He had asked James Power to hold up publication of the seventh number of the *Irish Melodies* until he saw how his long poem went. 'I still have my fame in the lyrical way to retire upon—but, if I should so unluckily contrive it as at the same time to fail in *both*, I am *bedevilled*, and you with me altogether . . .'

Twenty years later writing to Thomas Longman, whose treatment of Moore was hardly less than noble, Moore anticipated the verdict of posterity.

'Dear Tom,

'With respect to what you say about *Lalla Rookh* being the "cream of the copyrights", perhaps it may in a *property* sense; but I am strongly inclined to think that, in a race into future times (if *anything* of mine could pretend to such a run), those little ponies, the "Melodies" will beat the mare, *Lalla Rookh*, hollow.'

Scott gave the signal that the day of the poem for narrative purposes was over. Moore is later to be found turning an idea, conceived originally as a poem, into a novel. The result was *The Epicurean*—admired at the time, but proof that for Moore there was no future if he tried to follow in Scott's footsteps.

Moore got the idea of using the story of Robert Emmet in one of the four sections into which the four-hundred-page *Lalla Rookh* was divided. *The Fire Worshippers* describes the conflict between the Ghebers with their Persian religion and the Moslems. Lalla Rookh is the daughter of Al Hassan, the Muslim tyrant. She is loved by Hafed, leader of the Ghebers. Lalla tries to warn her lover of his danger, but he stays in his citadel and she—in opera fashion—joins him to die with him.

As Moore said that he had the Emmet parallel in mind there is no point in arguing with learned scholars who have claimed because the poem was hailed in Poland, it could not have had a merely local inspiration. The theme is universal; but Moore was able to kindle some fire by thinking of Emmet. His interest in the Ghebers was strictly academic.

There are fine lines in the poem, but it is all weighed down by lack of inspiration. One verse lives, if only in parody:

> Oh! ever thus from childhood's hour
> I've seen my fondest hopes decay;
> I never loved a tree or flow'r
> But 'twas the first to fade away.
> I never nursed a dear gazelle.
> To glad me with its soft black eye,
> But when it came to know me well,
> And love me, it was sure to die!

Nothing reveals more the long-term failure of Moore's enterprise or his own perspicacity than the fact that the only portions of the poem which have ever had the semblance of life are the songs with which it was sprinkled. He reserved the right to publish these separately through Power.

> There's a bower of roses by Bendemeer's stream
> And the nightingale sings round it all the day long;
> In the time of my childhood 'twas like a sweet dream,
> To sit in the roses and hear the bird's song.

That was made for light opera or musical comedy. Rogers, whose high contemporary reputation is inexplicable now, is to some extent responsible for misdirecting Moore.

There was the article of money, so badly needed. *Lalla Rookh* had provided £3,000 but, as we have seen, Tom used the bulk of this to help his family—it was soon to be called upon to meet debts. The sudden affluence made no difference. Moore was always short of cash.

When he set off with Rogers to celebrate in Paris, he wrote to his mother to say that he had taken a letter of credit for three hundred pounds for form's sake 'and the dash of the thing' but he expected to spend only thirty. She must have nodded her head when she read that.

Charles Greville, who knew the world, describes a dinner given for the Hollands; Melbourne was among the guests. Greville was sitting beside Luttrell, a wit whose good things were often recorded in Moore's Journal. Luttrell was talking of Moore and Rogers—the poetry of the former so licentious, that of the latter so pure; much of its popularity owing to its being so carefully weeded of everything approaching indelicacy; and the contrast between the *lives* and the *works* of the two men —the former a pattern of conjugal and domestic regularity, the latter of all the men he had ever known the 'greatest sensualist'.

To point his paradox Luttrell may have been too severe to Rogers. When he died Greville wrote at length about him. It is the best picture we have of one who played a beneficent part in Moore's life. Greville and Rogers had fallen out because Greville explained, he was not a patient listener. Rogers's voice was feeble, and it has been said that his bitterness and the caustic nature of his remarks arose from the necessity of his attracting attention by the pungency of his conversation.

Moore, we may be sure, listened to Rogers. That was one of Moore's charming qualities. When he first appeared in society he was slow to hold forth; and he is never accused of monopolising the conversation. The acid test was Macaulay. He expressed his delight in Moore's company, which shows with what exquisite tact Moore must have waited for those 'flashes of silence'.

Russell's editing of Moore's Journal, according to Professor

Dowden, has falsified the relationship between Moore and Rogers. Russell, for instance, cut out a passage which Dowden supplies showing how Rogers behaved when he heard Moore describe the success of his *The Epicurean.*

'I was foolish enough to pour out a little of my prosperity on him. A silence ensued, & at last he said "You *stop* very strangely in your book". "Oh then" I said, "You've read enough of it, to find out the bad stopping?" "No",—he answered, "I merely turned over a page of it at a bookseller's yesterday". The next time I saw him about the middle of the week, he said "Well, I have read the last three lines of your book & think it very pretty". The only set-off against all this is that if my book had not been succeeding, he would have been foremost to give it a lift.'

Hobhouse in his Journal for 25 January 1826 reports Rogers deprecating Moore's writing the *Life* of Byron, saying that he was 'a wretched fellow'. Rogers urged Hobhouse to undertake the task. Moore—again I rely on Dowden—listened to Allen (the Hollands' librarian) comparing Rogers unfavourably with Monk Lewis, calling him a social climber. And Moore in his Journal complained of Rogers's lack of consideration for his 'little businesses' and described 'ridiculous exhibitions of his with Lady Louisa Vane' when Rogers concealed himself in a gallery niche and jumped out upon her as she passed.

For his part, in letters to his sister, Rogers is found complaining when Moore fails to call on her when he is abroad, visiting great houses. He was a man who liked others to be under an obligation to him. Some of his anger with Moore was occasioned by the other's refusal to turn to him more frequently for help. The great thing is that the friendship, for all these fractures, survived for as long as Moore lived.

Rogers had cardinal merits as a travelling companion: he was not encumbered with a wife; he had lots of money; he was free with his purse. It was worth giving him his head in conversation and, wherever Moore was, he would discover unlimited diversionary opportunities, an endless round of calls.

He wrote ecstatically to James Power. 'Paris is the most delightful world of a place I ever could have imagined; and, really, if I can persuade Bessy to the measure, it is my intention to come and live there for two or three years.'

Before the end of the month he was home again. Barbara, the Moore's eldest child, had had a fall and was seriously ill. Bessy tended her day and night. Telling his Derbyshire friend Strutt of this sad news, he copied out the verses Byron had addressed to him and which had arrived in a letter. Certainly Moore shared to the full his correspondents' interest in himself. And when the little girl died, Moore's letter to his mother reveals this artless self-preoccupation.

'It's all over, my dearest mother; our Barbara is gone. She died the day before yesterday, and, though her death was easy, it was a dreadful scene to us both. I can bear such things myself pretty well; but to see and listen to poor Bessy makes me as bad as she is. Indeed, my dearest mother, you can only conceive what she feels by imagining *me* to have been snatched away from you at the age of Barbara. It will be some time before she can get over it; but she is very sensible and considerate; and her love for us that are left her will, I know, induce her to make every effort against the effect of this sorrow upon her mind.'

A few days later he can report that Bessy is somewhat more composed, and lets fall that he will 'go down as soon as possible to Lord Lansdowne's, who (I think I told you) wrote most friendly to me to say he had been looking out for a house in his neighbourhood for me. It would certainly be an object to be near such a man; his library, his society, all would be of use to me; not to mention the possibility of his being some day or other able to do me more important services. Lady Donegal is very anxious that I should take the house he talks of'.

Lord Moira had been replaced; and Moore was on the move again.

Moore was not impressed by the house near Devizes in Wiltshire; but Bessy went to inspect it with James Power, and was 'not only satisfied but delighted with it; which shows the humility of her taste, as it is a small thatched cottage, and we get it furnished for £50 a year'.

Bessy had, no doubt, approved the project from the start. The chief consideration was to keep Tom away from the expense and distractions of life in London. Lady Donegal would have been in one mind with her on this. And now that the rat-infected houses at Hornsey was haunted by the ghost of the dead child, any change could only be a blessing. Within a month they were installed. 'Our maids (servants being always the hardest to please) look a little sulky at the loneliness of the place; but I dare say they will soon get reconciled', he told Power.

As there was room for the Moores (who were to add two small boys to the family) and the servants, the thatched cottage was more commodious than Moore's description would suggest. In later years he made extensive repairs and additions to it, among others slating the roof. It is today a charming, cheerful house.

'I dare say we shall find it dreary enough through the winter', he confided to his new friend Strutt after Power sent a present of the piano he had offered Moore in Derbyshire. The death of Barbara, he said, left 'a want of confidence in the blessings that still remain'.

Moore's recent trip to Paris had excited his imagination. He settled down at once to a new work, *The Fudge Family in Paris*. It took the form of letters between members of the family, in rhymed couplets, altering the metre from anapaests to tetrameter when the father Fudge writes. The lighter verse of the young Fudges has lasted better. Phelim O'Connor, a cousin of the Fudges, is joined in the correspondence to represent the views of an Irish patriot. The scheme allows for a mixture of comedy and satire. It was an extension of the *Twopenny Post-bag* formula which had been so unexpectedly successful.

In spite of the family sadness, Moore, after the birth of *Lalla Rookh*, was in high spirits, and this is still apparent in what is the most readable today of Moore's satires. When he published the poem in the following year, he added for good measure a long diatribe in verse against Canning, who had joined the Government that handed Europe over to reactionary governments. Canning had referred to a man of seventy who had been injured in riots as 'revered and ruptured Ogden'. Had Canning eaten his children he could hardly have inspired harsher invective than Moore poured out in too many quatrains. Unrepentantly sympathetic to Napoleon (Louis XVI is described as 'a Royal craven') the various reception of the

Fudges by the press was largely coloured by political alignments. It was paid the most genuine compliment by an immediate flow of imitations and parodies.

Blackwood's, which had been favourable to *Lalla Rookh*, raked up Moore's licentious past and advised him to stay away from polemics, he was encouraging sedition. Palmerston was one of the contributors to a counter-blast, *The New Whig Guide*, in which some of Moore's Irish songs were parodied. Moore, according to the *Literary Gazette*, was 'pandering to the basest passions of the multitude'.

The most enthusiastic of all the critiques the verses received came from the redoubtable Hazlitt.

'The spirit of poetry in Mr Moore', he wrote, 'is not a lying spirit. "Set it down, my tables"—we have still, in the year 1818, three years after the date of Mr Southey's laureateship, one poet, who is an honest man. We are glad of it: nor does it spoil our theory, for the exception proves the rule. Mr Moore united in himself two names that were sacred, till they were prostituted by our modern mountebanks, the Poet and the Patriot. He is neither a coxcomb nor a catspaw,—a whiffling turncoat, nor a thorough-paced tool, a mouthing sycophant, "a full solemn man", like Mr Wordsworth—a whining monk, like Mr Southey, —a maudlin Methodistical lay-preacher, like Mr Coleridge,— a Merry Andrew, like the fellow that plays on the salt-box at Bartlemy Fair, or the more pitiful jack-pudding, that makes a jest of humanity in St Stephen's Chapel. Thank God, he is like none of these, he is not one of the Fudge Family.

'Mr Moore calls things by their right names: he shews us kings as kings, priests as priests, knaves as knaves, and fools as fools. He makes us laugh at the ridiculous, and hate the odious. He also speaks with authority, and not as certain scribes we could mention. He has been at Court, and has seen what passes there . . .

'But he was a man before he became a courtier, and has continued to be one afterwards; nor has he forgotten what passes in the human heart. From what he says of the Prince, it is evident that he speaks from habits of personal intimacy; he speaks of Lord Castlereagh as his countryman. In the epistles of the Fudge Family, we see, as in a glass without a wrinkle, the mind and person of Royalty in full dress up to the very throat, and we have a whole-length figure of his Lordship, in the sweeping, serpentine line of beauty, down to his very feet.'

Hazlitt was never to be so pleased with Moore again.

In a letter to Strutt, dated November 1817, Moore speaks of 'a little triumph' he had had. Murray had invited him to write a poem as a preface to an edition of Sheridan's collected works. Moore refused when he saw that the book was dedicated to the Prince Regent. But he agreed to write an essay if the publisher sacrificed 'his R.H. to me'.

The Sheridan essay led to the idea of a full biography. Moore hesitated. Murray offered £1,000 for it. And when Moore asked for half the amount as an advance, he had committed himself. In the event the book was not published for seven years, and then by Longmans.

The Moores were settling down at Sloperton Cottage, as it was called. Lady Donegal was given a long description of their life. Moore's only regret was that there was not some 'near and plain neighbour for Bessy to make intimacy with, and enjoy a little tea-drinking now and then, as she used to do in Derbyshire. She continues, however, to employ herself very well without them; and her favourite task of cutting out things for the poor people is there in greater request than we bargained for . . .' But someone was found.

One of the Moores' neighbours was Robert Hughes, once a fellow of King's, but reduced in circumstances, having failed at farming—these were bad times—and dependent for a living upon the sale of licenses to hawkers and pedlars—a monopoly which was threatened. Moore interceded on his behalf on more than one occasion. Bessy found Mrs Hughes congenial—no doubt she could not afford to give herself airs. Often when Moore was going to Bowood to dine, he dropped Bessy off at Buckhill, the Hughes's house. And Lady Lansdowne, in an extremity, snatching Moore away from home for a dinner at Bowood, employed Mrs Hughes as a Bessy-sitter.

Bessy enjoyed herself when she hadn't to live up to high-life assumptions. She was happy with Rogers for instance, although he was considered a cynic. He gave the Moores presents of fine furniture, and from the first took to Bessy and she to him.

Strange, because his face was so habitually gloomy that Alvanley, a wit of the time, asked him once, why, when he could afford it, didn't he keep his own hearse. One evening when Tom was reading *The Vicar of Wakefield* aloud a young Irishman called with a tale of woe that his wife had been delivered of twins on the road and was without provision of any kind. Bessy responded at once, made a large jug of caudle, raided her larder, and gave two shillings. One of which Moore claimed as his gift, because the visitor was an Irishman. When the pitcher was not brought back next day, Moore went out to find he had been cheated. 'Sad hardness of the heart these tricks are.' But he bore no resentment, nor did Bessy. And the entry in the diary he had begun to keep reads:

'Walked my dear Bessy for the first time into the garden; the day delightful. She went round to all her flower beds to examine their state, for she has every little leaf in the garden by heart. Took a ramble afterwards by myself through the Valley of Chitoway, and the fields. Exactly such a day as that described so beautifully by the sacred poet Herbert:

> Sweet day, so cool, so calm, so bright,
> The bridal of the earth and sky;
> Sweet dews shall weep thy fall to-night,
> For thou must die.

'Wrote some more of my flashy epistle; and, in the evening, finished *The Vicar of Wakefield* to Bessy; we both cried over it. Returned thanks to God most heartily for the recovery of my darling girl, and slept soundly.' The tears of a happy man.

Bessy never changed. A diary entry fourteen years later fixes her character and explains the durability of that marriage. 'An invitation from Lady Lansdowne to Bessy to dine at Bowood on Monday and go with her to Mrs Heneage's ball. After a long discussion with the dear girl, in which I in vain persuaded her to get a new gown for the occasion, she consented to if I would allow her to go in the old one which, she assured me, was quite good enough for a poor poet's wife. Took her answer (accepting the invitation) to Bowood, where I dined.'

Moore was perfectly situated. All his grander London friends came at one time or another to stay at Bowood, and he dined there regularly. Bessy could only be persuaded to go when the Bowleses (the parson poet and his wife) were invited, and she had the old lady 'to protect her'. But it was not a success, and Moore had resolved not to put her to the torture of it often. 'In addition to her democratic pride—which I cannot blame her for—which makes her prefer the company of her equals to that of her superiors, she finds herself a perfect stranger in the midst of people who are all intimate; and this is a sort of dignified desolation which poor Bessy is not at all ambitious of. Vanity gets over all these difficulties; but pride is not so practicable . . .'

However, it was better when the Lansdownes called at the cottage bringing with them Pamela, Lord Edward Fitzgerald's daughter, when they lunched together and listened to music and rambled together to see the church on the other side of the valley. Lady Lansdowne, 'frank and sensible, unaffected, and certainly very pretty', was 'all heartiness and good-nature'. Bessy 'whose element is home, was seen, I flatter myself, to much advantage'. As for the new patron: 'He is delightful: and if I could but once forget he is a Lord, I could shake his hand as heartily as that of any other good fellow I know.'

Soon Moore was writing to tell his mother that the seventh edition of *Lalla Rookh* was going to press and 'poor Bessy is ailing with *her* new edition, and is often very low-spirited; but she keeps up for my sake, and does her utmost to make me happy and comfortable'.

At the very moment when his circumstances were at their meridian, his reputation established, a patron installed, *The Fudges* running at once into five editions, his mind at its most inventive, and the prospect of a child, the best cure for recent heartbreak—Fate struck Moore her worst blow to date.

The deputy whom he had appointed in Bermuda defaulted and Moore was held responsible for the amount involved which was reckoned at £5,000. He had hoped Sir John Sheddon, the deputy's uncle, who had recommended him to Moore, might feel obliged to make good the loss. But no offer was forthcoming.

Before he realised the worst Moore went to Dublin for three weeks to see his mother and to collect Sheridan material from the Rev. Thomas Lefanu, who had married Sheridan's sister.

On the previous visit to Dublin Moore had been complacent and rather unpleasantly derisory of the efforts to honour him; but now it was different. Rogers heard from him that there had never been anything like the reception he got. 'It was even better than Voltaire's at Paris.' There was more 'heart' in it. In the theatre he had been hailed with applause which broke out again on several occasions during the performance. It was 'overwhelmingly gratifying' as well as 'proof of the strong spirit of nationality in my countrymen'. With the success of the Fudge family and his appearance as the satirist-in-chief of the British Government, Tom was at last accepted as a national political force.

At a public dinner in Morrison's Great Rooms in Dawson Street, Lord Charlemont was in the chair. There were as many lords as Moore could have desired, and Maturin and Lover, and Daniel O'Connell. Moore made several speeches, and did not forget to pay a tribute to his father, who sat on one side of the Chairman. It must have been a proud night for John Moore. Keats, reading of this, wrote to his brother and sister in America that 'the most pleasant thing that accured was the speech Mr Tom made on his Father's health being drank'.

When Moore came back from Dublin, Bessy was in the garden waiting to greet him. There was the usual panic about smaller matters. His portmanteau had gone astray. An order for fish was sent to James Power—the Bowleses were coming to dinner.

By July Moore was promising Murray he hoped to have 'Sheridan' completed by Christmas. It proved a rash prophecy. But, in any event ,a task of this kind was an irresistible temptation to Moore. It gave him a valid excuse to be on the go. He had to collect material.

In the *Journal* which he now began to keep with the idea of creating a literary property for his family he describes a visit to Mrs Lefanu, Sheridan's sister at Bath. He found her 'the very image of Sheridan, having his features without the carbuncles, and all the light of his eyes without the illumination of his nose'. If only Moore could have retained his diary manner in the biography when it eventually appeared it would have been alive now, but the urge to experiment in metre did not attach to his prose.

The birth of Thomas Lansdowne Parr Moore in October 1818 was an occasion for rejoicing. Moore, always confident that his friends were on tiptoe for news about him, wrote at once to Lansdowne, Rogers and others. The choice of names for the heir was not without significance. 'Thomas' went without saying; 'Parr' was in honour of the great Greek scholar, whom Moore met with Mrs Lefanu; he had taught Sheridan at Harrow. Lansdowne was not inevitable. Moore had hesitated to presume; but when his patron called and discovered Moore and 'the little things were in the very thick of boiled beef and carrots' (Bessy was not on view), the 'long-thought of request' rose to his tongue. He let it out. Lansdowne consented 'with much kindness, saying he was proud to be elected to the office'.

At times Moore is caught complaining about the society in Wiltshire, but he got on very well with his neighbours and Bessy came to be regarded as a local Florence Nightingale. After Bowood the next great house was Lacock Abbey with its attendant mediaeval village, all still miraculously intact today (only a wing of Bowood has been left standing). Other neighbours, as well as the Hugheses, were the Phippses at Wans House, the Houltons at Farley, the Benets at Pyt House, and the Vicar of Bremhill, the poet Bowles. To these was to be added Napier, historian of the Peninsular War.

Coleridge was an admirer of Bowles's sonnets; the Vicar-poet was a thorough eccentric, but with conservative opinions. Turning his sheep bells in to thirds and fifths, he dressed as a druid and appeared at Stonehenge on the fourth of June. His absent-mindedness exceeded even Moore's; he engraved his own poems on the tomb stones of parishioners, and on one occasion presented a friend with a Bible inscribed 'with the author's compliments'. Moore, he wrote to his sister, was 'an example, in private life, of domestic happiness, and irreproachable conduct'. Of the parson, Moore recorded many strange accounts, but with amusement. On one occasion 'Bowles came after breakfast, more odd and ridiculous than ever. His delight at having been visited yesterday by the Prime Minister and Secretary of State, Lord L. having taken them both to Bremhill.

The foolish fellow had left his trumpet at home, so that we could hardly make him hear, or, indeed, do anything with him but laugh. Even when he has his trumpet, he always keeps it to his ear when he is talking to himself, and then takes it down when anyone begins to talk. To-day (17th October 1837) he was putting his mouth close to my ear, and bellowing away as if I was the deaf man, not he. We all pressed him to stay to dinner, but in vain; and one of his excuses was, "No, not indeed, I cannot; I must go back to Mrs Moore". Rogers very amusing about this mistake. "It was plain" he said, "where Bowles had been all this time; taking advantage of Moore's absence etc etc".'

Moore walked about with an abstracted air, the privilege of poets; but he entered fully into local affairs. There was nothing pompous about him; he went into town to buy breast-guards for Bessy when she was sore from suckling one of the infants; when Phipps got involved in a foolish duel, Moore was all concern; and there is a pleasing account in the Journal of his meeting the Phippses at one of the Lansdownes' London parties, and walking about with them, pointing out the celebrities present. Complaints about and references to servants are not often to be met in the Journal: it always comes as a surprise when even a children's nurse is mentioned. This must be a tribute to Bessy's management. One of the first entries in Moore's Journal describes the preparations for a Christmas party for the staff; food and drink coming down from London; Moore singing for them, and the two Moores joining all evening in the dancing. And these parties were not confined to their own staff. Guests were invited; up to twelve, on one occasion, which Moore described as 'a large party and most uproariously jolly in the evening'.

Moore was great fun. His more scholarly biographers have failed to stress this, and have left unintentionally an impression of an afflicted man.

He describes in his Journal in June 1828 how Bessy had written to tell him that young Tom had shown symptoms of fever. 'This news filled me with anxiety; the idea of his having typhus, and communicating it to the other two children, dreadful. Read the letter over and over again to try to extract comfort from it; read it also to Mrs Houlton who thought I had no reason to be alarmed. In the evening had all sorts of gaieties, in which I joined, I think with the more *abandon* from the exalted state of my mind during the day. Played at magical music and then blindman's buff.'

Next day he treated no news as good news, and went to look at the young beauties of the previous evening practising archery, and 'did not like it; the exertion unfeminine, and distorts both their figures and faces'.

He wrote one of his best lyrics at this time in the new series of National Airs, *Oft in the Stilly Night*.

> Oft, in the stilly night,
>   Ere Slumber's chain has bound me,
> Fond Memory brings the light
>   Of other days around me;
>   The smiles, the tears,
>   Of boyhood's years,
>   The words of love then spoken;
>   The eyes that shone,
>   Now dimmed and gone,
>   The cheerful hearts now broken!
> Thus, in the stilly night,
>   Ere Slumber's chain hath bound me,
> Sad Memory brings the light
>   Of other days around me.

In the summer of 1819, Bessy's sister Anne married William H. Murray in Edinburgh. Bessy and the children travelled by sea from London for the occasion. Dining out and theatre-going, Moore was the most active member of a committee to organise a Burns dinner, the proceeds to go to the erection of a memorial. The Duke of Sussex presided, and Moore found himself in a quandary when he was allotted only seven places at the high table. He had invited ten guests. 'Put down some of them to a lower table. Murray, one of them, not at all pleased, came to me, and said that the object of his coming was merely the pleasure of my company, and as it was rather inconvenient to him to stay, he would leave me a draft for his donation (ten guineas) and be off. This would not do, so

I promoted him to the top table. Phillips, too, very cross; but what could I do? Seated Crabbe next myself.'

That, at least, was as it should have been.

However, the dinner was a triumph for Moore when he rose to speak ('the people crowded from their seats round my table'). The Irish present were particularly enthusiastic. Moore's guest's subscribed a fourth of the subscriptions at the table; and Corry was too drunk to walk home.

On the following evening Moore proposed himself to dinner at Lady Holland's. In the middle of dinner she said to him 'I hope you mean to sleep here tonight; you are never agreeable when you are on the wing for your Lady Corks, etc., you haven't the *esprit present*'. And a man was thereupon dispatched to fetch Moore's 'things'.

Next day there was a frantic round of calls, hiring a fancy dress for Lady Darnley's ball, cancelling a dinner at Lord Dunmore's, a concert at the Philharmonica. This was too much; and had a Pooter ending. 'The ball a most beautiful spectacle, but I had left my glass at home; besides I was rather ashamed of my dress; and the little girl at my lodgings had stitched my stockings to the trunks so ill, that they came asunder, and threatened every minute to make a Highlander of me. To add to my annoyance, the Duke of Sussex, whom I was hiding from behind a pillar, took me by the hand, and drawing me forth into the full light of the room, said, "Come, let us look at you; why, you're very smart".'

It was not his first humiliation of this kind, to judge by a verse he had written in 1810:

Between Adam and me the great difference is,
Though a Paradise each has been forced to resign,
That he never wore breeches till turn'd out of his,
While, for want of my breeches, I'm banished from mine.

In the next few days there were dinners to meet William and Caroline Lamb, a ball at Lady Grey's, working over the National Melodies with Power and Bishop (who had replaced Sir John Stevenson). And Phillips, recovered from his annoyance at the Burns dinner, started to paint Moore's portrait.

The poet's fortunes had never been so prosperous. When

Bessy, from Edinburgh, wrote for fifteen pounds, he sent twice that sum and raced back to London to plunge into dinners again.

Bessy arrived in London to hear hopeful news of the progress of the Bermuda affair. The birth of a second Thomas Moore seems to have agreed with her health; she came back from Scotland happy, and even went out with her husband. They visited the theatre. The Lord of Misrule is always at the elbow of a man in a hurry; dining with Lord Lansdowne, Moore recited Byron's attack on Lord Romilly before he discovered that he was facing his son at the table. But he recovered from the shock at Covent Garden, after dinner, where *Mother Goose* was being performed.

And a similar confusion marked Bessy's departure with the little ones: 'Was mortified sadly at finding that I had by mistake taken their places in the six-inside coach, and that they were crammed in with a legion of disagreeable people, and a pile at the top quite terrifying. Wanted Bessy to forfeit what I had paid and give up going; but she would not. Worried myself about it all the evening, Richard Power and I went to the Lyceum to see the Jovial Crew; from thence to Covent Garden behind the scenes.'

Moore did not hug grief. It lighted on him, and took off after making the bough tremble.

Two days after Bessy's departure, 'the truth came upon me like a thunder-clap'. He learned that the Bermuda case had been given against him and an attachment was being put in force against his person. The letter telling him this had been misdirected; leaving Moore in a fool's paradise. He called on his publishers, wrote to tell Bessy the awful news, and 'dined with R. Power at the George and went to *Don Juan* in the evening'.

The fact that he could do so helps to explain the charm that he exercised over the people who now came forward to help. We may be sure that breakfasting next morning with Rogers, calling later at Holland House, dining in the evening at Lord Blessington's, Moore was the most cheerful person present.

Rogers was not the only one to advise a retreat out of the law's clutches; a compromise of the claim might be manoeuvred.

Longmans offered to pay any sum that was arrived at; Burdett suggested an appeal to the Crown to relinquish the claim. Perry, editor of the *Morning Chronicle*, had put in a paragraph with the object of arousing sympathy; Leigh Hunt answered it, and suggested opening a subscription list, offering himself to sell the piano upon which Moore had played; Rogers had £500 ready to put down, so had Richard Power of Kilfane, and Jeffrey in Edinburgh. Lord Lansdowne offered to underwrite the whole sum; Lord John Russell wrote to say that his brother Tavistock wanted to help, while he himself would give Moore the proceeds of his recent book; an unknown friend, Mrs A, offered her house as a place of concealment, adding that as her husband was unaware of the offer, would Moore please be tactful in the form of his reply; Miss F—author of 'Come, Stella, arouse thee'—offered the copyright in a volume of poems then in preparation. From Venice, Byron wrote to Murray. 'Talking of blunders reminds me of Ireland—Ireland of Moore. What is this I see in *Galignani* about Bermuda—agent—deputy —appeal—attachment etc? What is the matter? Is it anything in which his friends can be of use to him? Pray inform me.' Lord Strangford was another who wrote asking if he could come to his old friend's assistance.

And all this while Moore was discussing Sheridan, looking through Sheridan's papers, arguing the relative merits of Virgil and Milton. Lord Lansdowne congratulated him on being the first Irishman of his acquaintance not to make mistakes about 'will' and 'shall'. Back at the cottage there was much visiting and being visited, walking in woods, picnics, a *fête champêtre* at Devizes with musicians playing on an island in the water. 'Dined in the tower; very merry; the dancing, too, very pleasant.'

Pride forbade Moore to take any of the assistance offered; there was a plan to lodge him in Holyrood House; escape was urgent—Lord John Russell proposed a visit to Paris. Bessy at first had not taken kindly to this; but later was reconciled. She 'bears all so sweetly, though she would give her eyes to go with me; but, please Heaven! we shall not be long asunder'.

There were tears from all the women, and then Moore set out for London where Lord John had his coach in readiness to start.

Bessy came up to town for a day to have a last long look at her lord. 'God send I may meet her again in health and happiness, a nobler hearted creature never breathed!'

LORD JOHN RUSSELL's brother, the Duke of Bedford and his Duchess, took the travellers in their packet from Dover; the Bedfords were going to the Rhine. Moore's manner on his journey into exile can be guessed from the Duchess's expression of regret that she 'wished they had some one with them, like Mr Moore, to be agreeable when they got to their inn in the evening'.

Lord John was regarded as a rather awkward person socially; but this is not the impression Moore gives of his new friend. Once again he was fraternising with a young nobleman (Russell was twenty-seven) who had literary ambitions; he consulted Moore about giving up politics for literature. A future Prime Minister, it would have been a foolish choice. There is no evidence that he had literary talent of an original kind; but originality was not at the time valued highly. The idea of correctness prevailed. Moore's *Lalla Rookh* was most warmly praised for the wealth of detail he had amassed and his patient slogging to avoid mistakes in describing places he had never been to and scenes he had never witnessed.

Russell's affection for Moore was the most sincere compliment ever paid him, because Russell found human contacts difficult. During Moore's Paris sojourn, Russell came over from England on several occasions and spent much of his time with Moore. He was outwardly stiff, but kind. On hearing a tale of distress, he offered Moore £500 to relieve it, although the person concerned was a stranger. This friendship lasted up to and beyond the grave, and it was unique in Russell's withdrawn life. Gallois, one of Moore's Parish acquaintances, complained about Russell's apparent coldness of manner and 'indifference to what is said by others'. Moore understood a Frenchman's attitude to such reserve and silence. But, even in England, Russell was usually an uncomfortable person in general society. He was staying for a fortnight in Paris to do research work for a second edition of his *Life of Lord Russell*, then he proposed taking Moore in his coach over the Alps.

Here is an entry in Moore's Journal on his second day in Paris. It is a fair example of his life for the next three years.

'Sept. 10th 1819

'Saw Lord Lansdowne: drove about in Lord John's *caleche*. Went to the church of St Sulpice; the organ very beautiful. Dined with Macdonald, who has just married Lord Albemarle's daughter, Lady Sophia. Company: the Lansdownes, Lord Auckland, Lord John and myself. Went to the Théâtre-Français to see Mdlle. Mars in the *Misanthrope* and *Les Étourdis*, but got squeezed down nearly under the stage, and saw only a scene or two, but these were admirable. The scandal scene, where they all sit to cut up characters, which certainly, one would think, had given the hint to Sheridan, and Célimène's retort upon Arsinoe (I think), the Mrs Candour of the piece. Not able to stand the pressure: went off to the Opera, to a box which Lord Auckland had, and sat by a pretty little girl, Miss Herbert: the pieces, my old friends *Anacreon chez Polycrete* and *Flore et Zephyre*.

'Lord Lansdowne mentioned at dinner the practice which they have in Ava of annually squirting water at each other— King, Court and all. Eat ice at Tortoni's afterwards. Lord John to-day mentioned that Sydney Smith told him he had an intention once of writing a book of maxims, but never got further than the following: "That generally towards the age of forty, women get tired of being virtuous and men of being honest".'

While Lord John was taking notes in the library, Moore's days were very like his best times in London, and it is remarkable how many English people were in Paris at this time, enjoying no doubt the sensation of novelty after the years since the Revolution and war with France put an end to visiting the French capital.

On the 18th of September the two friends left Paris in Lord John's coach. They looked at the table on which Bonaparte had signed his abdication at Fontainebleau, with the marks of his penknife dug into it. Lord John repeated verses he had written,

which Moore found 'very good indeed'. He read on the journey
and kept a record of Russell's better anecdotes.

In his Journal Moore records his sensations when they arrived
at the Jura. 'When we arrived at La Vattay, Lord John and I
walked on, as the sun was getting very low. It was just on the
point of sinking when I ran on by myself, and at the turn of the
road caught a sight of the stupendous Mont Blanc. It is impossible to describe what I felt. I ran like lightning down the steep
road that led towards it, with my glass in my eye, and uttering
exclamations at every step.'

Crossing the Alps on the return journey from Switzerland
(where relics of Voltaire had absorbed the travellers' attention)
he does not search for words to describe the Simplon pass. 'It
baffles all description.' Close to the summit he walked on by
himself. 'All was magnificent to a degree that quite overpowered
me, and I alternately shuddered and shed tears as I looked
upon it.' Coming down new wonders are recorded as 'All
grand beyond description'.

Russell, remembering this excursion, more than thirty years
afterwards, fills in the picture.

Moore on the journey, 'leaving his country, embarrassed by
an unforseen incumbrance, and with but an uncertain hope of
an early return' was 'as cheerful as if he had been going for a
few week's amusement to the Continent, and we amused ourselves with imaginary paragraphs, describing his exile as "the
consequence of an unfortunate *attachment*". His sensibility to
happy and affecting emotions was exquisite'.

In Milan the inevitable round began again—from library to
dinner, to opera, to supper; and in the cathedral, if the music
was not very good, there were one or two pretty girls among
the congregation. As if Moore travelled with a touring company, even in Italy the scene is filled with 'Lord Kinnaird,
Lady Oxford, etc.'. He parted with Russell there to their
mutual regret, and proceeded on his way towards Venice and
Byron. Architecture meant nothing to him apparently, and
painting very little. He passed through Verona and Vicenza,
noticing certain antiques, with nothing to say about the beauty
of these cities. But he was in a hurry, and with his constitutional
restlessness had little time to spend on the way to the accomplish-

ment of his mission. 'Left Padua at twelve, and arrived at Lord Byron's country house, La Mira, near Fusina, at two.'

Moore arrived at a happy time; Byron was involved with his Countess Guiccioli, his days of dissipation were over; the meeting found them at once on their old laughing friendly footing.

If Byron had perused Moore's Journal notes, he might have been disappointed. Their encounter is laconically described.

'He was but just up and in his bath; soon came down to me: first time we had met these five years; grown fat which spoils the picturesqueness of his head . . . Found him in high spirits and full of his usual frolicsome gaiety.' Of the Guiccioli Moore observed that she was blonde, and young, but not very pretty. Moore had not been able to go into raptures about Venice because his companion's conversation, though 'highly ludicrous and amusing, was anything but romantic'.

Byron put Moore up in his own rooms in Venice; he had to stay with his Countess out of town for the sake of her health, but they met every day. Lord John removed from Moore's Journal, when published, Byron's 'I say, Tom, you might have been my salvation—for if you had come here a little sooner, I'll be damned if I would have run away with a red-haired woman of quality'.

If Moore was always cheerful with friends and spared them his woes, he never seems to have liked anyone better than he liked himself; Byron, by contrast, according to Moore, had a 'fixed hostility to himself'. The description of their meeting in Moore's biography of his friend reveals the nature of Moore's regard. 'The delight I felt in meeting him once more, after a separation of so many years, was not a little heightened by observing that his pleasure was, to the full, as great, while it was rendered doubly touching by the evident rarity of such meetings to him of late, and the frank outbreak of cordiality and gaiety with which he gave way to his feelings. It would be impossible, indeed, to convey to those who had not, at some time or other, felt the charm of his manner, any idea of what it could be when under the influence of such pleasurable excitement as it was most flatteringly evident he experienced at this moment.'

The Countess Guiccioli helped Moore when he was writing the biography, and the encomium on her charm and beauty in that is inconsistent with the note taken at the time. Byron's exuberant gaiety made their course through the Venetian canals one of 'uninterrupted merriment and laughter'. Moore preferred to stay at an hotel if Byron wasn't going to be at home, but Byron insisted on putting him up and promised to dine with him every day.

'As we now turned into the dismal canal, and stopped before his damp-looking mansion, my predilection for the Gran Bretagna returned in full force: and I again ventured to hint that it would save an abundance of trouble to let me proceed thither. But "No—no" he answered,—"I see you think you'll be very uncomfortable here; but you'll find it not quite so bad as you expect".'

'As I groped my way after him through the dark hall, he cried out, "Keep clear of the dog"; and before we proceeded many paces further, "Take care, or that monkey will fly at you;"—a curious proof, among many others, of his fidelity to all the tastes of his youth . . . When we had reached the door of the apartment it was discovered to be locked, and to all appearance, had been so for some time . . . I again sighed inwardly for the Gran Bretagna. Impatient at the delay of the key, my noble host, with one of his humorous maledictions, gave a vigorous kick to the door and burst open . . . "here", he said, in a voice whose every tone spoke kindness and hospitality,— "these are the rooms I use myself, and here I mean to establish you".'

They stood out on the balcony to look at the scene on the canal. Moore began to talk about Italian sunsets, 'that peculiar rosy hue'. Byron interrupted him. 'Come, damn it, Tom, don't be poetical.' Some English-looking men passed in a gondola. 'Lord Byron, putting his arms akimbo, said with a sort of comic swagger, "Ah, if you, John Bull, knew who the two fellows are now standing up here, I think you would stare".'

They had enormous fun. Moore's letters extant and his Journal (in which he was only note-taking most of the time) do not convey the pleasure of his company. It was not on account

of his domestic character that Byron pined for his presence. In
the midst of his wildest dissipations he had written

> What are you doing now,
> Oh Thomas Moore?
> What are you doing now
> Oh Thomas Moore?
> Sighing or suing now,
> Rhyming or wooing now,
> Billing or cooing now,
> Which, Thomas Moore?

That was when he was in love with his Venetian, Marianna,
of whom he wrote such intimate details to his publisher and
friends at the time. He was happy—for the moment—and it
set him off on another impromptu.

> But the Carnival's coming
> Oh Thomas Moore,
> The Carnival's coming
> Oh Thomas Moore,
> Masking and humming,
> Fifing and drumming,
> Guitaring and strumming,
> Oh Thomas Moore

They went by gondola to a former Jewish cemetery where
Byron had horses waiting. And proceeded—not very fast—
along the sands of the Lido after picking their way among the
fallen tombstones; they each wished to prolong the pleasure and
enjoy the sea air. One day Byron, always unpredictable, took
offence at the attentions of admirers, spurred his horse into a
gallop, and left Moore far in the rear. If the watchers had been
women, Moore objected, Byron would not have taken umbrage
or galloped away so fast.

In company Byron was gay, but afterwards, when they were
alone, the chief subject of conversation was Byron's marriage.
He was most anxious to hear the worst that was said about him,
admitting that 'on one or two occasions during his domestic
life' he had let 'the breath of bitter words escape him'. During
one of their few intervals of seriousness he pledged Moore

(whom he was sure would survive him) to surrender him up to 'condemnation where he deserved it, to vindicate him where aspersed'.

Moore recollected this, but pronounced Byron's apprehensions groundless when the time came. He was not aware of the extent of Lady Byron's machinations, and he had had experience of Byron's suspicious temper.

He had once written to Byron to say, 'When *with* you, I feel *sure* of you, but at a distance, one is often a little afraid of being made the victim, all of a sudden, of one of those fanciful suspicions which, like meteoric stones, generate themselves (God knows how) in the upper researches of your imagination, and come clattering down upon our heads, some sunny day, when we are least expecting such an invention'.

Once Byron had flown—to Moore's knowledge—'into one of his fits of half humorous rage' against him for a fanciful allusion to Byronic heroes in the Fudge verses. Byron admitted the truth of this and that he had planned retaliatory measures. 'But when I recollected what pleasure it would give the whole tribe of blockheads and blues to see you and me turning out against each other, I gave up the idea.'

Moore had hoped that Byron would come to Rome with him and Byron was eager to go; but Moore said he advised against it because at this time the husband of the Guiccioli was making himself unpleasant and had asked Byron for £1,000, which Byron was reluctant to give.

The Guiccioli gave him a holiday for Moore's last day in Venice; they went to the opera and then to a cabaret in the Piazza and sat beside the Palace of the Doges, drinking hot brandy and laughing over old times, 'till the clock of St Mark struck the second hour of the morning. Lord Byron then took me in his gondola, and, the moon being in its fullest splendour, he made the gondoliers row us to such points of view as might enable us to see Venice, at that hour, to advantage. Nothing could be more solemnly beautiful than the whole scene around, and I had, for the first time, the Venice of my dreams before me'.

Byron caught his companion's mood. 'His voice, habitually so cheerful, sunk into a tone of mournful sweetness, such as I

had rarely heard before from him, and shall not easily forget.'

Next day Moore called at La Mira on his way to Ferrara. 'A
short time before dinner he left the room and in a minute or two
returned carrying in his hand a white leather bag. "Look here,"
he said, holding it up. "This would be worth something to
Murray, though I dare say you would not give sixpence for it."
"What is it?" I asked. "My Life and Adventures," he answered.
On hearing this, I raised my hands in a gesture of wonder. "It
is not a thing," he continued, "that can be published during
my lifetime, but you may have it—if you like—there, do what
ever you please with it." In taking the bag, and thanking him
most warmly, I added, "This will make a nice legacy for my
little Tom who shall astonish the latter days of the nineteenth
century with it". He then added, "You may show it to any of
our friends you think worthy of it"—and this is nearly, word
for word, the whole of what passed on the subject.'

Byron tried to persuade Moore to stay longer in Venice; and
when he found him determined to move on remonstrated with
him. 'At least, I think, you might spare a day or two to go with
me to Arqua. I should like to visit that tomb with you'—(the
tomb where Petrarch is buried)—'A pair of poetical pilgrims—
eh Tom.' But Tom had set his mind on reaching Rome. The
fidgets were in the ascendant again. Afterwards he was amazed
at himself foregoing 'an excursion which would have been
remembered as a bright dream'. Byron went with him for some
miles, his horses following the carriage. And then 'I bade my
kind and admirable friend farewell'. They were never to meet
again.

A GOOD night's sleep lifted Moore's depression. He was making the Grand Tour, and there is no indication in his Journal that the parting from Byron left him sad. After his brilliant visit, his mind had turned at once back to the safe domestic anchorage where Bessy was in charge. Now he was ready to see all that could be seen. His church and gallery-trotting reveal his taste to be that of his time. The marbles of Canova, whom he was to meet in Rome, were praised as highly as any of the greatest of the Renaissance sculptors; sweetness was much in request, and theatrical effect. 'The sublime' is the aim, and naturalistic work—Caravaggio, for instance—an offence. A Magdalen by Van Dyck sent him into transports. 'The upturned eyes almost dissolved in tears are exquisite.' But when he went to the Sistine Chapel to see the Universal Judgement, he could not understand it or feel its beauty. 'Some of the dead *aspirants* are pulled up by rosaries, others are putting on their flesh for the trip.' Bernini's baroque fussed him; he did not understand his painter friend Jackson (to whom he was giving sittings) when he said Bernini's St Catherine in ecstasy looked 'equivocal'. Byron would have known what he meant.

Jackson and Chantrey the sculptor were Moore's guides, and Sir Joshua's sayings were always uppermost in his mind. Even at this date (1819) Turner's name cropped up when looking at a Claude. Excursions were made to Tivoli and elsewhere.

It was all breathless, but the glimpses of Moore are more precious than his reflections on his orgy of sightseeing. Inevitably there are people. His countrywoman, Lady Morgan, was having a social triumph. Lady Davy offered to take him out in her carriage. Bartolini insists on sculpting his head. He does Lady Burghersh an honour which became his complimentary stock-in-trade from this time forward—he lent her the Byron manuscript to read. When she admitted that she had copied out extracts, he insisted on being present while she burnt them. He heard music whenever he could; it was always and everywhere Rossini whose merits were the subject of endless debate. Sir Thomas Lawrence was in Rome. Moore saw his remarkable portrait of the Pope, but failed to be impressed. At an evening party at the Borghese palace he met the Princess (Napoleon's sister), 'a fine creature in her way: delighted to find that I knew her friends Ladies Jersey, Holland and Lansdowne. Showed her beautiful little hands, which I had the honour of kissing twice, and let me feel her foot, which is matchless'. Whether this was done in the presence of other guests or alone, he failed to mention.

At the Duchess of Devonshire's assembly, the famous beauty Mrs Dodwell was among the guests. Her husband had been a great favourite with the Pope, who called him 'Caro Doodle'. Moore asked the Abbé Taylor to introduce him to Mrs Dodwell, 'but he would not; said it would not be proper, and forced me instead into an introduction to her husband'.

He acquired a hundred books as well as Goldoni's *Memoirs*, which he had taken away from Lord Byron, leaving him an *Ariosto* in its place, and 'by the bye, have left the first volume behind me at Ferrara'. His mind began to run on the plan for a *Fudge Family in Italy*. It began with his recollecting Byron's saying 'What do you think of Shakespeare, Moore? I think him a damned humbug.' Moore had heard Byron speak slightingly of Shakespeare on other occasions and put it down to jealousy.

'Among my epistles from Italy must be one of the exaggerations of travellers, and the false colouring given by them and by drawings to the places they describe and represent. Another upon painting; the cant of connoisseurs, contempt artists have for them. To a real lover of nature the sight of a pretty woman, or a fine prospect, beyond the best painted picture of them in the world. Give, however, the due admiration to the *chefs d'oeuvre* of art, of Guido, Titian, Guercino etc. Mention the tiresome sameness of the subjects on which the great masters employed themselves; how refreshing a bit of paganism is after their eternal Madonnas, St Francises etc; Magdalen my favourite saint. Introduce in a note a discussion about the three Marys. Another epistle must touch upon the difference between the

Italian women and the German in love: more of *physique* in the feelings of the former: the Italian would kill herself for a living lover, whom she would forget if he died; the German would pine away for a dead one. The senses of the latter are reached through her imagination (as is the case very much with the Englishwoman), but the imagination of the Italian woman is kindled through her senses etc etc. Spent a miserable night at Covigliaio, bitten by fleas, bugs, and all sorts of *animaletti*.'

But the Fudge family's Italian journey never was committed to paper.

Urgent messages arrived from Lord John. He had been summoned to parliament and must return. Moore was to join him at Genoa without delay. The call was not obeyed. And Bessy?

'A letter today from darling Bessy;' 'some rows of Roman pearls for my darling Bessy'; 'bought a few cameos for my dear girl, and wished that the moment for giving them to her was come'; 'went to Torlonia's and got letters from my sweet Bessy, more precious to me than all the wonders I can see'; 'Miss Scroope gave me the two pretty Venetian bracelets for Bessy'; 'went to Bodoni's printing-house, and bought a copy of Gray's Poems (printed here) for Bessy'; 'bought Parini's works and a little mosaic of the Coliseum for Bessy, this being the dear girl's birthday. Heaven send her many happy returns of it; and may she always make me love and value her as intensely as I do at this moment.'

When, on the 11th December, he arrived in Paris, he went as soon as he could 'with a beating heart, to inquire for letters from home. Found only one from my darling Bessy . . .'

Longmans had also written to say that it was not safe for Moore to come back as yet to England. He decided to send for Bessy and the children, and plunged at once into the social life of the English in Paris. Chantrey and Jackson had accompanied him on the journey from Rome, and he was exercised to return their good offices on his Italian journey.

Their reaction to Voltaire's bust by Houdon, the resemblance which has given the world their idea of the philosopher, throws a sharp light on Moore's attitude to art. 'Though quite contrary to Chantrey's theory of what is beautiful in art, from its enter-

ing into all the common details of nature, yet he has confessed
that it has something very admirable in it, and that he never
tires of looking at it . . . It would be frightful to have the image
of any person one loved with such a true and ghastly resemblance to life.'

If 'life' was ghastly, Moore put its horror to good purposes in
Paris. On one of his evenings out

'Flahault sung, and so did I, very nervous about it. If I had
given way I should have burst out a-crying; as I remembered
many years ago at a large party at Lady Rothes's. No one
believes how much I am sometimes affected in singing, partly
from being touched myself, and partly from an anxiety to
touch others.'

There was an unaccountable absence of news from Bessy.
Moore rented 'a little *faery* suite of apartments' in the Rue
Chantreine, but he found housekeeping for himself 'a disagreeable operation' even though he was abroad most of the day
and night. A letter came from Bessy at last. Little Tom had
been very ill, but was now recovered.

Lady Morgan noticed a trait which was quite as characteristic of Moore as his restlessness and perpetual motion—he was
forever changing plans, making provisional arrangements to
dine, cancelling one engagement in favour of another, and
hesitating to commit himself so that he had options open for
dinner or supper on as many days as possible. This was not a
precaution intended only to save himself from having to refuse
a more attractive alternative to a previous engagement,
although it must have been so interpreted by many, including
Lady Morgan. It arose from anxiety about being tied down.
Sometimes he broke an engagement to eat alone.

Bessy and the family had not arrived in time for Christmas
1819. Moore was invited to dinner by the Feildings. He preferred
'faute de mieux' to pass the day with the Granards, 'who are
the oldest acquaintances I have here, and old recollections have
always something domestic about them. Resolved to invite
myself to dinner there, and called; but Lord G. anticipated me
by asking me himself. Told him, however, my intentions'.

But there was no anchoring him even for Christmas. 'Went
to Lady Giffard's in the evening, and heard Blanzini and his

wife sing some very pretty things. Mrs Fitzherbert, too, who I thought had cut me, gave me a very kind greeting.' His paper war against the Prince of Wales had not been taken to heart as much as he thought.

Bessy arrived with the family at Calais where Moore had travelled to meet them, well but for a broken nose from a fall off her pony. Her appearance had suffered, her 'beautiful nose too, that might have vied with Alcina's own, to have been so battered'. He hoped it would 'come right again', but never recorded its recovery or whether her shape which she began to lose after one of the children's births was ever restored.

The 'dear girl' set about settling the apartment on arrival, but her ignorance of French presented a difficulty. 'Rather hard upon me to be the interpreter on these occasions: indeed, housekeeping, millinery, everything, falls upon me just now and I fear there is but little chance of leisure for writing; besides there is this infernal young lady learning the pianoforte over my head. Dined in the evening; the first time I had attempted anything like study for some months.'

The note of grievance is rather hard on Bessy, but Moore was more disorientated by the move to Paris than he admitted to himself.

Longmans had accepted the idea of a 'Fudge Family in Italy', on which he had started work. 'Have made a resolution (in which Bessy joins me with pleasure) not to go into society here, excepting a few quiet friends to dinner sometimes. They relieve my fears both about time and purse; and I shall, I trust, get on more industriously from henceforward.'

The resolution was hardly made than the inevitable round of visits and dinners; calls and excursions got into full swing. On the 11th of October, nine months later, he was to record in the Journal: 'We dined alone with our little ones, for the first time, since the first of July, which was a very great treat to both of us; and Bessy said, in going to bed, "This is the first rational day we have had for a long time".'

The 'faery suite' had proved a sad disappointment, and the Moores were relieved to escape from a harridan landlady who fleeced them to a cottage on the Champs Elysées. There was continuous uncertainty about the time it would take to settle the Bermuda business. For a man of his temperament this uncertainty was the worst stimulus to work; but he felt under an obligation to the Longmans. Days passed with no work done. Then he would settle down to one project after another, all to prove false inspirations. The first was the *Fudge Family in Italy*. Longmans advertised it, but Moore had to confess that he could not work up the humorous elements and sent only political satires to his publishers, later to appear, but suppressed at the time because Longmans were advised they might prejudice Moore's chances of settling his case.

Napoleon's Egyptian campaign caught his interest. He began to buy books on the subject. Denon, who had accompanied Napoleon on his expedition, lent Moore the volumes of his history, the most authoritative work on the country. Moore spent hours with Denon inspecting drawings. Then he announced his intention of writing another *Lalla Rookh* with an Egyptian background. Denon told him that Savary had never been further than Cairo and 'had that kind of imagination which is chilled by the real scene, merely taking it from the description of others'. Without realising how fatal the confession was, Moore recorded complacently that this was 'very much the case with myself'.

Since his inspiration came from books, it was not surprising that he found Chateaubriand had anticipated what seemed like an original inspiration. However, he was not deterred. He was 'delighted with his subject': the adventures of an Epicurean who goes to Egypt in search of the Elixir of Immortality, sees the girl who disappears into the Catacombs and is later discovered dancing in a spectacle in the 'subterranean elysium of the Pyramids'. They meet and love: he is imprisoned; she rescues him; a persecution of Christians takes place; she is martyred. He tries to rescue her, is nearly killed, becomes a Christian, and devotes the rest of his existence 'to repentance and remembrance of the beloved saint who had gone before him'. Moore had adumbrated this fantasy in his diary before he left England. 'If I can't make something of all this, the devil's in it.'

With all the fervour a writer conjures up in the light of a false dawn, he set to work and wrote several lines almost every day.

To complete the dreariness of the scheme the story is told in rhymed letters. It all proved a sad waste of time. Some of the verses were later published, and the poem several years later was worked into a novel, *The Epicurean*. Meanwhile Moore was 'much harassed and depressed'.

The best thing to happen to the Moores during this period was their cultivation of the friendship of the Villamils, a Spanish couple. Tom described them as 'plain excellent people', and she sang. They owned a large property at La Britte, Coaslin, hanging over Sèvres, with magnificent views of Paris and St Cloud.

Moore's description suggests what happily proved to be the case; they were suitable friends for Bessy. Although she was often ill. Moore's wife led a gayer life in Paris than ever before. But her idea of friendship was as thorough as her notions of wifely duty. Mrs Villamil had two children during the Moore's time in Paris. Bessy was always there to help, getting out of a sick-bed to nurse one of the Villamil children, sitting up two nights running with another little one who died on the day before a party the parents had arranged. They refused to let the Moores take over the entertainment when it was apparent that the child couldn't live. And these were kind, good people. A child dying was an insufficient excuse to upset a social occasion—death in the nursery was not a matter of such great moment.

The Moore's were given a pavilion in the Villamil's grounds, which they occupied during the summer months. But Moore's writing went no better even in ideal surroundings. He was taken aback when Power advertised the eighth number of *Irish Melodies*. He had written none. However, he could always rise to this demand, although the lyrics in this number were to be the least inspired of all his melodies.

The favoured few were lent Byron's *Memoirs* to read; a supplement arrived from Ravenna while Moore was in Paris. At different times Moore was paying three people to make a copy of them. The original was beginning to suffer from the number of fingers that had handled it.

Russell came and went, eventually persuading Moore to come on a visit to England disguised with a false moustache.

(He would have been recognisable at quarter of a mile distance, even with a beard.) The trip gave him an opportunity to cross to Ireland to see his parents, to call on his publishers and to try to hurry on a settlement of the Bermuda imbroglio. While he was in England he was informed that the case had been settled. Lord Lansdowne had put up the money.

Even then Moore did not return to England immediately. But Sloperton Cottage was available, and the Moores were installed again in time to celebrate Christmas 1822.

The Paris diaries contain interesting accounts of Wordsworth and Canning. The latter, although the object of so much radical satire, was the more attractive. Moore met him walking with his daughter, 'a very pretty girl. I remember, when I saw and walked in company with this girl at Rome, I made a resolution (on observing not only her beauty, but feeling all those associations of an elegant and happy home which her manner called up), that I could never write another word against her father. His cordial reception of me has now *clinched* this determination'.

Wordsworth did not make such a romantic impression. Lady Frederick Bentley sent an invitation to Moore and Wordsworth to come to her box at the Comédie Française. Wordsworth had already invited his wife and sister to the theatre. 'The struggle . . . between nobility and domesticity was very amusing. After long hesitation, however, and having written one note to say he must attend his wife, *my Lady* carried it, and he wrote another accepting the seat. I should have liked well enough to have gone myself, but this was our dear little Tom's birthday, and I had promised to pass the evening at home.'

Dining with Canning next day, Moore got excited and feared he talked too much. Wordsworth, also present, was 'rather dull. I see he is a man to *hold forth*; one who does not understand the *give and take* of conversation'.

Wordsworth called on Moore at half-past eight on the following morning and stopped to breakfast. He accused Byron of plagiarising him and expressed his conviction that Scott was the anonymous author of the Waverley novels, although he was shocked to find in them 'such bad vulgar English as no gentleman of education ought to have written'. The only person he praised unequivocally was Burke. 'By far the greatest man of his age.'

Moore's influence was in request. Madame de Souza, widow of Flahaut, who had been guillotined in the Revolution, insisted on reading the manuscript of her latest novel to him and then tried to get him to persuade Murray to publish an English translation. Moore, unwisely, broke a rule of his own, and agreed to write a review in the *Edinburgh*. This, when it appeared, led to a coolness. Stendhal wrote to say that he had just read *Lalla Rookh* for the fifth time and enclosed an order on a bookseller (signed 'Aubertine') for three free copies of his own *Histoire de la Peinture*, hoping Moore would distribute them among suitable friends.

Stendhal in another mood was to 'note Lord Byron is to be handed over to a wretched hypocrite like Moore'.

A pleasant acquaintance of this period was Washington Irving. The young American writer had made his mark; he read aloud his forthcoming book to Moore, and was frequently in his company. 'Scarcely a day passes,' Irving wrote to a friend, 'without our seeing each other, and he has made me acquainted with many of his friends here. He is a charming, joyous fellow, full of frank, generous, manly feeling . . . His acquaintance is one of the most gratifying things I have met with for some time; as he takes the warm interest of an old friend in me and my concerns'.

Lord John Russell expressed his regret when he read the account of his Paris life in the Journal that he 'had some hand in persuading Moore to prefer France to Holyrood. His universal popularity was his chief enemy'.

The struggle to compel himself to write must not have been apparent in his manner and he juggled with appointments, provisional and promised, sending excuses to the Duke of Orleans in one mood, eating an ice alone in another. He still writes twice a week to his mother. In general he is a bad correspondent, and feels remorse for his neglect. He presents a sunny face to the world. An extrovert and an optimist, only occasionally does he experience a 'burst of devotion. . . . Tears came fast from me as I knelt down to adore the one only God whom I acknowledge, and poured forth the aspirations of a soul deeply grateful for all his goodness'. When little Tom was born, he went down on his knees to pray and then was embarrassed at the thought that a servant girl might catch him in the act.

Barnes, the editor of *The Times*, was ill; he invited Moore to write leading articles during his absence for a fee of £100 a month. The offer was refused. It is an interesting indication of Moore's political status. Barnes must have regarded him as a serious thinker. And yet Lansdowne, his loyal and generous friend, seems never to have contemplated Moore in any situation other than writing at home or dining out. A few years before, when Moore was offered the editorship of a new monthly magazine, he recorded in his Journal: 'I declined, of course; told him that, as long as the little originality I possessed remained, I should not take to reviewing, but when I become invalided, I shall look upon the editorship of a review as a good sort of Greenwich Hospital to retire to.'

He was never unhappy for long because of the ease with which he made friends. The Storys—Mrs Story in particular—come into the Paris Years very frequently, a couple with young children who were obviously devoted to the Moores since Kegworth days. Tom got on particularly well with Mrs Story, one surmises; and there were other acquaintances, some of whom were poor, to whom Moore was kind. When one of these asked for money and was not at home when Moore called with three napoleons, Bessy insisted that he should send again.

Bessy's mother, who had not hitherto been mentioned in the Journal, is sent three pounds. Perhaps mother and daughter kept up a regular correspondence. Moore never gives any hint that Bessy had a life of her own except a disposition to do little charitable acts to the poor. But in later years he mentions visits to Bessy's mother when he is in London. On one occasion he listed his dependants—his father, mother, sister, and Mrs Dyke.

Bessy travelled to England to make arrangements for the family's return; there was no question of their settling in Paris, and Ireland was never considered, although Moore toyed with an offer to become librarian of the Royal Dublin Society. A group of pretty English girls 'as refreshing to the eyes in this country as a parterre would be in a desert' reminded him where his home was now.

BEFORE HIS return to England Moore settled to the composition of what was to be his last long poem. *The Loves of the Angels* was founded on the passage in the Book of Enoch—'It happened, after the sons of man had multiplied, in those days, that daughters were born to them, elegant and beautiful; and when the angels, the sons of Heaven, beheld them, they became enamoured of them.'

The allegory was to exemplify the descent of the soul of man from its original purity. Once again Byron had entered the field before him. His *Heaven and Earth* was a verse drama, which he never completed, on precisely the same theme. Composed in Ravenna in October 1821, the first part was published the following year, but Moore was not put off and, for him, composition proceeded swiftly. He began to write in May 1822, and three thousand copies had been subscribed for when the poem was published in December of that year.

One day was pleasantly filled arranging his books; on Christmas Day, Bessy not feeling well enough, he took the children to church. On St Stephen's Day he felt suddenly 'rather fidgetty' about the fate of his poem. Lady Lansdowne sent toys to the children with a note, but said nothing about the *Angels*. 'Rather ominous this.' He wrote to Lady Donegal about silver tissue for a dress for a fancy dress ball. Her answer came upon him 'like a thunderbolt'. She had been 'vexed and disappointed' with the poem and was 'not allowing Barbara to read it'. Never, Moore reflected, had anything given him more pain than this. At once his mind was invaded by doubts and fears. This explained the dead silence from Longmans, the non-announcement of a second edition, Lord Lansdowne's reserve —everything. Bowles, who was with him at the time, did his best to set his mind at rest; but the poetical clergyman was under the disadvantage of not having read the poem.

It was necessary to prepare old Mrs Moore in Dublin for the worst, and Longmans were written to for a candid opinion. Bowles took his departure. And then Lord Lansdowne called— 'like an avatar'. In his warmest manner he praised the poem. Not only was it beautiful, but it was 'exceptionally pure'. He preferred it to anything Moore had ever written. With him on the visit was General Byng, who, some weeks previously, had 'expressed some alarm about the title'. Now that he had read the poem he had written off to some friends who had felt the same apprehensions as himself to say that 'it might be safely trusted in the nursery'. Not, one might think, words to bring rapture to a poet, but infinitely musical to Moore's anxious ears. Bessy, who had been trying to counteract the effects of Lady Donegal's letter with her own good sense and sweetness, was also relieved.

It is impossible to reconcile this picture of a hardened soldier behaving like a nervous hen with the prevailing tone in, say, Byron's correspondence. Where did the moral balance lie in society? This is the world of *Mansfield Park*, in which the Oxfords and the Lambs had no place, at which Lady Holland would sneer. Soon the tone of society would be heavily moralistic and daughters would deplore the books their Regency mothers took out of the libraries. The intense righteousness was an off-shoot of the political reaction against Jacobinism. The days of Fox and Sheridan had fled. In Paris a girl who wore a tricolour ribbon in her dress was arrested and sent to prison. The change in moral tone reflected the growth of the middle class. It would soon dictate.

The reviews that came in were favourable enough; and a clerical magazine, *The Museum*, saw traces of a moral design. Moore was to quote from this when writing to Lady Donegal to tell her about Lord Lansdowne's good opinion.

Lord John Russell had written to say that he was delighted with the poem. Lady Jersey, the witty Luttrell—there was a phalanx of admirers—but Moore was not in shape to take the strictures of *John Bull*, a Tory sheet. The attack ran into two numbers, and Moore was alarmed because it lent weight to the opinion that the poem had a character of 'impiety and blasphemy'. His agitation was now of quite a different order. To

Murray, with whom he was negotiating a sale of the Byron *Memoirs*, he wrote to inquire what *The Quarterly* was going to do. If that journal joined in the cry of irreligion it would leave him 'carried away down the current of cant without redemption'. With one exception, all his friends had approved, but what was the support of Bowood, Middleton, Holland House etc if 'the d—d sturdy saints of the middle class should take it into their heads not to buy me, for *you* know well, how they can send me to Coventry—so, pray, take care of me on this point—this one point—and I forgive everything else printed that even Croker can produce—if Croker has *indeed* had the good nature to undertake me as half promised the other day at Kensington'.

In February he wrote again to enquire: but nothing happened. *The Quarterly* never spoke, although Croker in the meanwhile had been 'very kind upon the subject'.

Charges of irreverence and impiety in *Blackwood's* and other magazines, and the inevitable raking up of 'Thomas Little', upset Moore so much that he made the suggestion to the publishers of altering the text for the fifth edition, then in preparation. He would make the angels Turkish and change God into Allah. Longmans were agreeable to the suggestion.

It was an extraordinary concession, a plea of guilt, and after the damage, if any, had been done. Writing to congratulate Byron on a new production and his success with the public, Moore admitted that he regarded his 'Angels' as having been a failure in the impression they made, although he agreed with 'the select few' that he never wrote anything better.

When he was the busiest man in Ireland, O'Connell wrote to his wife to say that 'Moore's *Loves of the Angels* is come out. I got it a while ago and read it in half an hour. It is only an account of three angels that fell in love with three ladies and although the subject is not very promising it is really an exquisitely beautiful little poem . . . a mere trifle for such a poet, but exquisitely sweet and not stained with a single indelicate thought. The poetry is full of Moore's magic. In spite of the *Edinburgh Review* Moore is the very prince of poets. There is more melody and harmony in his versification than in any other poet I ever read.'

There were still in Moore's possession the political squibs which he had been advised not to publish when his Bermuda business was before the courts. These had been intended for the Fudge family's Italian tour. Now he collected them together and Longmans published them as *Fables for the Holy Alliance, Rhymes on the Road, and Miscellaneous Poems.* The author was 'Thomas Brown, the Younger', Moore's device which deceived nobody, nor was intended to, made him feel exciting. But Longman's legal adviser expressed some anxiety, and the advice of the future Lord Denman was sought. As a judge he was to make a phrase that has never been forgotten when he decided that Daniel O'Connell should be released from prison. On this occasion he made light of the publishers' fears, and the verses came out while *The Loves of the Angels* was still going through its several editions in this successful year of Moore's return.

Hazlitt was in Switzerland, full of reverence for Rousseau. It was not a happy moment to stumble upon Moore's *Rhymes*. Always inflammable, his indignation took fire at once. He began a long essay:

'I was sorry to find the other day, on coming to Vevey, and looking into some English books at a library there, that Mr Moore had taken an opportunity, in his *Rhymes on the Road*, of abusing Madame Warens, Rousseau, and men of genius. *It's an ill bird*, as the proverb says. This appears to me, I confess, to be *pick-thank* work, as needless as it is ill-timed, and considering from whom it comes, particularly unpleasant . . .'

The verse to which he took exception was certainly lamentable.

> 'And doubtless 'mong the grave and good
> And gentle of their neighbourhood,
> *If known at all*, they were but known
> As strange, low people, low and bad,
> Madame herself to footmen prone,
> And her young pauper, all but mad.'

'What would he say if this method of neutralising the voice of the public were applied to himself, or to his friend Mr Chantrey; if we were to deny that the one ever rode in an open carriage tête-à-tête with a lord, because his father stood behind a counter, or to ask the sculptor's customers when he drove a milk-cart what we are to think of his bust of Sir Walter? *It will never do . . .*

'There is something more particularly offensive in the cant about "people low and bad" applied to the intimacy between Rousseau and Madame Warens, inasmuch as the volume containing this nice strain of morality is dedicated to Lord Byron, who was at that very time living on the very same sentimental terms with an Italian lady of rank, and whose Memoirs Mr Moore had since thought himself called upon to suppress, out of regard to his Lordship's character and to that of his friends most of whom were not "low people" . . .'

And on and on. It was Hazlitt's way. He called the essay *On Jealousy and Spleen of Party*. Towards the close it becomes apparent that the inspiration was not chivalry unalloyed. Moore's unhappy lapse recalled another feud.

> 'At the time that Lord Byron thought proper to join with Mr Leigh Hunt and Mr Shelley in the publication called the LIBERAL, Blackwood's Magazine overflowed, as might be expected, with tenfold gall and bitterness . . . Mr Moore darted backwards and forwards from Cold-Bath-Fields Prison to the Examiner-Officer, from Mr Longman's to Mr Murray's shop in a state of ridiculous trepidation, to see what was to be done to prevent this degradation of the aristocracy of letters, this indecent encroachment of plebeian pretensions, this undue extension of patronage and compromise of privilege. The Tories were shocked that Lord Byron would grace the popular side by his direct countenance and assistance— the Whigs were shocked that he should share his confidence and counsels with any one who did not unite the double recommendations of birth and genius—but themselves! Mr Moore had lived so long among the Great that he fancied himself one of them, and regarded the indignity as done to himself . . .'

On the principle that the style is the man, Hazlitt was put off by what he epitomised in the phrase 'Mr Moore's Magdalen Muse'. 'For my own part', he declared, 'I hate . . . this alternative of meretricious rhapsodies and methodist cant, though the one generally ends in the other.' Contemplating Titian's *Loves of the Gods* he compares it with Moore's *Loves of the Angels*. One is in 'living blood colour', the other calls to mind 'pink silk stockings'.

The two men were temperamentally incompatible—Hazlitt's disastrous loves, Moore's prosperous one—Hazlitt accustomed to being thrown out of houses, Moore invited by lords to lodge at their gates. Hazlitt's antipathy to Moore's 'cosmetic' art pushed him into extremes. To make up for his condemnation of his serious verse he overpraised his satires. To say that nothing in Pope or Prior ever surpassed 'the delicate insinuation and adroit satire' of a verse which—disastrously for his comparison —he quotes, showed a signal failure to anticipate the process of weathering. Hazlitt had a painter's eye, Moore a musician's ear; it explains Hazlitt's failure to appreciate verses that required music and a singer's voice to bring them fully to life.

It was sad because Hazlitt began on such good terms with Moore, before Hunt, disappointed by Byron in his efforts to get the latter to go into partnership, discovered Moore's advice against the project, the only advice a friend could have given. When Hunt enlisted Hazlitt, who was fired at once by a grievance (never himself being without one), Moore lost favour, and his failings monopolised Hazlitt's attention.

Only a year had passed since Hazlitt published *The Spirit of the Age*, in which he gave a more balanced account of Moore. As a poet 'He ought to write with a crystal pen on silver paper . . . It has been too much our author's object to pander to the artificial taste of the age; and his productions, however brilliant and agreeable, are in consequence somewhat meretricious and effeminate . . .' Having demolished his claims as a serious poet, Hazlitt acknowledged that 'Mr Moore is in private life an amiable and estimable man'.

In another place, when describing Tivoli, he said that it called for the pen of Moore, his pen being 'not more light and evanescent than the fountain'. Evanescent was the word Bessy used to describe her husband's disposition.

But we need not suppose that Moore was greatly upset by Hazlitt's strictures. He never referred to them; he was only cast down when he failed to please his friends. Russell explained this when he analysed the element of vanity in his make-up. It was not the envious sort. There is another kind of vanity which takes for granted the world's good opinion, ascribes sneers and depreciation to the malignancy of the few, and goes on happily in spite of it. Moore's love of praise was joined with 'a most generous and liberal dispensation of praise to others'. It did not require much cogitation to arrive at this conclusion. Moore in his Journal had anticipated his noble editor.

Another who refused to be drawn into the charmed circle was Henry Crabb Robinson. In his copious diaries Moore's name appears quite frequently, and he repeats anything he hears to his discredit from Hunt and other tainted sources. Robinson was a sound man without frills, very plain to look upon. His heroes were Goethe and Wordsworth. He acted as Wordsworth's disciple and thought no inconvenience too great to put up with if suffered in the great man's company. His account of a European holiday with Wordsworth is almost comical, so resolutely did the poet refuse to enter into the spirit of his enthusiastic cicerone. Moore, quite unintentionally, ruffled Robinson by not recognising him when they met; from the time that he began to salute him Robinson's diary tone noticeably sweetened. He, rightly, regarded Wordsworth and Coleridge as Moore's superiors. Moore agreed with him, certainly, in Wordsworth's case. Few, at that time, gave Coleridge full justice as a poet. When Moore praised his *Genevieve* to Wordsworth, saying it was 'a beautiful thing', Wordsworth disagreed. There was 'too much of the sensual' in it; and he said Coleridge's prose was better than his poetry. That Coleridge was a genius nobody who met him at his best could doubt. 'The only person I ever knew', Hazlitt wrote, 'who answered to the idea of genius . . . He talked for ever and you wished him to talk for ever . . .'

An opium addict; when off form, the effect might be blurred and the magic fail. Robinson and Lamb agree that Coleridge was in excellent health and spirits at Mr Monkhouse's dinner on the 4th April 1823. It was a remarkable occasion, 'dining in Parnassus', as Lamb described the day to his friend Bernard Barton. 'Half the poetry of England constellated and clustered in Gloster place'. Wordsworth, Coleridge, Rogers and Tom

Moore. That is the order in which Lamb placed the company. Wordsworth knew only monologue or silence and, on this occasion, is not reported to have said a word. Coleridge's subject, according to Robinson, was 'metaphysical criticism on words'. Not one upon which many could embark confidently without previous preparation; and Lamb said, 'not one there but was content to be a listener'.

Moore, according to Robinson, 'seemed conscious of his inferiority. He was very attentive to Coleridge but seemed also to relish Lamb whom he sat next'. Lamb 'kept himself within bounds', and was not noticeably drunk until the party's end.

The beginning of Moore's Journal entry for that day is given over to Lucy Drew (of whom, more later). He had called on her in the morning to go to Chantrey's to see some medals; then off in the hackney coach to show her Murray's rooms and pictures, then to the Foreign Office.

He was far too much accustomed to meeting celebrities to be as much impressed by the company at Mr Monkhouse's as a book-lover, with hindsight, would expect him to have been. Wordsworth had invited him to the party. Monkhouse, the host, was connected to Wordsworth by marriage and the poet stayed with him whenever he was in London. Moore had never seen his host before. 'A singular party' was his description; and there is nothing in his account to suggest that he was aware of any personal inferiority. Had he been invited to sing he would have enjoyed himself better, and so might have the ladies present (not mentioned by the other recorders of the feast). With Lamb 'the hero at present of the *London Magazine*' was his sister, Mary, 'the poor woman who went mad with him in the diligence on the way to Paris'. Mrs Wordsworth was there and Mrs Monkhouse. 'Coleridge told some tolerable things', the host 'a Maecenas of the old school, contributing nothing but good dinners and silence'. Lamb 'a clever fellow, certainly, but full of villainous and abortive puns'. As for Coleridge's 'metaphysical criticism of words'—Moore thought one of his pronouncements 'absurd'. And he recorded that Coleridge talked much of Jeremy Taylor.

Robinson was described by Moore as 'one of the *minora sidera* of this constellation of the lakes'. Robinson read this

thirty-two years later; when the Russell edition of Moore's
Memoirs was published, he rushed into print at once; but he
had mellowed towards Moore in the interval and explained that
he was at a disadvantage with the other guests at the dinner,
not knowing his company so well. At least, Moore was polite to
Coleridge and attentive to Lamb, who, Robinson remembered,
when 'he could not articulate very distinctly', called on Moore
to drink a glass of wine with him—'suiting the action to the
word and hob-nobbing'. Then he went on, 'Mister Moore, till
now I have always felt an antipathy to you, but now that I have
seen you, I shall like you ever after'.

Rogers, who 'occasionally let fall a remark' (he hated to have
to listen for long to anyone) invited Lamb to breakfast next day
to meet Moore without any of the present company.

Shortly before Coleridge's death, Moore was to meet him at
a party given by Lockhart, Scott's son-in-law and biographer.
Not realising that it was a special occasion, Moore arrived with
his young Tom (he was always anxious to show him off). Too
far from Coleridge at table 'to hear more than the continual
drawl of his preachment', he moved up to him when the ladies
retired. He found his discourse difficult to follow in places.
Coleridge spoke of Daniel and the Revelations and Irving the
new religious leader. He had tried, he said, to bring Irving to
some sort of rationality on these subjects 'to steady him', but his
efforts had been unsuccessful and Irving, after many conversations, confessed that the only effect all Coleridge had said was
'to stun him'. After that, Coleridge began to recite his own
poetry. It was 'very striking and in the same, mystical religious
style as his conversation'. On this occasion the host did not
repeat Mr Monkhouse's mistake, and called upon Moore to
sing.

When he had finished Coleridge spoke eloquently of the
perfect union (as he was pleased to say) of poetry and music
which it exhibited: 'The Music, like the honeysuckle round the
stem, twining round the meaning, and at last over-topping it.'
A remark which struck Moore as 'not a little applicable to his
own style of eloquence'.

Great men do not usually shine in general society. Moore
was not a great man, but one of extraordinary natural talents.

How happily Coleridge described his method at the piano is proven by a description given by William Gardiner, a professional musician: 'He might be compared to the poets of old who recited their verses to the lyre; his voice, rich and flexible was always in tune and his delivery of the words neat and delicious; his manner of touching the instrument was careless and easy; his fingers seemed accidentally to drop upon the keys, producing a simple harmony just sufficient to support the voice.'

There were other performances; and as a Scottish woman sang, Moore thought sadly of another evening like this in the same room when Walter Scott was present. That was his sort of man. He wanted little Tom to be able to say he had shaken Scott's hand. Moore did not approve of family-deserting Coleridge, but when, after his death, he said so to Wordsworth, when they were dining with Rogers, Wordsworth defended his old friend without taking offence. Wordsworth, who made to Keats's regret such a bad impression in London on account of his 'egotism, vanity, and bigotry', seems to have had a liking for Moore's company. Moore was 'very well pleased to be a listener' while Wordsworth described what happened on the rare occasions when he went out to dinner in his own neighbourhood. 'The conversations may be called cathecetical; for, as they do me the honour to wish to know my opinions on the different subjects, they ask me questions, and I am induced to answer them at great length till I become quite tired.'

Only then, Moore remarked, was it possible, indeed, to edge in a word.

With Landor, who seemed more formidable, Moore had unexpected success. They met in 1838 at breakfast, their host Monckton Milnes. 'A remarkable party', Moore records, 'consisting of Savage Landor and Carlyle (neither of whom I had seen before), Robinson, Rogers and [Spring] Rice. A good deal of conversation about German authors of whom I knew nothing, nor (from what they paraded of them) felt that I had lost much by my ignorance. Savage Landor a very different person from what I had expected to find him. I found in him all the air and laugh of a hearty country gentleman, a *gros réjoui*, and whereas his writings had given me rather a disrelish to the man, I shall take more readily to his writings from having seen the man'.

When Moore depreciated his own writings to the older poet he was told, 'I think you have written a greater number of beautiful poems than any one that ever existed.'

Crabb Robinson described it as 'a delightful breakfast'. Rogers, he said, was angry 'at being forced into Landor's company' and Moore was 'very civil to me, whom he on other occasions had cut . . .' He noticed that Moore had never heard of Blake.

From the first Moore appreciated the genius of Dickens, upholding the merits of *The Pickwick Papers* against Sydney Smith's criticisms; but then, Smith was critical of every contemporary. Curiously, although he was in Dickens's company on a few occasions, Moore had very little to say about him. It was not through any lack of sympathy. In the Dickens novels there are five allusions to Burns; thirty to Moore; to other authors no more than two; but Byron's *Farewell* to Moore appears in three books.

There was a good deal of Dickens in Moore (but not the dark side from which Moore instinctively fled). They were at one in the sentimental and humorous vein—illustrated in *Bleak House* when Mr Bagnet says 'Believe me, if all those endearing young charms' was 'his most powerful ally in moving the heart of Mrs Bagnet when a maiden and inducing her to approach the altar'.

According to the Irish artist, George Mulvany, Moore scarcely ever sat down; and his conversation was more brilliant than profound. He never indulged in sarcasm or ill-natured remarks. Lady Becher (a celebrity of the stage as Miss O'Neil) said that with the single exception of Chief Justice Bushe, he was the most attractive of companions. In Abraham Hayward's correspondence edited by Henry E. Carlisle, a letter of 22nd April 1837 gives what must have been a familiar picture. 'It is a pity you were not here last week, for Moore dined with me, and it was not a little amusing to see Lady Vincent and Mrs Stanhope scratching for him. They almost quarrelled. Of course I decided the matter by putting him next to my own favourite, which put the others in a rage.'

That was Moore's life. Lady Holland's occasional sharpness only lent flavour to what might otherwise have been too sweet a diet.

Moore remembered evenings with Byron when they talked down the sun, evenings which, when they recalled them in Italy, made the Countess Guiccioli long to understand English so that she might listen to 'the boyish wordy frolic Byron and Moore enjoyed together'.

When Moore met Maria Edgeworth, a lion in other circles, in early days in Ireland, she had listened to Moore's singing, and when tears came into her eyes he was glad to think that he could move 'higher spirits'. (Alas, in later years, in London, 'Miss Edgeworth with all her cleverness, anything but agreeable. The moment anyone begins to speak, off she starts too, seldom more than a sentence behind them, and in general contrives to distance every speaker. Neither does what she says, though of course very sensible, at all make up for this over-activity of tongue'.)

There were happy days at Bowood where sometimes Moore slept the night so as not to break up the party. Mrs Piozzi (Johnson's Mrs Thrale) provided fun on one occasion; her prediction of the ultimate perfection of the human race 'when Vice will take refuge in the arms of Impossibility' tickled her audience.

The atmosphere there had become more relaxed ever since Lady Lansdowne offered Moore the use of her shower-bath (Moore's health was giving him quite serious trouble). 'It was delightful to see that cold uncertainty which first hung upon her manner to me is clearing away and giving place to a friendly, frank familiarity which is both more becoming to her and far more comfortable to me.' She took the trouble to write from London to describe the battle for the copies of his new poems at Holland House. He was in his cottage, where Bessy's next (and last) baby was born. His children's names as always were an index to Moore's friendships. 'John Russell' was chosen on this occasion. (Did Rogers resent the fact that his own name never was?)

In Paris Moore had shelved the Sheridan task. He now resumed it. The inspiration for the *Melodies* had died down.

Henceforth verse was to be occasional; for his living he must depend on the more pedestrian Muse.

Once again he was offered a post. Constable, the publisher, tried to persuade him to move to Edinburgh as a first step to taking over the editorship of the *Review*. Jeffrey was finding it hard to devote his time to it, and would welcome Moore's appearance in his place. But he did not take up the offer. He should not have been worried about his financial position. Longmans had placed £1,000 to his credit from the earnings of the *Angels*, and the *Fables* had brought him in £500. But he had become restless again. Russell talked about a trip to Ireland and then backed down. He was always indecisive in making arrangements. Then the Lansdownes suggested that Moore should join them at Killarney; they were going to visit their Irish estates in Kerry. Bessy, who had had another fall, was upset at the thought of Tom's departure, but, as always, encouraged him to go.

MOORE'S TRIP to Ireland in July 1823 was unlike any he had paid before; and his Journal entries show a more serious concern for his country. His parents were ageing, and there is less about them than formerly; but it was on this visit that a domestic incident which has won a niche in Moore legend took place. 'My mother expressing a strong wish to see Lord Lansdowne, without the fuss of a visit from him, I engaged to manage it for her. Told him that he must let me show him to two people who considered *me* as the greatest man in the world, and him as the next for being my friend. Very good naturedly allowed me to walk him past the windows, and wished to call upon them, but I thought it better thus.'

Everywhere on their travels Moore asks gravely about the state of the country. His manner was altogether different from the time when he stayed with his sister and her husband in Tipperary, and talked of armed force as the only way to settle disturbances. In Callan in County Kilkenny, on the journey south, he saw 'for the first time in my life some real specimens of Irish misery and filth; three or four cottages together exhibiting such a naked swarm of wretchedness as never met my eyes before'.

In Lord Lansdowne's train they stayed at great houses, but the conversation at dinner was tame because the Lansdownes were not at their ease with strangers. (Moore's first recorded impressions of Lady Lansdowne were unfavourable. He preserved them as proof of the injustice one may do to character till better acquainted with it.)

The travellers were told that the forty-shilling freeholder was the curse of the country and one of the obstacles to Catholic emancipation. Since 1793 Catholics could vote at parliamentary elections if they held property to this value. As they couldn't sit in parliament, it paid a landlord to create as many voters in

his interests as possible; but these would be a legion against him
if Emancipation came and they could vote for Catholic candi-
dates. There was much talk of tithes, greatly resented by the
peasantry, who had to support clergymen not of their own
faith. And there were gloomy murmurings about the growth of
irreligion among the populace. Deeply though Catholics were
mistrusted, it was admitted that they were restrained by their
priests.

In Lord Lansdowne's company, Tom Moore made an almost
royal progress, but he was sometimes on his own, and he
stayed in Cork in order to visit his sister Kate, letting his
friends go on to Kenmare where he hoped to join them.

John O'Driscoll, a Cork friend of T. C. Croker, described
Moore's spectacular setting out on the steamboat. 'Moore went
down the river (which he as truly as poetically termed "our
noble sea avenue") to see his sister, Mrs Scully, at Cove, and
the steamboat and quay were crowded to get a glimpse of the
"Irish lion", as Lord Lansdowne called him. As you well
know Moore dresses with peculiar neatness, and looked that
morning, I think, particularly well in his smart white hat, and
gloves, brown frock coat, yellow cassimere waistcoat, grey duck
trousers, and blue silk handkerchief carelessly secured in front
by a silver pin; he carried a brown silk umbrella.'

The dinner was good and Lady Kenmare 'very pleasing', so
that it was not surprising to find that when it came to the time
the Lansdownes were to depart Moore was in a dilemma
whether to stay for a stag-hunt or to go on with his friends. He
slept on it; but the Lansdownes won.

O'Connell came to dinner there, and although Moore kept
a note of some of his conversation he gives no description of the
man himself. This is one of the sad lacks of his method. We
rarely *see* any of the people Moore meets. His first interest in
them is how they respond to him. But it is evident that O'Connell
was at his ease, and Moore came away from Ireland in a very
different state of mind than on previous visits. Tales of a Captain Rock caught his imagination. Before returning to Sloperton, having been fêted in Limerick, he spent a few days in
Dublin where a letter from Russell was waiting him to say he
had changed his mind and would be very happy to accompany

Moore to Killarney. This was a very typical occurrence—
Russell's irresolution and Moore's restlessness led to frequent
confusion, but they never fell out over it.

In Rome Lady Morgan had been a sensation, now in
Dublin she invited Moore to dinner; 'quite *comme il faut*', he
recorded. She was to complain about him in her *Memoirs*—if
she did lead the call for a statue to his memory when he died—
sensing condescension in his manner. And she lived long enough
to read this example of it. Moore's attitude towards others who
had made social progress in life was not unlike that of a retainer
in a noble family, apprehensive for its dignity and alert to spy
strangers. It was a feature of his character that annoyed
Hazlitt who heard about it from Leigh Hunt. He complained
of Moore's 'carrying a slide rule by proxy for Byron . . . Mr
Moore vindicates his own dignity; but the sense of intrinsic
worth, of wide-spread fame, and of the intimacy of the great
makes him perhaps a little too fastidious and *exigeant* as to the
pretensions of others. He has been so long accustomed to the
society of Whig lords, and so enchanted with the smile of
beauty and fashion, that he really fancies he is one of the *set* to
which he is admitted on sufferance, and tries very unnecessarily
to keep others out of it'.

Apart from that unhappy flash of condescension to Lady
Morgan, Moore's visit to Ireland seemed to affect him with a
new seriousness. It is incredible that he knew his own country
so little; but we have his admission that he had never seen rural
poverty before, an indication that he hardly travelled at all out
of Dublin. When asked where precisely in the 'sweet vale of
Avoca' was the Meeting of the Waters, which he had immortalised, he was not able to say with certainty. He was short-
sighted, and unlike Tennyson who looked the closer for that
reason, he was not deeply interested in natural appearances. For
all his tears in the Alps, his descriptions of scenery—the
beauties of Killarney included—are trite and conventional. He
continued to send anonymous 'squibs' to *The Times* for money,
but a reforming spirit was abroad, and Moore took his tone from
the new seriousness. His patriotic enthusiasm, sometimes
dormant, was awakened again.

The Sheridan biography was put aside and, after a few weeks, he scrapped the factual account of the tour that he had begun on his return. Instead, he embarked on a fiction. But *The Memoirs of Captain Rock* is not a novel so much as an extended pamphlet setting out the long history of British misgovernment; for chapters at a time the hero is forgotten. His presence and the jesting manner in which the book begins is the merest pretence of jam on the powder which the reader is about to consume. At the end Rock is arrested on a charge of walking in the moonlight and being unable to account for his movements, is transported but not executed because his identity is not discovered, although many present in the court could have identified him. 'But the only virtue which the Irish Government has been the means of producing in the people is a fidelity to each other in their conspiracies against it.'

As a book *Captain Rock* suffers from extreme haste in its composition, but as a statement of British misrule it is devastating. Why it is so seldom referred to in Irish books can only be explained by the tacit conspiracy to denigrate Moore's patriotism and confine his activity to drawing-room singing. It was— for a man in Moore's circumstances—a brave book, and it won him his place at Irish cottage firesides.

The success of *Captain Rock* was not to occupy Moore's mind for long. On 14th May 1824, when he called at Colburn's library to check an address, the shopman told him Lord Byron was dead. The young Tennyson when he heard the news in a rectory in Lincolnshire went out and wrote it on a rock; the forty-four year old Moore 'hastened to Murrays'.

At what was to prove their last meeting, at La Mira on 11th October 1819, Byron, it will be recalled, gave Moore the leather bag containing his *Memoirs* to do whatever he pleased with, provided he did not publish them in Byron's lifetime. By May, Moore is having a copy made because the original has suffered from 'passing through so many hands', and he is a witness when Lady Burghersh burns extracts she made when the manuscript was on loan to her. In November Moore made enquiries about how to get Byron's next instalment to Paris (where he is still) from Ravenna. It arrives within a month, with a letter from Byron suggesting that Moore should raise money on the manuscript. Presumably Moore's Bermuda debt was what prompted Byron to act so generously in the first instance.

In July 1821, although the *Memoirs* contained some unflattering allusions to her, Moore lent them to Lady Holland. Having been refused by Longmans, he had written to Murray who offered 2000 guineas for them in August, if Moore would consent to edit them at Byron's death, should he survive him. In November 1821, on a visit to London, the purpose of which was rather vague, Moore signed over the papers by deed to Murray in exchange for the cash.

Byron had agreed to this by letter, but no sooner was the transaction completed than Moore began to be assailed by doubts. Lord Holland described the sale as the deposit of a quiver of poisoned arrows for a future warfare upon private character. Moore pressed him for details—the references to Lady Holland were not mentioned—there seemed to be very little to substantiate the objection; but Moore 'lay awake thinking of it'. He was always susceptible to the least suggestion from some one he respected that he had not acted exquisitely in any given circumstances. It would seem that Lord Lansdowne had also questioned the propriety of the sale.

We can get some idea of the context of the *Memoirs* from Byron's letters. Like other famous letter writers, he had the habit of repeating himself to various correspondents. It requires no great effort of imagination to see him sitting down when the mood took him and rushing off one letter after another, not pausing even to punctuate; dashes doing for all.

The *Memoirs* were given to Moore on 11th October 1819; on the 26th Byron writes to Kinnaird to say 'Moore has been here —we got tipsy together—and were very amicable—he is gone on to Rome—I put my life (in M.S.) into his hands—(*not* for publication) you—or any body else may see it—at his return.— It only comes up to 1816.—He is a noble fellow—and looks quite fresh and poetical—nine years (the age of a poem's education) my Senior—he looks younger—this comes of marriage and being settled in the Country.'

Three days later he is writing to Murray whom he tacitly appointed publisher of his Venetian gossip as well as of his poetry. 'I gave Moore who is gone to Rome—my Life in M.S.

in 78 folio sheets brought down to 1816— —But this I put into
his hands for *his* care—as he has some other M.S.S. of mine—
a journal kept in 1814—&c.—Neither are for publication
during my life—but when I am cold—you may do what you
please.—in the mean time—if you like to read them—you may
—and show them to anybody you like—I care not.— —The Life
is *Memoranda*—and not *Confessions*—I have left out all my *loves*
(except in a general way) and many other of the most important
things—(because I must not compromise other people) so that
it is like the play of Hamlet—"the part of Hamlet omitted by
particular desire".— —But you will find many opinions—and
some fun—with a detailed account of my marriage and its
consequence—as true as a party concerned can make such
accounts—for I suppose we are all prejudiced . . .'

To Hoppner, the scandal-monger, he writes that he wishes he
had been in Venice when Moore was there. 'We were very
merry and tipsy—he *hated* Venice by the way—and swore it was
a sad place.'

In December he tells Murray the same story, with an injunc-
tion '*not* to *publish*' on any account; he says Moore has been told
to show it to whomsoever he pleased. And he would wish Lady
Byron to read it 'that she might have it in her power to mark
anything mistaken or misstated'. Later in the month he writes
to Lady Byron, telling her about the *Memoirs*. He has omitted,
he says, 'the most important and decisive events and passions
of his existence', but his account of their marriage is 'long and
minute'. His reason for writing his *Life* is to show that those who
had 'traduced and blasted it—and branded me—should know
—that it is they—and not I—are the cause'.

We have, therefore, a reasonably clear picture of what the
world will never read. Those who feel that they have been
deprived of references to sodomy may comfort themselves with
the knowledge that if this were so Moore would certainly not
have handed the *Memoirs* to every new female acquaintance.
And there would have been busy talk at the time if Byron had
accused himself of a capital crime.

In April of the following year (1822) Moore approached
Murray and said he wanted to cancel the deed of sale and to
substitute for it a mortgage giving him the power to redeem the

Memoirs whenever he paid off the loan. Murray 'agreed with the best grace imaginable'. Moore's motive, he records in his Journal, was 'an over-delicate deference to the opinion of others; but it is better than allowing a shade of suspicion to appear within a mile of one in any transaction; and I know I shall feel happier when rid of the bargain'.

John Cam Hobhouse, one of Byron's executors, in his account of the proceedings described the arrangements as 'this most extraordinary agreement (by which Lord Byron made a present of himself to Mr Moore, and Mr Moore sold his Lordship to the booksellers) . . .'

At the time, when Moore met Hobhouse in London, and no doubt assured him that he would soon redeem the mortgage, he was confirmed more and more in his own satisfaction at 'having rescinded the bargain'. He hadn't, of course, until he paid back the money, but the secret of Moore's happy manner lay in his capacity to take the will for the deed.

Hobhouse 'an upright and honest man' said 'I know more of Byron than any one else, and much more than I should wish anybody else to know'. His devotion to his friend was undoubted, he had never flattered him and often disagreed with him, but there was a curious inconsistency, the result of his possessiveness, which made him hint at depravities when, at the same time, he was being so zealous to protect Byron's reputation by the destruction of his papers. He recorded his hints on his copy of the biography for the benefit of posterity.

There followed a testy correspondence with Murray: one of the publisher's grievances was the failure to return the original deed assigning the *Memoirs* to him which was the basis of his security. This was in the possession of Kinnaird, who held Byron's power of attorney. He was hoping that Moore would pay Murray off, and had entered into negotiations with Longmans for that purpose. Rees, one of their directors, urged Moore to hurry up, the money was available. On the following day (14th May 1824) Moore heard that Byron was dead.

There was then the sort of flutter that always attended Moore in a crisis; more time spent canvassing opinions than getting down to business. Kinnaird offered at once, on behalf of Lord Byron's family, 2000 guineas to get the manuscript into their hands (this was after a call from Hobhouse). Brougham's opinion was sought on Moore's legal rights. The lawyer was not encouraging. Moore stood up to Kinnaird at first, insisting that he was the person who should redeem the *Memoirs* and he would then submit them, not to Lady Byron, but to a 'chosen number of persons'. If they, after examination, pronounced them unfit for publication, he would burn the manuscript.

At this point Moore's vanity went into the ascendant. It became enormously important to him that he and not Murray should be the person to hand the *Memoirs* to Augusta Leigh, Byron's half-sister and residuary legatee (Moore was determined not to give them to Lady Byron).

Moore's fears that Murray would prove obdurate were false. He was more anxious than anyone that the manuscript be destroyed—than anyone, that is to say, except Hobhouse. *He* was fanatical on the subject. It was his opinion, in which he persuaded Kinnaird to support him, that Mrs Leigh should burn the papers without looking at them. Moore objected that 'this would be throwing a stigma upon the work, which it did not deserve'.

An appointment was made to meet Murray at Mrs Leigh's rooms where he was to be paid 2000 guineas and the manuscript taken from him and handed to Mrs Leigh. To be burnt, Hobhouse said, but Moore demurred.

It was after this that Moore remembered a circumstance which 'independent of any reliance on Murray's fairness' set his mind at rest. On Luttrell's advice he had directed that a clause be put in the agreement giving him three months after Lord Byron's death to raise the money and redeem the pledge. 'This clause I dictated as clearly as possible both to Murray and his solicitor, Mr Turner, and saw the solicitor interline it in the rough draft of the agreement.' This—as it proved— imagined happening buoyed Moore up. Until then he had depended, characteristically, on Murray's indulgence, that he should neglect the letter for the spirit of the agreement. In the last painful scene when the *Memoirs* were destroyed, a reference to Shylock's bond was among the insults exchanged between the parties.

Moore went off on a predictable circus of calls, eliciting

opinions. Luttrell strengthened Moore's resolve to appeal to Mrs Leigh at the meeting not to destroy the papers. The two men called on Wilmot Horton, whom Murray had involved originally as representing the family. He was joined by Colonel Frank Doyle, Lady Byron's representative. In fact Wilmot Horton was close in that lady's counsels, and Colonel Doyle spoke of himself as representing Mrs Leigh. Hobhouse adopting a Pontius Pilate attitude when invited to join in the work of destruction that he was responsible for. He had—was it because of thwarted literary hopes?—a dislike of writers and their thirst for copy. There is always this war between those who put the reputation of the dead above the right of posterity to know the truth about them and supporters of the legal maxim that makes truth a defence in an action for libel: a man is not entitled to damages for injuries to a character to which he is not entitled.

When Lady Byron sent a message to Hobhouse that she wished him to give out that he was going to write Byron's biography in conjunction with the family and Lady Byron, he turned down the suggestion and remarked: 'Poor Byron! Here is his dear friend Tom Moore, his publisher Murray, and his wife: the first they think of is writing his *Life* or getting it written. Such are the friendships of great authors!' He had despised Moore when he said, 'I hope, after this sacrifice, that if any *Memoirs* are to be written, the family will give me the preference'.

Mrs Leigh's house was to have been the scene of the surrender; but her representative, Wilmot Horton, preferred to go to Murray's office. Here took place a final flare up between Moore and Hobhouse, Moore protesting against the burning, Hobhouse holding him to his written agreement. Then came the final dramatic moment. Colonel Doyle said to Moore, 'I understand then that you stand to your original proposal to put the MSS. at Mrs Leigh's absolute disposal'. Moore replied, 'I do, but with the former protestation'.

'Well then,' said Colonel Doyle, 'on the part of Mrs Leigh I put them into the fire.'

With the original was burnt what Moore said was the only copy.

If blame is to be apportioned for what now seems an act of sheer vandalism, it attaches most to Hobhouse, who was the prime mover, secondly to Murray, who acquiesced for prudish motives. Lady Byron, in fact, controlled Mrs Leigh's nominal representatives. She saw herself as doing an unpleasant duty.

Hobhouse ostensibly was acting on Augusta's behalf but, in fact, he unduly influenced that unhappy and weak woman, who was not apprehensive on her own account, being quite sure that Byron would not have left evidence against her in any writings that might be published. It was Augusta's fate to act on the dictates of stronger characters; her conscience had no self-starter, it had to be cranked up by someone with a moral handle. Byron's widow had one, the guilt of Augusta's association with her brother. Hobhouse had another, his dedication to Byron's fame and passionate concern for his reputation.

As Byron's executor, Hobhouse was the prime mover. Moore, ever pliant, had agreed at first to the destruction—he was over-eager to match Hobhouse in devotion to their friend's memory —but he thought better of it almost immediately, and his sensible wish was that the *Memoirs* should be read and a decision taken after reflection as to what should be destroyed and what preserved. But Hobhouse, who had never seen the *Memoirs*, got his way. He was possibly more hurt than he cared to admit even to himself that Byron had given the *Memoirs* to Moore without stipulating that he should be one of the select few to read them.

Byron's widow was no doubt glad to think that his account of the separation would not now be available; but she had refused to read the *Memoirs* when Byron gave her the opportunity in his lifetime.

Moore said that there was one objectionable passage in the first volume and a few obscene pages in the second. He was alluding, it is believed, in the first instance, to Byron's admission that he had his bride on the sofa before dinner on the first day of the honeymoon.

Moore was inconsistent throughout; his motives were mixed, and he was confused by guilt. His dilatory behaviour had been the immediate cause of the crisis. He was to suffer a final humiliation when it was disclosed that the clause in the deed he had described in such detail was not there. Worse, there *was* one he had forgotten about which said that the reason for withdrawing from a sale of the *Memoirs* outright to Murray was 'Lord Byron's and Mr Moore's not now inclining to make the said MSS. public'. He had insisted during the discussion that Lord Byron's wishes were being contravened. Now, when Hobhouse asked what he had to say to that, he pleaded forgetfulness. Probably sincerely. When in London, as his diary shows, it was nothing for him to have three engagements in the morning and afternoon and four, perhaps, at night. As he composed while walking, his mind can never have been concentrated on any matter of business unless when he lay awake at night. His habitual state of mind is demonstrated by his habit of leaving whatever he was carrying behind him, an embarrassment which grew with time as did his confusion about engagements. He was for ever turning up at the wrong house, and early in his social career he began to accept conflicting invitations from which he had later to extricate himself.

When the *Memoirs* were in the fire and Hobhouse went home, he found a letter from Moore awaiting his arrival.

> 15 Duke Street,
> St James's

'Dear Hobhouse,

Though it is difficult to suppose (particularly after the friendly manner in which you parted from me) that you could have seriously intended to insult me during the conversation of to-day, yet there was something in your manner and certain expressions which looked so very like it, and which haunts me so uncomfortably, that it would be highly satisfactory to be told by yourself that you had no such intentions and I trust you will do me [the] favour as soon as possible, to set my mind at rest on the subject.

> Yours truly,
> Thomas Moore'

Hobhouse refused to meet this request, and Moore, on being so informed, had 'nothing more to say'. He continued to live in a condition of moral inferiority towards Hobhouse, gratified by any concession, resentful of his aloofness.

Hobhouse was the paradigm of the Englishman whose reserve used to inspire a sense of inferiority in less self-sufficient races. It seemed to indicate superiority to human weakness and supreme confidence. He was in fact incensed by finding critical references to himself in Moore's letters to Byron; and they did not upset him so much as the thought that Byron had not shown any resentment. Hobhouse was not above letting Moore know of suppressions of matters hurtful to him. In his recollections, written in old age, as Lord Broughton, he let the curtain down a little in one paragraph: 'Sam Rogers told me that Byron told him at Pisa that he, Byron, had only one friend in the world, and that was Tom Moore. "I thought of you" said Rogers. Now this was so truly in the worthy man's usual style that I was aware what to do, and only said "I am sure Kinnaird is the best friend he ever had in the world".'

THE CRISIS of the *Memoirs* did not end with the burning. Murray had accepted payment; Moore now insisted that he should not be recouped by the Byron family for his loss. As usual, he consulted his friends, and got conflicting counsel. Lord and Lady Lansdowne were strongly for his taking the money, so was Lord John Russell. Luttrell who, at first, had been in favour of taking the money, 'with a candour that did him much credit', changed his mind. They were with Hobhouse at the time. Luttrell had persuaded Moore to call on him, 'assuring me that no one could be more kindly disposed towards me than Hobhouse was'. The latter, after a discussion, looked earnestly at Moore and said 'Shall I tell you, Moore, fairly what I would do if I were in your situation'? 'Out with it', Moore answered ('eagerly well knowing what was coming'). 'I would not take the money', he replied; 'the fact is, if I wished to injure your character, my advice would be accept it'.

This, Moore told himself, was 'an honest and manly triumph of good nature over the indifference (to say the least of it) to my reputation, which must have dictated his former advice'.

There were then to be considered the references to the matter which were appearing in the newspapers. A suitable reply was drafted and agreed upon for insertion. There, with anyone other than Moore, the matter might have ended, but we see him hurrying off, like the White Rabbit in *Alice in Wonderland* to consult Lord Lansdowne about what he had done. There was a party in progress when Moore arrived, but in the short time available for conversation on the subject, he saw that the Lansdownes were still in favour of his taking the money. He called again next day; they held to their opinion, and advised him to consult Abercrombie and Lord John Russell. On the way home he met Murray, who was worried by rumours that he was being criticised by Lord Lansdowne.

'Mr Murray', Moore assured him, 'you need not fear any injustice from Lord Lansdowne, who is well acquainted with every particular of the transaction between you and me from beginning to end. As to this last affair, I am ready to bear testimony that your conduct has been very fair.'

It is the measure of Moore's attraction that his self-centredness, to which his letters and diaries so abundantly testify, did not repel his friends. So far from trying to escape him, Lord John Russell called to persuade him to take the money. Russell had been pressed into service by Wilmot Horton, acting for the Byron family. Moore and Russell had a long inconclusive talk and arranged to meet again. When he left, Moore went off to see Rogers. That crusty bachelor was at home with the sister, to whom he was devoted. They listened attentively while Moore went over the ground again. Rogers said that while he in Moore's shoes would not take the money, he thought that Moore as a married man ought to. 'More mean things have been done in the world under the shelter of "wife and children" than under any other pretext', Moore assured him. His mind was quite made up. But it had been made up hours before when he left Hobhouse. Why had he to monopolise so much time and attention with his problems? He shared them so liberally with others that they did not give him sleepless nights.

From Rogers he went to dinner at Lord Bellhaven's on his way to the Opera, and so affected 'that beautiful person, Lady Fullerton', with his singing of *Poor Broken Heart* that she was obliged to leave the room, sobbing violently.

And then *The Times* published its own account of the proceedings.

'Since the death of Lord Byron it occurred to the sensitive and honourable mind of Mr Moore, that by possibility, although the noble author himself had given full authority for a disclosure of the document, some of his family might be wounded or shocked by it. He appointed, therefore, a time for meeting a near connexion of the noble Lord (not Lady Byron), and after a deliberate and joint perusal of the work, finding that the lady apprehended from it much pain to the minds of many persons still living, though no sort of imputation on her brother's memory, Mr Moore, with a spirit and generosity which the better part of mankind will be at no loss to appreciate, placed the manuscript in the lady's hands, and permitted her to burn it in his presence. This sacrifice of self interest to lofty feeling was made the day before yesterday, and the next morning the £2000 was repaid to Mr Murray by Lord Byron's self-destituted legatee.'

In Moore's Journal this colourful report is noticed briefly: 'true as to the leading facts of the destruction of the MS. and my repayment of the money to Murray, but incorrect as to other particulars'. But he expressed no anxiety about correcting it, nor was he embarrassed by the fulsomeness, judging by his next observation: 'Occupied about the insurance of my life'.

Hobhouse and his friends waited to see what Moore would do. When he did nothing, Wilmot Horton put a corrective into an evening paper. In the meanwhile Moore had been told by Lord Mansfield's son-in-law that he had 'done the finest thing man ever did—you have saved the country from a pollution'. Moore assured him that this was a mistake; but at Lansdowne House when the Duke of Gloucester said, 'You have done the handsomest and finest thing ever man did', Moore's reply is not recorded.

Moore, at Hobhouse's persuasion, made a statement in *The Times*, and Horton and others published accounts in other newspapers.

Hobhouse's merits were marred by his manner. Acting in what he thought his dead friend's interests, he showed Moore the very side of himself that had often discouraged Byron, and made him turn to the ever pleasant Moore to escape from Hobhouse's obtrusive conscience. Perhaps Byron, with his uncanny prescience in divining the true character of his friends, realised that Hobhouse would try to stifle publication of the *Memoirs*. Otherwise it is difficult to understand why, when Hobhouse was his executor, he didn't give him instructions.

Righteousness is often a cover for ill-will; and Hobhouse used his position as executor to punish Moore for his familiarity with Byron and to emphasise his unworthiness. To this Moore was all too willing to lend himself.

As a rule, Moore avoided funerals. He had gone to Curran's (did he know how harshly Curran had treated his daughter after

Emmet's death—locking her up, driving her away from home?).
And it would have been extraordinary if he hadn't attended
Byron's.

In the first week of July he 'began to think whether it would
be necessary' to go up to the funeral. He wrote to Hobhouse for
advice. Hobhouse replied that he had wished for an Abbey
burial, but Mrs Leigh had decided for Newstead, and therefore
the only mark of respect would be sending carriages. But when
Moore read in the papers that the friends of Lord Byron would
accompany the funeral out of London, he decided he must be
there.

It was naïve of him to look to Hobhouse for advice in anything to do with Byron; but he continued to do so, unable
apparently to understand that jealousy can poison even the
purest wells. Moore could do nothing without consulting someone. Rogers had to be written to; but when he realised that if
he waited for a reply the funeral would have taken place Moore
set off for London.

Rogers, when he called on him, thought the trip had been
unnecessary. He had himself been invited by Hobhouse to
travel in one of the coaches, and was not disposed to. Moore
however persuaded him to come. Rogers liked to be persuaded.

The day and evening were spent in making calls; Lord
Lansdowne was surprised by a visit. In the afternoon Rogers
took Moore out to Highbury to dine at his brother's house.
When Moore returned late at night to his lodgings there was an
invitation from the undertaker that he should go as a mourner
to the funeral.

Next morning he was with Rogers at half-past eight. They
set out together. 'When I approached the house, and saw the
crowd assembled, felt a nervous trembling come over me,
which lasted till the whole ceremony was over; thought I should
be ill. Never was at a funeral before, but poor Curran's. The
riotous curiosity of the mob, the bustle of the undertakers, etc.,
and all the other vulgar accompaniments of the ceremony,
mixing with my recollections of him who was gone, produced a
combination of disgust and sadness that was deeply painful to
me.'

He bore Hobhouse no ill-will, watched him take charge of

the proceedings, and admired his 'manly, unaffected feeling'. Moore shared a coach with Rogers; Campbell, the poet; Colonel Stanhope and Orlando (the Greek deputy). 'There were however few respectable persons among the crowd; and the whole ceremony was anything but what it ought to have been.'

The mourners discussed Byron, Stanhope speaking of the strange mixture of avarice and profusion which he exhibited. Campbell's conversation was 'in very bad taste'. He discussed Moore's neighbour, the poetical parson Bowles, and described him as a rascal, 'upon which Rogers took him up very properly'.

As soon as the carriage 'was off the stones' Moore got out. He was at Hyde Park Corner, where the country road began. He hurried back to his lodgings 'to get rid of my black clothes, and try to forget, as much as possible, the wretched feelings I had experienced in them'.

Rogers was available for a walk in the Park, but as luck would have it, they met a soldier's funeral. In the state Moore's heart was in, the sight affected him strongly. He walked down Paternoster Row to the Longmans' office and dined with Rees, one of the partners. They talked about a Byron biography; but Rogers had entreated Moore not to broach the subject to the family at the present time. From this Moore deduced that Rogers knew of a plan to settle the much-discussed two thousand pounds on 'little Tom'. If so, he was not going to interfere.

Leaving Paternoster Row he called on Lady Morgan, found her half-dressed, and had 'the felicity of seeing the completion of her toilette'. This was gallantry; 'the wild Irish girl'— always plain—was by this time as ugly as a monkey. Moore admits that he looked 'much more at her handmaid (Morgan's pretty daughter) than at herself'. From there he went to Mrs Story's and supped with her. The Story girls were at home, and after supper he took them to Vauxhall. 'A most delicious night.'

What is to be said of this performance? Mrs Langley Moore, speaking for Byron lovers, sees it as a revelation of Moore's shallowness. He, true to his mother's example, saw no merit in nourishing grief. He kept it at bay. It was not insensibility. It showed consideration for the living. It showed a sort of courage. He was defying the foul fiend.

Douglas Kinnaird saw the pressures of poverty and vanity behind Moore's conduct over the *Memoirs*. Proust and Kafka in collaboration could not have devised a more complicated state of mind than his as he twisted and doubled to avoid the hounds at his heels. There was a third which Kinnaird could not see: conscience was panting in the rear. In comparison with Moore's at this time, Hamlet's was an easy conscience. Moore would have said, most probably, that his friendship with Byron had cost him dear, that he had borrowed two thousand guineas to pay back Murray in order to demonstrate that he had not profited by a penny out of the friendship, that he had been subjected to abuse and criticism and—when the time came— refused their assistance in making a worthy record of Byron's life by the very people he had injured himself to propitiate.

He could not have known that his friendship with Byron would eventually become his second-best assurance of immortality. The fascination of Byron is perpetual, and whoever looks at that bright sun must always see Moore among its brightest satellites. Of his prose books his biography of Byron is the only one that anyone reads today. In life he took pleasure and pride in the letters (not always answered) that poured out from one of the best letter-writers in English; and he had known familiarly the delight of his company.

As we watch Moore hurrying hither and thither, consulting this one and that one, asking for advice what to do and approval of what he had done, it is not always easy to remember that this is the Moore Byron described in his dedication in *The Corsair* as 'The poet of all circles and the idol of his own', that this is the Moore whose appearance in a theatre in his native Dublin (or in Edinburgh) brings the house to its feet.

Only in the Byron circle was he vulnerable. There his friendship with their star had been resented. Fighting between themselves, they closed ranks to snub Moore. His need was his weakest point. Byron had given him the *Memoirs* to help him financially. His vanity (or pride) compelled him to take a stance that pretended he was not influenced by money. His high-minded patrician friend Lansdowne was unable to understand his difficulty. Mrs Langley Moore has put it baldly: 'Moore's most persistent foibles were snobbery and the kind of defensive pride that is found chiefly in men who lack security. An Irishman in an epoch when the Irish were still an oppressed people, a grocer's son who had magically won a foothold in the world when birth was usually indispensable to acceptance, his position was rendered still more vulnerable by his being poor . . .'.

Lansdowne, who refused places in Cabinets, the office of Prime Minister, and a dukedom, found it hard to enter into the perplexities of one who wanted to demonstrate that his conduct was not influenced by his need when his need was the only cause of the trouble.

Under a compulsion to prove that he was disinterested, he was impressing nobody but himself. By concentrating on a quittance on the score of self-interest or pecuniary motives, Moore was trying to deafen himself to what his conscience was telling him: that he had betrayed Byron's trust. Byron had urged him to make money out of the *Memoirs*: there was therefore no need to be squeamish on that score. Byron had told him he might show them to people without stipulating to whom; Moore could rely on that when he was attacked for having shown the *Memoirs* almost indiscriminately. What Byron did ask was that the book should be published; and Moore's final words of self-exculpation at the fire were an acknowledgement that Byron's intentions had been defeated. We know now that Moore had no power to prevent this. The property in the manuscript was Murray's. If there had been a competent solicitor advising the publisher, he would have made this clear at the outset; and then Moore would have been excluded from the arrangements. He had sold the *Memoirs*; and if Murray chose to burn what was his own property, that was his affair.

Instead, by persuading himself (and everyone else) that he had rights over the disposition of the papers, Moore had not only saddled himself for ever in the eyes of posterity with responsibility for having been at least an accomplice in the burning, he burdened himself with a debt to Longmans in order to have the satisfaction of repaying Murray a debt he didn't owe him.

Moore was subsequently at pains to persuade himself that Hobhouse's story was true—it flattered Hobhouse's vanity to think so—that Byron regretted giving the *Memoirs* to Moore and would have recalled them if he could have done so without hurting his feelings.

At ease in Scott's encouraging company, Moore gave what by then (October 1825) had become his own version of what happened and why:

'In talking of my sacrifice of the *Memoirs*, said he was well aware of the honourable feelings that dictated it, but doubted whether he would himself have consented to it. On my representing, however, the strong circumstances of not only the sister of Lord Byron (whom he so much loved) requiring it, but his two most intimate friends, Kinnaird and Hobhouse, also insisting earnestly upon the total destruction of the MS. and the latter assuring me that Lord Byron had expressed his regret for having put such a work out of his own power, and had said that he was restrained only by delicacy towards me from recalling it; when I mentioned these circumstances (and particularly the last), he seemed to feel that I could not have done otherwise than I had done. Thought the family, however, bound to furnish me every assistance towards the life of Lord B.'

Scott had listened to a total distortion of the facts by the person who would seem to be in the best position to report them aright; Moore persisted in the delusion that he had something to sacrifice, and he was as blissfully unaware of Mrs Leigh's antagonism towards himself as he was to her true disposition towards the *Memoirs*—indifference as to their contents with no desire to destroy anything of her Byron's.

Where Moore did fail Byron was in his treatment of his letters. These he bowdlerised freely, and then, apparently, destroyed. If he did not, Russell is the most likely culprit. Bessy, we may be sure, was meticulous in handing over to him all the papers she found intact.

Byron's friends would not have criticised Moore on this account. They were all in agreement that their duty was to leave to the world the most favourable picture of their friend, and to achieve this it was not only a duty but a pleasure to tamper with the evidence and to destroy incriminating letters.

What is pathetic in the story is the utter failure of Moore to impress the people he was so anxious to propitiate. He was himself so little given to malice or capable of sustaining hard feelings that he could not conceive that any others could nourish hostility towards himself. Murray, to whom he insisted on paying the money in spite of his protest (in the upshot he presented a bill for interest and expenses), complained about Moore's subsequent conduct. Hobhouse's journals are full of expressions of contempt for Moore; and Kinnaird was not impressed. No friend of Byron could have hoped to please his widow. But of all the friends and family the gentle Augusta was most resolutely opposed to Moore. 'I detest his very name', she said when the question of authorising a biography came up. But she thought Moore ought to have his money because Byron had intended to enrich him. She was kinder than Hobhouse, who did not want Moore to get any benefit. Murray was opposed to the plan to compensate Moore; he saw it as a reflection on himself for allowing Moore to reimburse him. Lady Byron chose to regard Murray as the loser—he could have made a profit out of the *Memoirs* had he not burnt them. This was true.

It was then agreed between the family to give Murray the money and let him offer it to Moore—the most humiliating way in which he could be repaid. Walter Scott, ready with cheerful and encouraging advice, told Moore to ask Lansdowne to intervene.

Over a year had passed since Moore had discussed over breakfast at Bowood the project of writing a *Life* of Lord Byron. Longmans had been pressing Moore to attempt it as their only means of recovering the money they had lent him to give to Murray. Lansdowne quite agreed with Moore when he said the subject had become so tarnished that perhaps he ought not to undertake it. Moore underlined '*ought*' in his Journal. He had stood on a point of principle and Lansdowne had left him up there. His lordship would have been surprised to read the next line in the diary entry: 'It is my intention, however, to leave both the Longmans and the public under the impression that I *do* mean to write the life.'

Since then Moore's *Sheridan* had appeared. Now Lord Lansdowne 'expressed a strong wish that I should undertake the life of Grattan', but Moore brought the subject round to Byron and to Scott's advice that he should employ Lansdowne to negotiate between him and the family. The entry is yet one more of Moore's ingenuous recordings of his disingenuousness in dealing with anyone he looked up to. 'This brought him to tell me (what he had hitherto, very much at my own desire, kept a secret from me) the nature of the negotiations which he had in that quarter last summer. It seems that Wilmot Horton consulted Lord L. with respect to the question of paying me back the money, and Lord L. gave it as his opinion that the obvious step for the family to take was (without any reference to me, who was decided upon refusing it) to settle it upon my family . . . On proposing it, however, to the family they refused to pay the money otherwise than making myself take it. From all this it appeared that Lord Lansdowne has no channel of communication (as I supposed) with the family . . . Walked nearly home with me. All this conversation . . . threw me into a state of nervousness and depression on my return home, for which it required all the efforts of my natural cheerfulness to recover me. Bessy, too, did much for me by her own sweet womanly fortitude, bless her!'

For Moore to write the *Life* and Murray to publish it was the obvious way of settling all the vexing questions about money, and this was eventually what was to happen.

THERE WERE to be alarums and excursions about the Byron *Life* for many years; but in the meanwhile Moore busied himself to complete Sheridan's biography, which he had set about so sanguinely before his removal to Paris and abandoned there. He had begun this task cheerfully; but his enthusiasm waned. His account of Sheridan's working methods as a writer are interesting—Moore was a very intelligent man. But he seems to have become disillusioned by his better acquaintance with the dramatist's personal character. Professor Dowden, who is working on Moore's Journal,* so casually bowdlerised by Russell, has come across a reference to Sheridan which throws a strange light, not only on him, but on Lady Holland, and suggests that the tone of Moore's conversation with her was of another character to that which prevailed at Bowood.

'Lady Holland thinks the first Mrs Sheridan "a little mad", and that the life of the Sheridans "from continual love, jealousy and infidelity towards each other must have been a series of scenes". She repeats the rumour that Mrs Sheridan had a child by Lord Edward Fitzgerald, and, amazingly, reveals her own involvement in their lives:

'Lord Lorn was also a lover of hers—"at the time he (Sheridan) was making love to me" said Lady Holland "and she was flirting with Lord Lorn, they would, both of them most willingly have given us up for each other, if they could have come to some explanation together".

She then proceeds to recount a sordid tale of Sheridan's infatuation with her, including a threat to blackmail her over "a person, for whom I certainly did not care the least", and, when this failed, taking "another most extraordinary method". Disguising himself as a servant who had a message to deliver to

* It was damaged by water during the London Blitz.

her, he gained entrance to her room and "rushed at [her] with
a ferociousness quite frightful" and bit her cheek "so violently
that the blood ran down [her] neck". Afterwards she was
afraid to go into society for fear of meeting him. She relates
other unsavoury examples of Sheridan's conduct, which
prompts Moore to express his doubts in his Journal: "I wonder
are all these stories of my Lady's true".'

Everyone who knew Sheridan had one of his funny sayings
to recount; most of these died on the printed page. What
Moore was chiefly interested in was the politics of Sheridan's
last years. They had a poignant significance for Moore because
they were the background to his days of expectation from Moira.

Sheridan, on one occasion, behaved so dishonestly that Moore
had to disclose it; in general he covered up for him, and wherever
the Prince Regent crossed Sheridan's path became a partisan,
so much so that when the book came out the Prince sent for
J. W. Croker and made an elaborate statement contradicting
some of Moore's assertions and giving details of Sheridan's
indebtedness to him. The Prince's alienation from Sheridan
was brought about by the dramatist, he affirmed. Sheridan
borrowed £4000 from him to buy a seat in parliament and then
used it to pay private debts.

Some of Moore's verses arraigning the false friends—the
Prince in particular—for neglecting the dying Sheridan were
reprinted in the biography. It was very recent history, and for
Moore dangerous ground because he was so closely associated
with some of the leaders of Sheridan's party. Lord Holland
told him that Sheridan attributed his moral lapses to his having
ideal standards so impossibly high that nobody could be expected
to live up to them. It must have hurt Moore to discover that
Sheridan was responsible for the failure of the Whigs to form a
government in 1812 when George III was suffering from one
of his recurring bouts of insanity. All this part of the story
brought back painfully the Moira phase of his own career. The
Regent was prepared to ask Lords Grey and Grenville to form
a Whig administration and thus realise the long-cherished hope
of a party which had put too much faith in the Prince's liberal
views. The noble lords refused to take office because they
understood the Household was not going to be changed, and

the Regent would be surrounded by the same entourage. Commissioned to tell them that this was not the case, Sheridan not only withheld this information, he affirmed the contrary. Consequently the Tories retained power for fifteen years and all hopes of reform were dashed.

It is sad to relate that Sheridan is usually seen acting selfishly, playing his own hand. Even so, Moore left out a great deal, and the book has very much a Hamlet without the Prince of Denmark air; its style in general rather turgid. It was a chore, and it reads like one. But there are some splendid passages.

There was, of course, the usual wave of praise and congratulations from Longmans who had sold 1000 copies straight off. The *Quarterly Review* contained 'the long-threatened cannonade'. Lord Lansdowne, for once, had criticisms to make, but only on statements of fact. The Hollands were not happy. He was too genial to say so, but nothing ever put constraint upon his wife, and years later, she was to tell Moore the book lacked 'taste and judgement'.

Lord John Russell, full of praise, suggested a trip to Paris— the Lansdownes were also going—then, as so often, changed his mind. Moore hesitated—on account of 'the expense, Bessy's health, the idleness, and one or two more things', but 'Bessy would not hear of my staying at home: insisted that if I did not go to France, that I must go either to Scotland or Ireland, to amuse myself a little. Dear, generous girl, there never was any-one like her for warm-heartiness and devotion. I shall certainly do no good at home, for the daily fidget I am kept in about my book . . .'.

He decided to visit Sir Walter Scott.

Scott was a genial host, and his hospitality was such that Lady Scott was heard to say that except in the item of revenue Abbotsford had all the character of an inn. But Scott's letter to Moore breathes more than conventional politeness. Moore had written to him not long before to excuse himself for not having been there to greet him on his visit to Ireland. Scott in his cordial reply extended an invitation to Abbotsford to Moore and added—not knowing his man—'Bring wife and bairns'.

On November 11, 1825, Moore, on the wing, announced his coming, and Scott in his reply—'My dear Sir—Damn Sir—My dear Moore'—regretted not being able to meet him en route, and advised him to approach on the south side of the Tweed. He would come himself a few miles in that direction on the chance of meeting him. There was accommodation for any fellow-traveller Moore might have with him.

This was in keeping with the spirit of his earlier letter, when he spoke of claret in store and the prospect of talk about 'poor Byron, who was dear to us both . . . I very often think of him almost with tears. Surely you who have the means, should do something for his literary life at least'.

Moore's full Journal entry of the visit was made use of by Lockhart when writing his celebrated *Life* of his father-in-law. Scott gave himself up completely to the entertainment of the visiting Irishman, whom he was meeting for the second time; and he delighted Moore by putting a hand on his breast on the second day, saying, 'Now, my dear Moore, we are friends for life'. A visit to Wordsworth would not have provided any experience like that! Scott's naturalness of manner particularly delighted Moore. He regretted that he had not had Scott's education; his own had been too much of a 'boudoir' kind, the want of manly training showed in his poetry. Scott politely disagreed. But he remarked how the poetry he read in magazines was so much an improvement on what was written thirty years before. 'Ecod, we were in the luck of it to come before those fellows.' Scott's own note of the visit is worth giving in full. It is taken from his Journal.

'November 22 Moore—I saw Moore (for the first time, I may say) this season. We had indeed met in public twenty years ago . . . Not the least touch of the poet or the pedant. A little— very little man—less, I think, than Lewis, and something like him in person; God knows, not in conversation, for Matt, though a clever fellow, was a bore of the first description. Moreover, he looked always like a schoolboy. Now Moore has none of this insignificance. His countenance is plain, but the expression so very animated, especially in speaking or singing, that it is far more interesting than the finest features could have rendered it.

'I was aware that Byron had often spoken, both in private society and in his Journal, of Moore and myself, in the same breath, and with the same sort of regard; so I was curious to see what there could be in common betwixt us. Moore having lived so much in the gay world, I in the country, and with people of business, and sometimes with politicians; Moore a scholar, I none; he a musician and artist, I without knowledge of a note; he a democrat, I an aristocrat—with many other points of difference; besides his being an Irishman, I a Scotchman, and both tolerably national. Yet there is a point of resemblance, and a strong one. We are both good-humoured fellows, who rather seek to enjoy what is going forward than to maintain our dignity as Lions; and we have both seen the world too widely and too well not to contemn in our souls the imaginary consequence of literary people who walk with their noses in the air, and remind me always of the fellow whom Johnson met in an alehouse and who called himself "the great Twamley— inventor of the flood-gate iron for smoothing linen". He also enjoys the *mot pour rire*, and so do I. It was a pity that nothing save the total destruction of Byron's *Memoirs* would satisfy his executors;—but there was a reason—*Premat nox alta*. It would be a delightful addition to life, if T.M. had a cottage within two miles of one. We went to the theatre together, and the house being luckily a good one, received T.M. with rapture. I could have hugged them, for it paid back the debt of the kind reception I met with in Ireland.'

Scott had stood back in the box in the theatre to allow Moore to take the applause of the house alone. His name had been called, and the greeting was spontaneous.

From Scott's house Moore went to stay with the Murrays in Edinburgh—Bessy's sister and her husband. Jeffrey of the *Edinburgh Review*, now a Law Lord, came in his coach to fetch him out to his house, where he returned for another dinner before making for home again. Scott took part in one of these festivities; and Moore noticed that he was more inert and less amusing than when he was the host in his own house.

*   *   *

Moore's next meeting with Scott was in London. Sir Walter was on his way to Paris in connection with his biography of Napoleon, one of his less memorable productions. In the course of conversation, Moore said 'How I should like to go with you'. Scott pressed him to come. There was room in the carriage, 'only you must take care and not rumple Anne's frills'. They were off on Thursday, and Moore said he would make up his mind definitely by Wednesday.

Immediately Moore was thrown into the perplexities that inevitably accompanied his making any decision. Rogers was consulted. He—as was his way—'threw a little blight over it, said it was an extraordinary frisk, but that it was like me; nobody else would think of it; that it would never surprise him (even after hearing me complain, as I did eternally, of pressure of business and want of time) to be told of my having set off on a party of pleasure *any where* and with *any body*'.

Longman was asked to consider; he thought the trip was an excellent plan. Moore wondered if it might injure Scott to travel with such a political reprobate as himself. Longman thought Scott above such considerations.

At a breakfast party where they met, Scott made no allusion to the trip; Moore interpreted this as evidence of second thoughts; but when he met Scott later in the day, Sir Walter said that it was all fixed, he had Moore's passport. Moore asked for further reassurance and was given it.

Bessy meanwhile had been consulted by letter and replied to say she left the matter to his own decision. He had now 'almost made up his mind to go', and called on Scott to say 'he would make an effort to start with him on Thursday'.

'That's right; but what will you do about your passport?'

He had forgotten, he said, to put down Moore's name, but, it was not too late. Moore, however, decided not to go. He thought he detected 'a *little change*' in Scott's manner.

SPEAKING TO Lansdowne on 12th December 1825, Moore
agreed that he was not going to write about Byron. Writing to
Hobhouse from Dublin nine days later he begins 'You have
heard, I dare say, that I am at last about to occupy myself
seriously with some Memorial of our friend Byron. Whether,
however, it is to be a regular biographical Memoir, or merely
such a sketch as my own knowledge and materials afford must
depend entirely on the assistance I receive from his family
executors'. He went on to ask Hobhouse to write the book with
him, humbling himself further by suggesting that Hobhouse did
'not think much of the *Life of Sheridan*; but I may improve as
I go on . . .'.

Hobhouse replied, 'I do not see what good end can be
answered by writing a life of our late friend . . . You will write,
there can be no doubt, a very clever and a very saleable book.
But I shall be most agreeably surprised if you accomplish those
higher objects which you must propose to yourself by becoming
the Biographer of such man as Lord Byron . . .'.

There was something insufferable in this use of borrowed
plumage, but Moore kept his temper.

'However flattering it might be to my vanity to find a person
like you entertaining the same partial opinion of my talents
that others do, be assured that you cannot think much more
humbly of them than I do myself, and that nothing but the
want of means from any other source could have induced me so
long to avail myself of even that "saleable" quality (as you
describe it) which, however undeservedly, my writings have
hitherto possessed.'

Moore confessed that if he could see any other way of
discharging his 'heavy obligations' he would avoid the task.

Hobhouse relented a little, offering 'popular' as a substitute
for 'saleable' in his insulting paragraph. For which relief Moore

offered much thanks. He could never stand upright in Hob-house's presence; it went deeper than diplomacy (a fight with Byron's executor might have been fatal to the prospects of a book about him).

Moore asked Hobhouse to fulfil a promise and give a written acknowledgement that Byron felt regret at having put his *Memoirs* out of his own power and was restrained only by delicacy from asking Moore for them back. A request that Hobhouse ignored.

In November 1826, Moore wrote to Scott to ask him whether, in the event of Murray's agreeing to commission the *Life* (Rogers was acting as go-between), he would allow the book to be dedicated to him. (It was.)

Murray offered £2500 but declined to let his own Byron papers be used. He was keeping them for his children. Where-upon, Moore wrote to Hobhouse to say he was going forward with the book, but with Longmans, not Murray. Hobhouse had offered kindly 'to look over the book before publication': A kindness that in the circumstances might have seemed to threaten trouble.

Hobhouse met Moore in May. Because he was civil, Moore deluded himself that Hobhouse had become friendly. He was satisfied to have established a formula whereby Moore seemed equally to deprecate the project upon which he was venturing only from sheer necessity. He told Moore he 'wished it was not *necessary* for him to write such a thing, but the next best thing to *no* life was a short life'. They agreed together to destroy some parts of a journal Byron kept in Italy where he was about to tell of the 'violent though pure love and passion' he had for Edleston, the Cambridge choir boy.

Hobhouse suggested a reconciliation with Murray effected by walking up to him in the street and shaking hands. Murray 'seemed startled at first' but at Charing Cross parted saying 'God bless you, sir! God bless you, sir'.

Hobhouse hoped Moore would confine this book to an ex-tended preface to Byron's works; and Murray played with the idea of publishing some of his Byron papers in a separate book. Moore, hearing of this, took umbrage, and returned to Long-mans. There was a delay while Moore completed *The Epicurean*, and in mid-summer 1827, Moore began to collect material for the *Life*. The first person he turned to was Mary Shelley, the poet's widow.

Mrs Shelley had been drawn into the Hunt circle in Italy, and in spite of Byron's help joined in the canard against him. However, it was not an expression of her true feelings. She had a very soft spot indeed for Byron, and when Moore approached her in London entered wholeheartedly into the plan for the biography, offering not only to write down her own recollections and secure Byron's correspondence with the Greek committee, but to obtain a memoir from the Countess Guiccioli. Moore's scheme was to use letters, diaries, other people's recollections, and to confine the biographical office to writing linking passages and occasional comments.

Mary Shelley surrendered to Moore's attractions; her own fortunes were low, but she began at once to enter into his plans, not only helping with the work but interesting herself in his children. His Journal is full of excuses for broken engagements with her, none of which appear to have aroused her resentment. No doubt, like Bessy, she understood the sort of man she was dealing with. Moore could not appreciate her husband's poetry, but it must have helped their friendship that Shelley had always been an admirer of Moore. He had immortalised him in *Adonais*:

> . . . from her wilds Ierne sent
> The sweetest lyrist of her saddest wrong,
> And Love taught Grief to fall like music from his tongue.

But did he really *mean* it? Typically, Moore (who used to come sometimes to breakfast) expressed to a sympathetic woman his self-doubting. Mary was able to reassure him; and that she was not merely soothing his spirits is borne out by Shelley's letters; he never mentions Moore without respect. Mrs Shelley seems to have put her head on Moore's chest from the start. She was probably lonely and certainly poor. When he sent her a song, she questioned his awareness of the real pathos in his lines, and he was sincerely grieved 'to find such a tone of sorrow and hopelessness as pervades your last letter'. At Newstead, visiting the scenes of Byron's early manhood, 'next to

Byron, I thought of *you* during my visit there', he writes to her.

Work on the book was well under way when he wrote to Hobhouse later in the month; but he was dashed to hear in reply that Hobhouse refused to be associated with the biography, and repeated what he had told Moore some time before, when they met at a dinner: he had gone back on his offer to let Moore see the letters to Lady Melbourne, not that Hobhouse ever read into them—as later readers have—the suggestion that Byron was the father of his sister's child Medora. If he had he would have burned the letters at once.

Moore turned once again the other cheek, but this time with an irony which, apparently, Hobhouse missed, because he noted in his Journal that the letter was 'in proper terms'.

Moore begged him not to think that any expression of gratitude from him was to be construed as evidence of co-operation '. . . indeed the simple fact of my work being likely to appear without a single contribution of either paper or anecdote from any one of Lord B's immediate friends or relatives, would, of itself, sufficiently absolve them from any share of the responsibility attached to it'.

In his acknowledgement Hobhouse told Moore that he had struck out of an earlier memoir a threat by Byron to write a satire against Moore when something he had said in a letter incensed him. Moore replied effusively. 'It was very kind of you to suppress the passage and I may *now* tell you that I had occasion to perform the same service towards *you* (for which of his dear friends did he not sometimes make free with?) . . .'.

Hobhouse sat at home all morning answering this letter 'in the true Irish style, very malicious'. He was unable to conceal the motive for his curmudgeonly treatment of Moore. Moore 'had all the praise, I all the knocks'. He was hurt and jealous. 'Our correspondence is likely to have an ugly termination.' Did he foresee a duel? It would have been the most effective way to discharge such an accumulation of bile.

And then came Leigh Hunt's slimy and venomous book, *Lord Byron and Some of his Contemporaries*. That almost closed the ranks, but Kinnaird, who had not long to live, still stood out against the biography, even when Hobhouse reluctantly agreed that some answer was called for, and the calumnies against Byron should not be left to stand.

Kinnaird wrote with depressing logic, 'If on the one hand Mr Hunt's evident motives disqualify him from being a competent authority to judge of Lord B's character, the pen of a friend must be supposed to lie under an equal disqualification for fixing public opinion'.

In Moore's letter, to which this was a reply, he had castigated Hobhouse with others for their 'faithlessness to the memory of a common friend'. It was inconsistent with his long-suffering tone when writing to Hobhouse, to whom Kinnaird showed the letter (did Moore think he would?). Subsequently Hobhouse was to complain of Moore's coolness towards him when they met, when he had 'nothing to gain by caresses'. He decided that he had 'done him no injury—on the contrary much service— but then I did not contribute to his book, and besides he feels I know him—he is a poor creature'. Moore needed any cosseting he received from Mrs Shelley. They probably made between them a fair exchange.

The origin of Hunt's book went back to when, having drained all he could from the unworldly Shelley, he transferred his mendicant attentions to Byron. He paid for the Hunt family's transport to Italy and provided their lodgings there. Hunt's manner towards Byron was a deplorable show of effrontery, well described by Byron's biographer Leslie A. Marchand as 'tactless mock arrogance'. Inevitably Byron resented it, as he resented the rudeness of Mrs Hunt and the piggishness of their brood. He said so, and it was repeated to Hunt.

Byron, quarrelling at the time with his publisher, Murray, who had lost his nerve as successive instalments of *Don Juan* became more and more unrestrained, had gone over to the Hunts, contributed to their journal *The Liberal* and even ordered that his papers should be given to John Hunt.

Leigh Hunt came to Italy originally at Shelley's invitation. The object of the visit was to discuss a new periodical. Moore advised Byron against any business involvement with Hunt. It was wise advice, and Byron acted upon it, although he assisted Hunt in every other way.

In that circle there was no discretion; and Byron was most

culpable of all in the matter of showing letters. It seems to be a weakness of literary folk. The Bloomsbury group a century later enjoyed making mischief in this way. In Byron's case it led to incessant quarrels. Hunt attacked Moore in leading articles.

He had to nurse his resentment against Byron, on whom, after Shelley died, he became wholly dependent; but he enlisted Shelley's widow in his cause (she, too, had to take Byron's financial assistance).

When Hunt returned to England he was given £200 by Colburn, the publisher, to edit his own writings. Instead he published what Mrs Langley Moore has aptly described as a 'fearful book'. He was a mean sponge; and not the first to feel that his literary gift entitled him to exploit anyone whom he could flatter or impress.

When he came to deal with the Byron *Memoirs* Hunt wrote in a manner calculated to deflate all Moore's pretensions. He wished to bring home that Moore by accepting them was in the same position as anyone who took Byron's money. It must have maddened Moore to read: 'I should look upon myself as more tied, and rendered more dependent, by living as he does among the great, and flattering the mistakes of the vulgar, than by accepting thousands from individuals whom I loved. When I came to know Lord Byron as I did, I could no more have accepted his manuscript than his money, unless I could prove to myself that I had a right to them in the way of business.'

This from the man who had allowed Shelley to mortgage his expectations on his father's death to help him and who had taken from Byron all he could get in cash and kind!

In the Harold Skimpole fashion, Hunt coated this pill with sugar. He had a knack of glowing over his victims when they first presented themselves to his view, the implication being that they deteriorated when they exercised themselves outside his orbit. Moore did not defend himself; it was for Byron he hit back in *The Times*, with a verse *The Living Dog and the Dead Lion*, on 10th January 1828. It was signed 'T. Pidcock'. Pidcock was a man who kept a menagerie. Because the issues are as dead as the people who were concerned in them, it is no longer possible to appreciate much of Moore's satire; and those who profess to see in it his best work are contriving to bury his reputation. But here is one specimen where—as in his verses on Sheridan's funeral—all the persons and circumstances are familiar. In writing it, Mrs Langley Moore finely says, he recaptured the courage of his youth, 'the courage to make enemies'.

Next week will be published (as 'Lives' are the rage)
The whole Reminiscences, wondrous and strange,
Of a small puppy-dog, that once lived in the cage
Of the late noble Lion at Exeter 'Change.

Though the puppy is a dog of the kind they call 'sad',
'Tis a puppy that much to good breeding pretends;
And few dogs have such opportunities had
Of knowing how Lions behave—among friends.

How that animal eats, how he snores, how he drinks,
It is all noted down by this Boswell so small;
And 'tis plain from each sentence, the puppy-dog thinks
That the Lion was no such great things after all.

Though he roared pretty well—this the puppy allows—
It was all, he says, borrowed—all second-hand roar:
And he vastly prefers his own little bow-wows
To the loftiest war-note the Lion could pour.

'Tis indeed as good fun as the cynic could ask,
To see how this cockney-bred setter of rabbits
Takes gravely the Lord of the Forest to task,
And judges of Lions by puppy-dog habits.

Nay, fed as he was (and this makes a *dark* case)
With sops every day from the Lion's own pan,
He lifts up a leg at the noble beast's carcass,
And does all a dog so diminutive can.

However, the book's a good book, being rich in
Examples and warnings to Lions high-bred,

How they suffer small mongrelly curs in their kitchen,
Who'll feed on them living, and foul them when dead.

Moore was already engaged in collecting material for the
biography that Longmans had agreed to publish. Murray was
so enraged by Hunt's book that he wrote to Moore saying that
he had changed his mind and offering to put all his Byron
papers at his disposal.

At a meeting on February 7th in Albemarle Street, Murray
agreed to give Moore four thousand guineas for the biography.
Longmans, impeccable always in their treatment of Moore,
accepted £3000 from Murray—Moore's debt to them—and
released their rights. Hobhouse also came round—never
entirely, never other than grudgingly, but effectively insofar as
in his capacity as executor he could have put innumerable
obstacles in Moore's way. He was a cynic. Even when he met
Murray and listed to his indignation at the way Hunt had
defamed Byron, Hobhouse noted in his Journal that he pre-
sumed Murray 'cuts a poor figure' in the book. He could
reconcile himself to the idea of Moore's writing the book
when he had persuaded him to say he was doing so only for
money.

Given five hundred and sixty one of Byron's letters and his
journals, with the opportunity of publishing them for the first
time, it was almost impossible not to make a most readable
book in the teeth of any difficulties. Moore did better than that;
he allows Byron (and his other contributors) to speak for
themselves. But Moore is in attendance wherever he is needed,
never obtrusive, and with many luminous observations to make
on a man whom he understood very well. Certainly he must be
acquitted of any attempt to aggrandise himself by association.
He does not nudge the reader. This is not the book of a small
man. It was the best opportunity for a biographer since Boswell
undertook Johnson's life, and Moore wrote the best biography
since Boswell's.

In one respect he was to benefit by the attitude of the family
and the self-appointed caretakers of Byron's reputation—he
was released from the obligation to satisfy them, which weighs
heavily on most biographers when their victims are recently

dead. The family breathing down the neck has a paralysing effect on the pen.

Moore did a good deal of bowdlerising; and he gave throughout the more favourable interpretation of Byron's conduct where there was any doubt, but not in a dishonest way. It is an adult book; and as it was written by an intelligent observer, who knew his subject well, it must always have a freshness and immediacy which works of subsequent and more exact scholarship can never attain. If the widow (to whom Moore was kind) had helped, Moore might have been prevented from disclosing what Byron thought of his in-laws. Lady Byron, whose lips were sealed on principle, rushed into the fray on this account. She was at the time in a controversy with Augusta Leigh about an appointment of a trustee, insisting as always that Augusta must conduct herself like a convict on a ticket of leave.

When Augusta refused to capitulate, Lady Byron—against all responsible advice—prepared a pamphlet in which she revived Augusta's relationship with Byron. This, by implication, was the reason why Lady Byron's parents had influenced her not to return to her husband. Augusta, as a lady-in-waiting, stood to lose, if there was a scandal, her 'grace and favour' apartments, a pension of £300 a year and with her position in court, her position in society. She had been in danger at the time of the separation. Lady Byron was quite aware of this, and with an appearance of injured innocence, upon which she was to trade for all her long life, she was quite prepared to ruin her half-sister-in-law. She consulted Lord Melbourne and Lord Holland. They both advised her not to stir up trouble. While she was supposed to be considering her position, she took care that her pamphlet went to everyone that she wanted to influence, including the dying George IV. The recipients were enjoined to secrecy: nothing is calculated better to give a flying start to a scandal.

Moore, when the matter was brought to his notice by Lord Holland, offered at once to append Lady Byron's pamphlet to his second volume. Most reluctantly she was forced to agree to this, maddened to see herself promoting his sales. The steely-eyed Lady Holland saw exactly what was happening. She wrote to her son:

'Lady Byron is getting into a silly controversy with Moore upon some passages in his book. She will be the loser; as many suppressed passages will now be disclosed, and she will not like it. Your papa is doing his utmost to quell her restlessness, but in vain. I am afraid she is a cold, obstinate woman; but do not mention this opinion.'

Harold Nicolson, into whose possession it had come, gave Hobhouse's copy of the *Life* to a sale to raise funds for the London Library. It was copiously annotated. Inevitably Hobhouse came upon the inaccuracies he was looking for, even in the opening pages. But the book absorbed him, reopening old memories. Byron's friendship had gone deep with him. This was something Moore would never understand, whose friendships were the sparkle of sun on the surface of life's ebbing tide. But for all his growlings Hobhouse had to admit that Moore portrayed Byron's character fairly. What annoyed were the references to his early associates. 'In fact he had no friend till he knew Tom Moore', Hobhouse wrote on the wide margin. One can hear the pen scratching the paper.

By a curious perversity, in order to show that he was more intimate with Byron than ever Moore could have been, Hobhouse hints at depravity and seems to be most outraged by Moore's flattering references to his friend; charitable inferences are sneered at; in particular he deprecated Moore's references to Byron's accomplishments. When Moore made a sanctimonious reference to Lady Byron, Hobhouse wrote 'False and base' beside it.

If Moore intended to ingratiate himself with the widow he was soon to learn that he had failed. But it was in keeping with his own nature; if his loves were shallow, he was incapable of sustaining enmity. Hobhouse was saturnine in comparison. Moore knew that Byron had not treated his wife well, and the idea of any widow would have been sufficient to touch his surface sensibility. When a fund was collected to relieve Leigh Hunt's financial distress in later years, Moore subscribed. Was it a mere parade of magnanimity? Hobhouse would have said so, whose devotion permitted him to blacken Byron's character in his Journal. No wonder their friend preferred Moore's company and made the other executor of his will. They were dogs of a different breed, and each had the faults of his virtues.

After spluttering and raging Hobhouse was unable to sustain the attack. 'Excellent'; 'Admirable!', 'Quite right!', 'True!'. 'This is the man.' If the book wrung such epithets from that reluctant source it was certain to please disinterested critics.

The book was the talk of the town and, as was the fashion of the day, as well as ephemeral criticism (favourable or not according to the politics of the paper), it provided opportunities for considered re-assessments of Byron. The most celebrated is Macaulay's. It contained that best remembered of all his rhetorical sayings: 'We know no spectacle so ridiculous as the British public in one of its periodical fits of morality.' Macaulay's unstinted praise of Moore's work is its monument. Posterity has dispensed, among others, with the carping critic of the *Westminster Review*.

Moore was now at the zenith of his career. Murray engaged Lawrence to paint his portrait. There were thirty present when he sat down on the 6th February 1830 for the opening dinner of the Athenaeum, with Croker in the chair. A few days later he was approached to write the *Life* of Canning, an honour he declined because he would not be able to speak of the conduct of Lord Grey with the freedom the subject required because of his 'high opinion of him and gratitude for much kindness'. In fact he was already hard at work on the second volume of *Byron*, and at about this time the idea of a *Life* of Lord Edward Fitzgerald entered his mind. He was given a helpful start with a large bundle of papers; the book was written and published inside a year.

His chief concern about the second volume of *Byron* was how to deal with the Murray correspondence. He had always been shocked by Byron's choice of his publisher as a recipient of the news of his dissipations in Venice. Writing to Murray's son, Moore explained, 'It is a constant remark (which neither you nor he are likely to hear) how strange that a nobleman should write such letters to his bookseller'.

Not surprisingly the father, honoured by the confidences and communications, was sensitive on the point. Moore appealed to his 'honest manly good sense'. In the preface Moore explained that Byron wanted to keep his name before the public, and he used Murray's drawing-room, a centre of literary society, as a broadcasting house. Murray's attitude to Moore can be gathered from his Journal for 18th March 1830.

'Dined with Murray. Meant to have joined the Lansdownes at the play afterwards, to see Fanny Kemble, but had a note from Murray before dinner . . . to say "For God's sake do not go to Lord Lansdowne's this evening; you live with him, and it can be of no consequence to him, but to me it will be thrusting a knife into my feelings".'

Caroline Norton, one of the three beautiful daughters of Tom Sheridan, was a great beauty of the day, not at all like Lady Lansdowne or Moore's usual friends. Her association with Melbourne led to an action by her husband, which was settled in hugger-mugger fashion; her involvement with Sidney Herbert gave Meredith the plot for *Diana of the Crossways*. When Moore met her dining in June 1831 at the Feildings he told her that he was dedicating his *Summer Fête* to her, 'which seemed to please her very much'.

It was Moore's *Rape of the Lock*, but in a very minor key, and he called it a trifle. But, talking to Mrs Norton, he was in his new supremely confident mood. He had been invited by the Lansdownes and refused them on account of this engagement, whereupon the Feildings had asked the Lansdownes to come to meet *him*.

It was about this time that, walking with Russell, Moore said his life had been such a happy one, he wouldn't mind very much if he had to die.

We meet him again, calling on Mrs Norton at home, and finding her about to go out to sit for her portrait. 'Had accordingly a very brisk and agreeable walk across two parks, and took her in the highest bloom of beauty to Hayter, who said he wished that someone would always put her through this process before she sat to him.' He collected his inevitable compliment for the Journal before leaving artist and sitter together.

These pictures of Moore, and in particular his air of consequence in political matters in which his friends, not he, were active spirits, must be attributed to the effect on his soul of O'Connell's triumph for the Catholics. For centuries the Irish had been punished in their own country for the offence of being

Irish—Moore's ancestors may well have been driven out of Leix in Mary Tudor's reign—and ever since the victory of William III and the dishonouring of the terms made in the Treaty of Limerick Catholics had been persecuted. The Penal Laws have too often been invoked to recite them here. They were not merely harsh, they made Catholics an inferior caste. Emancipation in 1829 gave them the right to sit in parliament, to hold commissions in the army, to become senior barristers, magistrates and judges (they had only recently acquired the right to own land and not merely to hold it on lease).

That Moore was never ashamed of his social origins does not mean he was reconciled to the system that had ensured his being born over a shop. When seeking for a reason why he began at this time to write (unprofitably) about Ireland and Irish questions, the explanation lies, I feel sure, in that measure of parliament. A Catholic was now on a level with the next man.

Newman was not the only one to misjudge the effect of Emancipation on Catholics with social aspirations. These, he discovered to his chagrin, preferred to send their sons to Trinity College or across the Irish sea to Oxford and Cambridge than to support a new Catholic foundation.

Moore must have been infected by the new atmosphere and felt some moral cubits had been added to his stature. It helps to explain his attitude towards O'Connell; disapproval of his lapses into most ungentlemanly abuse of opponents, unconsciously jealous, perhaps, of one who burst his way through the barriers of centuries, conquering, not by wiles, but by sheer moral force.

ON RETURNING home from his visit to Scott, Moore found a letter from his sister Ellen to say their father was dangerously ill. He set off for Dublin as soon as he could get money from the bank.

In Dublin he met Corry, a very old, dear and true friend. Corry was at once engaged as messenger and interpreter. He had secured a room for Moore in Bilton's hotel; and while the poet stayed there, Corry called on Ellen to find out if Tom's appearance would be too much for his mother that night. As one might have supposed, his sister said her mother would be better for seeing her boy. He was glad to hear 'it was their strong wish I should not ask to see my father, as he was past the power of knowing me, and it would only shock me unnecessarily'. He comforted himself with the thought that 'it was Bessy's last wish that I should not arrive in time to see him alive, and her earnest request that I should not look on him afterwards. She knows how it would affect me'.

When he called at Abbey Street on the following morning, it was all over. In the evening the family found themselves able to converse. A priest had been sent for to attend the old man at the end; when he began to hear his confession Mr Moore called his wife. 'Auty, my dear, you can tell this gentleman all he requires to know quite as well as I.'

The Moores talked about their religious beliefs: Kate, the married sister, who, when Moore had last seen her, had been half inclined to declare herself a Protestant, now told her brother that she had taken his advice and 'remained quietly a Catholic'. (At this place in the Journal, Russell made a tantalising cut.) The entry continues, 'For myself, my having married a Protestant wife gave me an opportunity for choosing a religion, at least for my children, and if any marriage had no other advantage, I should think *this* quite sufficient to be grateful for.'

They went on talking, expressing sentiments, Moore observed, which would surprise or make ashamed those who believed Catholics were intolerantly attached to their faith. Mrs Moore was not one to nourish sorrow. 'The natural buoyancy and excursiveness of her thoughts' was his lucky inheritance. It 'affords a better chance of escape from grief than all the philosophy in the world'.

Unfortunately, there was still the grim matter of the funeral to be faced. Ellen and Kate, shocked and agitated by the attentions of the undertakers, wished to 'spare me the operation of the Mass in the morning, and advised me not to come until after the service was over; but thought it better for every reason to attend. Felt my heart full of sadness when I got to the bedroom, but was relieved by a burst both of tears and prayer, and by a sort of *confidence* that the great and pure Spirit above us could not be otherwise than pleased with what he saw passing within my mind. This, perhaps, not Christian humility, but let it be what it will, I felt consoled and edified by it'.

Moore was forty-six when his mother died; the next test of his sensibilities was when Anastasia took ill at her school in Bath. Her two elder sisters died before their personalities had developed sufficiently to impress themselves on their mercurial father; but Anastasia was now sixteen. She had become inexplicably lame in one leg; doctors were called in, seabathing was prescribed; by March 1829 all pretence of recovery was over. She was brought home to die. Her parents sat with her, talked to her, read to her—in nothing did Moore fail to do what he could to keep the poor girl as happy as possible. He had, according to Russell, seemed afraid of disturbing her with religious preparation, 'but Mrs Moore had long before inculcated in her daughter's mind those lessons of piety she was so well qualified to give'.

Anastasia asked if she might sing, and then began, 'When in death I shall calmly recline'.

Moore gives a detailed account of the child's gradual deterioration and Bessy's motherly fortitude. Towards the end it became all too much for the father. As he left the room Bessy ran after him with smelling salts, saying 'For God's sake don't *you* get ill'. Upstairs Moore sobbed, feeling as if his chest would come asunder while Bessy sat by the child, whose last words were 'Papa! Papa!'

Her dying wish would have been to see the household God. He need only have stood in the doorway.

Bessy went out next day and found a grave and prepared the child for her coffin, dropping in a bunch of snowdrops. Neither parent attended the funeral; Tom hired a chaise, and they went for a two-hour drive, 'each bearing up for the sake of the other'.

In August 1830 Moore decided to take Bessy and the boys to Ireland. Anastasia's death may have prompted him to let his mother meet her grandsons. Her coming to England never seems to have been contemplated. They found her in good health and spirits; sister Ellen ('Nell') inevitably 'sweet and gentle' (Moore's womenfolk might all have been invented by Dickens). Both women delighted in the boys—Tom good-looking and attractive; Russell, his mother's favourite. Bessy looked more handsome, Moore decided, than he had ever seen her. As the family sat together her face was full of the 'utmost sweetness and affection'. All for *his* sake. They had a most happy family dinner.

Moore resisted the first invitation to dine out, and instead took Bessy and the boys to the theatre in Fishamble Street. It was an evening to remember. There was continual fighting in the house; the Moores' box was invaded by a drunken man, but Moore persuaded him to leave when Bessy was handing Russell over to the actors on the stage for the child's protection. The Moores got home safely.

One of the excuses for the trip was to collect material for the *Life* of Lord Edward Fitzgerald. Major Sirr whose pistol-shot was the cause of the rebel leader's death was living in Dublin. He was most forthcoming when Moore called on him and gave a detailed account of the events that led up to Lord Edward's capture. The Major sent in his card when Moore was in conversation with the Duke of Leinster, Lord Edward's nephew. Moore marvelled at the changes wrought by time when the Duke described his uncle's killer as 'in his way, a good sort of man'.

Moore was saturating himself in the atmosphere of that

turbulent time when he had himself been playing with fire. Emmet's counsel, Burrowes, told him a tragic story. Emmet was no judge of character; he lived in the clouds; the man to whom he entrusted some money and a letter to Sarah Curran pocketed the money and gave the letter to a Government official. When Emmet heard this he offered to go to his death in silence if the letter were suppressed.

It was above all a nostalgic visit. Moore drove around the scenes of his childhood, trying to reconstruct the scene in the field at Dundrum where he had been crowned King of the Castle; and in this mood he travelled with Bessy and the boys to Kilkenny where 'my sweet Bess and I' recollected 'love-making days'.

Moore took young Tom to call on Mr Banim, father of the author, who kept a little powder and shot shop in Kilkenny. Mr Banim not being at home Moore left a note to say he had called out of respect to his son. 'Took care to impress upon Tom how great the merit of a young man must be who, with not one hundredth part of the advantages of education that he (Tom) had in his power, could yet so distinguish himself as to cause this kind of tribute of respect to be paid to his father.' A homily of a sort that is only heeded by children who don't need it.

And if young Tom had had access to his father's Journal he might have noted with some amusement that his father had read but one of Banim's stories, found it good and took the rest upon credit. A more likely motive for the call was Banim's good taste in dedicating his second series to Tom's father and calling him 'Ireland's free son and true poet'.

Back in town, the Moores dined with Lady Campbell (Lord Edward's daughter). She had misgivings about the prudence of writing the *Life*. But she gave Moore valuable information about her father's first escape from arrest. 'It is a very disagreeable task for a gentleman to be employed in', said Major Swan when he came to arrest Lord Edward. 'It is a task no gentleman would perform', Lady Edward replied.

The centrepiece of the holiday was a meeting to celebrate the recent Revolution in France. The room in the National Mart was large enough to allow more than 2000 to be present. Moore had been thinking about his speech during his trip in the country. Richard Lalor Shiel opened the proceedings. Second only to Grattan in renown as an orator, Moore was unimpressed by his performance, and thought he would not be a success in the House of Commons. His voice was a scream, with no medium tone; his actions theatrical, and of the barn order of theatricals.

But it did very well in Dublin. While he spoke a crowd burst through the doors completely filling the room. There were three thousand people present when Moore was called to his feet. The call for him had become 'obstreperous'.

'I rose. My reception almost astoundingly enthusiastic. For some minutes I got on with perfect self-possession, but my very success alarmed me, and I at once lost the thread of what I was going to say; all seemed to have vanished from my mind.'

He grew pale; but the audience attributed this to play-acting. And when he recovered himself, the applause made him 'feel capable of anything'. The cheering when he sat down lasted for some minutes.

'He is a most beautiful speaker', Sheil exclaimed. Bessy—when Moore broke down—decided that he was thinking of Anastasia. And she herself nearly fainted at the idea. 'It is true,' Moore wrote in his diary, 'I had often during the day thought with sad regret of our sweet child, and the delight she would have felt in witnessing my success had she been spared to us; but, of course, at the moment of my bewilderment I thought of nothing but how to find my way back again'.

He noticed that at private parties the audience was 'much colder' to his singing than in England. 'Nothing like . . . the crowding round the pianoforte, the eagerness for more which I am accustomed to in most English companies. This may be perhaps, from my being made so much more of a *lion* here, or from some notion of good breeding and finery, some idea probably that it is more fashionable and *English* not to be too much moved.'

Moore returned briefly to Dublin later in the year on receiving a bad report of his mother's health. But she rallied, and among other visits, was one to Lady Morgan's house where he expected to meet Lord Cloncurry, but found only his hosts. After dinner there was a large party, and he sang 'with no ordinary success'.

He talked a great deal of politics at this time and was unwavering in his criticism of O'Connell's methods. The Irish leader, having emancipated the Catholics, was employing the same tactics to further the cause of Repeal. Moore took the view that this only aroused useless antagonism; and that if individual Irish grievances were sufficiently pressed, England would grow tired and bring about separation herself. As the Irish peers in the House of Lords were always against remedial measures for Ireland, it is not easy to see on what Moore based his hopes.

WHEN LANSDOWNE and Murray were competing for his attendance at their tables, Moore was on a committee to choose out of a thousand possible members a nucleus of a hundred for the new Athenaeum Club.

As ever, he is impressed by the small change of civility; not, however, when the setting is dim. At Martin's (the artist) he met 'a large party of small literati. Flattered and talked at by them till I was sick and ran away'.

When Lady Lyndhurst, wife of the ambitious Lord Chancellor, invited him to a party, he promised to come 'if possible' (he would have looked for an escape hatch in Heaven). When he arrived he saw that it was an 'assembly of the most chosen'. The Duke of Wellington was there. He recognised Moore ('nothing more, however, than his blunt "How d'ye do" in passing'). At Holland House a representative group from the Cabinet were present. Lord Melbourne showed Moore a letter from Lady Byron deploring Thomas Campbell's review of the *Life*. Sydney Smith praised it, the first book by anyone that Moore had ever heard him speak well of. When he tells Lord Holland in July 1830 that he is going to write a *Life* of Lord Edward, his host seemed to welcome the idea and took him aside to hear what Holland had written about his rebel cousin in an *Account of His own Times*. He thought that Moore's *Oh, breathe not his name* was addressed to Lord Edward, and was surprised to hear the lyric was inspired by Emmet's speech in the dock. So little impression then, as always, did matters of Irish interest make even in sympathetic English circles.

None of Moore's Irish propaganda—if *Captain Rock* and *Lord Edward* may be so designated—got him into trouble with his English circle. He never encountered bigotry. Even his *Travels of an Irish Gentleman*, which was almost a Roman Catholic tract, was generously received by his Whig friends. They took him to task—gently—over *Sheridan*. That was because the book dealt with English politics and events in which they had been interested and involved, and when they found themselves in office they were embarrassed by Moore's decision to publish *Lord Edward* just then. But they remained friendly and polite even when Moore stood his ground.

By December 1830 the first volume was ready, but now Moore ran into opposition. Catholic Emancipation had been granted reluctantly in the previous year. It was a triumph for O'Connell and achieved by his unique capacity to enrol popular opinion and, at the same time, control it. So far from the reform leading to a union of hearts, it aroused all the bitterness of forced concession. O'Connell himself was meanly insulted when the first list of Catholic barristers called to be King's Counsels did not include his name—outstanding in Ireland, without a peer in his profession. In return he became more turbulent than ever, raising the question of repeal of the Act of Union and the injustice of tithes.

Lord Holland was the first to offer discouragement. He had two motives, as a cousin of Lord Edward and a leading Whig. The Whigs were now in office under Lord Grey, and with Ireland on their hands. Moore politely insisted on proceeding with publication. He would 'endeavour to keep the tone as cool and moderate as the nature of its subject would admit of'. In January 1831 a letter came from the Duke of Leinster, written, he said, at the request of Lady Campbell (Lord Edward's daughter) begging Moore to postpone publication. But he wrote back refusing to agree to this. Lord Lansdowne, whom he had been dining with every other night, must have avoided the delicate topic—Russell described him as 'honest as the purest virgin, Lansdowne was too yielding, too mild, and most unfit to deal with men in important political transactions'. Walking back with Moore to his cottage after he had slept the night at Bowood, he asked him how he was getting on with *Lord Edward*. Moore must have been dreading this. He wrote in the Journal: 'The book was a ticklish subject now between us, as, of course, anything likely to affect the present state of Ireland is, from his ministerial responsibility, of double interest and importance to him. If anything, indeed, could make me sacrifice my own views (and in some respects, I think character on the point), it would be the gentle and considerate delicacy with which he has refrained, not only from urging, but even from hinting, what I know must be his anxious wishes on the subject.'

The conversation became general. Lord Lansdowne refrained from expressing his disapproval.

Soon after this Moore was summoned to Dublin by his sister, fearful that their mother was about to die. March and April were devoted to the biography with occasional dinings out in the neighbourhood. The book was lingering 'like everything else I do' longer than Moore had anticipated.

Going up to London when Parliament had dissolved, he found everyone in a state of excitement. A chance meeting with O'Connell gave him an opportunity to defend himself. Longmans told Moore that they couldn't fit his manuscript into one volume, so he returned after a few days of visiting to Sloperton to get on with the second volume. But within a month he was back in London and much troubled by the noises overhead when he was trying to write. He was out every day and spent much of his time with Russell who was busy with the Reform Bill. He invited Moore to stay in his rooms in the Pay Office.

Lansdowne was reported to be deeply disturbed by the Fitzgerald project, or so said Sir John Newport, who tackled Lord John on the subject. Russell spoke to Moore at last. They were breakfasting together and meeting every day. Moore, it is quite clear, was unable to keep himself at Sloperton while so much was happening in London. And his Journal entries are full of politics.

Russell began by arguing that it was wrong of Moore to publish the book against the wishes of Lord Holland. Moore replied that he had undertaken the work with Lord Holland's approval (he had been quite enthusiastic when Moore broached the subject) and if he were to put it aside now, people would say it was because his Whig friends had come into office, and that he was looking for favours. The subject had become historical and could no more influence the public mind than Lord John's own biography of his ancestor Lord Russell. To which Russell replied that that was a quarrel long made up, not so the Irish Question.

But he ceased to tease Moore, who was not made to feel that he had fallen into any disfavour with his friends. When he met the Hollands he found her 'tolerably gracious' and thought him at first 'colder' than usual. But he admitted that he might have fancied it, 'and at all events no great matter'. Neither the Duke of Leinster nor Lord Edward's daughter, Lady Campbell, to whom Moore sent complimentary copies, acknowledged them.

Lord Edward is a loosely constructed book; Moore was satisfied in the Irish portion of that adventurous life to use letters to tell the story, and this, the most interesting part of the book, reads like notes for work in progress. But as in his *Sheridan* there are fine passages; one of particular interest for the light it throws on his own mind.

> 'On the right of the oppressed to resist, few in these days would venture to express a doubt; the monstrous doctrine of passive obedience having long since fallen into disrepute. To be able to fix, however, with any precision, the point at which obedience may cease, and resistance to the undue stretches of authority begin, is a difficulty which must for ever leave vague and undirected the application of a principle; a vagueness of which the habitual favourers of power adroitly take advantage, and while they concede the right of resistance as a general proposition, hold themselves free to object to every particular instance of it.'

So much for the spirit animating the United Irishmen; Moore took this opportunity to pay a tribute to Robert Emmet and other friends engaged in the 1798 rebellion. Of Emmet, whom he named, he said, 'Were I to number, indeed, the men, among all I have ever known, who appeared to me to combine, in the greatest degree, pure moral worth with intellectual power, I should, among the highest of the few, place Robert Emmet'.

This should clear Moore for all time of the charge that he was false to his past and lived in England currying favour with Ireland's oppressors. With his friends in high office, this was the time, if ever, to look for advantage. Instead, he made his most defiant stand as an Irish nationalist.

What was at work in his mind? Before he had finished *Lord Edward*, he was busying himself to collect material for his book *Travels of an Irish Gentleman in Search of a Religion*. This—a pot pourri of his theological researches—was a profession of faith in his Catholicism. Why did he embark on this unprofitable subject immediately after the other? Moore who was so anxious to please! He might have been expected to produce something to remove an unfavourable impression.

His silence in general about the most exciting year of his youth and his reference to an illness at the time of the 1798 rebellion mark what was probably the deepest inner conflict he ever experienced. But he overcame it (as his mother's son). He put it behind him; he went on to where glory awaited him. Buried deep, it erupted again when O'Connell defied the power of England and achieved Catholic emancipation. Now Moore could enter parliament without giving up his religion.

In July 1832, when Moore was waiting at Bristol for the steam packet to arrive with his sister Ellen who was coming on a visit, O'Connell was waiting at the quay. Moore at once began to discuss his prospects as member for Limerick; he had received a letter from the Irish leader earlier in the month discussing Moore's candidature in which he said there could not be the slightest doubt of Moore's return for the constituency 'were there not an impression entertained that from my friendship with Lord Lansdowne, I should consider myself bound to follow him in politics'.

With O'Connell towering over him on the quayside, Moore pleaded the evidence of his whole life that he would remain independent. So far from expecting any help from Lansdowne he doubted, knowing his views on Ireland, that Lansdowne would nominate him. He would most certainly not ask Lansdowne to give him his interest in Limerick. But he impressed on O'Connell that his dependence on his own daily labour made it unlikely in any event that he could ever come into parliament.

O'Connell's contemptuous snap of his fingers when Moore mentioned Lansdowne's interest was 'but too expressive, I fear, of the real facts of the case; i.e. of the impotence of any lord's interest, anywhere, opposed to himself and the people'.

What were Moore's settled views? Or had he any? On this

occasion he seems to disapprove of O'Connell's defiance of a noble lord, having himself taken the trouble to announce his own independence. At Brooks's, in conversation with two other noble lords, he deplored the Reform Bill which his closest friend Russell was putting through. How, he asked them, could such men as Lords Lansdowne, Holland, and Melbourne, to say nothing of the Canningites, allow themselves to be bustled into such a measure? For himself he had always been for 'improvement'. At this time he was staying with Russell who was talking with him at breakfast about coming into parliament, not, surely, to oppose the Bill upon which his hopes were set.

Having breakfasted with Russell, his 'kind and excellent host', on July 29th, and not being able to find himself a room in his usual lodgings in Bury Street, Moore thought Murray seemed 'highly pleased' when asked for a room for the night so that Moore could catch the coach in the morning. He dressed at Murray's and went out to dine with the Duchess of Kent; the party consisting of the Duke of Saxe Coburg, the Duchess of Cambridge and 'an abundant array of nobles and gentry'. Murray did not wait up to hear about it. Moore 'found supper' when he returned to get to bed in good time.

At home again, not having been able to put the final touches to *Lord Edward* in town, Moore worked diligently for three weeks. What his Whig friends might think of the book, he decided he didn't care. His recent insight into the views and leanings of the party had taken away his respect for them. There was as much selfishness and low party spirit among them as among the Tories without any of that 'tact in concealing the offensiveness of these qualities which a more mellowed experience of power and its sweets gives to the Tories'. Lords Grey, Althorp, Russell and Lansdowne, he believed to be exceptions; they had the public weal at heart, 'but even these are carried headlong through a measure, of which in their hearts they must see the danger . . .'

In October he called on 'Lord D—' *, and talked about politics to 'Lady D—'. Women drew Moore out—he was not

---

* Denham, Dudley, Durham? Possibly the first. Moore was meeting all three of the husbands at this period.

on his guard with them—and he confided in her his opinion of the Whigs and their 'vile practice of canvassing enemies and neglecting friends'. He had given up hope for many years of their ever *thinking* of doing him a service.

Even in the matter of franking his post, none of his Whig friends thought of offering this service. He had to rely on Croker and Greville. The only favour he had received was the Bermuda post, and that came from Moira when a Tory Government was in power. The Irish laureateship was offered by a Tory Viceroy, Hardwicke. 'Poor' Moira had given the barrack-mastership to his father. But from the Whigs, not 'even the semblance of a favour'.

Lady D— said flattering things. He had claims on all parties, in her opinion, and 'Oh dear', she exclaimed, 'if the Tories had such a person as you on their side, we should be made to feel the difference'.

For him every question was subjective. He confessed to Lady Donegal in 1808 that he thought by republishing his satires *Corruption* and *Intolerance* he 'might catch the eye of some of our patriotic politicians and thus be enabled to serve both myself and the principles which I cherish'. And his concern with the two great questions of the day—Reform and Emancipation—were never completely disinterested. In his publishing dealings he was never above giving false impressions, sometimes to the public, sometimes to his publisher, about the progress of current work and his plans for the future.

In politics, too, there was a confusion in his mind because, however he might deny any political ambitions (and when the opportunity came, he refused the chance of a seat in parliament) yet there is evidence that he did play with the idea of himself as a tribune. He refused a nomination for Limerick eventually, but he would probably not have refused a safe seat for Calne if Lord Lansdowne had thought of providing him with one. Lady Holland was certainly under this impression. Writing to her son, she said that she and Lord Holland had dined the previous day (13th October 1831) at the Pay Office (where Moore was staying as Lord John Russell's guest). Moore was 'not very friendly in the Govt, nor indeed to mankind, being very much nettled that half the Irish counties and towns did not ask him to be their representative, and that Lord Lansdowne did not bring him in for Calne'.

That uncompromising lady was Moore's most candid friend. She had told him once that she had no intention of reading *Lallah Rookh*. 'Mr Moore, I have not read your Larry O'Rourke. I don't like Irish stories.' And when he wrote his 'little dog' verses against Hunt, she told him she thought them vulgar. Perhaps this explains why he let her read Byron's *Memoirs*, in which she was abused. He had snubs to avenge.

What Lady Holland saw may not have been apparent to the high-minded Lansdowne or the impractical Russell.

Writing to Murray, after the granting of Catholic Emancipation in 1829, Moore described the measure as the limit of his own political demands. 'I little thought I should ever live to see the *end* of my politics—but so it is—the Duke has had the merit of exorcising the devil of rebellion out of me and I am now (at your service) as loyal and as well behaved an author as you could desire. In this feeling, too, I rather think I am the representative of the great mass (or rather mass-goers) of my countrymen. All we wanted was fair treatment, and God forgive you and your *Quarterly Review* who so long grudged it to us.'

But revolution in France roused his rebel blood. On 7th December 1830, soon after the Whigs came into office, he had written to Lord Lansdowne describing the campaign for parliamentary reforms as the beginning of the end, a coming crash. He went on to say, 'As to my own poor poetical politics they are the same, God help them, as they have ever been since I can remember them. At the time of our Catholic triumph I thought their task, like that of the "tricking Ariel" was done and that I should have no more occasion for them. These late events, however, in the world have affected me, as they have other people, and have given a new shake to the bottle which has brought up all the Irish spirit (or sediment, if you please) again into ferment. The author of the *Green Flag* and *Captain Rock* would prove himself to have been but a firebrand of the moment *then* if he did not go on burning a little *now*. The Union I always detested the very thought of it, and though I resent most deeply the introduction of the question now, and under auspices that would disgrace a far better cause, I never could bring myself so far as to sanction the principle, origin or mode of carrying that measure as to oppose myself to any steps taken for its repeal.'

One morning in November 1832, Moore was surprised by a visit from the Irish novelist, Gerald Griffin, and his brother. They stayed for dinner, and although Moore was 'obliged to leave them a great part of the day to themselves' they had a good deal of conversation. If Moore would consent to represent the Limerick constituency a fund would be raised for his support calculated to produce about £400 a year.

At dinner Moore gave the young visitors his political views. He saw Repeal of the Union as leading almost inevitably to separation, but thought that the risk was worth running, Ireland having fared so ill under both Whig and Tory governments. A Catholic House of Commons would instantly set about disposing of Church property and the estates of absentees. There would be at some time or another a contest between England and France as to whom Ireland was to belong—that was another 'awful question'.

Next day the Griffins called on Moore for an answer. Moore refused the offer. Between them they settled the form of the letter that they carried off 'across the fields on their way to Devizes, and the warm-hearted fellows parted from me, I must say, with tears in their eyes'.

Gerald Griffin wrote his own account of the meeting. It is familiar but indispensable.

'We found our hero in his study, a table before him, covered with books and papers, a drawer half opened and stuffed with letters, a piano also open at a little distance; and the thief himself, a little man, but full of spirits, with eyes, hands, feet, and frame for ever in motion, looking as if it would be a feat for him to sit for three minutes quiet in his chair. I am no great observer of proportions, but he seemed to me to be a neat-made little fellow, tidily buttoned up, young as fifteen at heart, though with hair that reminded me of "Alps in the sunset"; not handsome, perhaps, but something in the whole cut of him that pleased me; finished as an actor, but without an actor's affectation; easy as a gentleman, but without some gentleman's formality; in a word, as people say when they find their brains begin to run aground at the fag-end of a magnificent period, we found him a hospitable, warm-hearted Irishman, as pleasant as could be himself, and disposed to make others so.'

Moore's letter to the electors of Limerick, suitably high-flown in tone, explained that he depended on the labour of the day for his daily support, and if he were to take advantage of the provision that was being made for him he would lose his valuable freedom.

Predictably, the next few days were sweetened by 'a visit from Bowles, full of delight at my letter; "manly, affecting, etc."; had made him cry in reading it'. Lord Kerry called: 'The best letter ever written.' A letter from John Russell. A note from Lord Lansdowne: 'It was,' he said, 'really perfect for the occasion.' A letter from Corry quoting plaudits from Irish admirers, including Chief Justice Bushe: 'I rejoice with you at Moore's farewell: he was right: What would the Muse do in a Pandemonium?'

O'Connell was fond of Moore's poetry and introduced quotations into his speeches. Moore's disapproval of his methods was probably unknown to him. He had affectionate feelings for the writer of the *Melodies* and showed it in several instances. O'Connell attended a public dinner given to Moore on his Dublin visit in 1818. Sixteen years later, when O'Connell was in parliament—a Radical in policy in contrast with Moore who had deplored the Reform policies of his patrons and friends, Russell and Lansdowne—the Irish leader was described as being 'in a state of indescribable excitement at the perusal of one of your last melodies'. And no wonder. Here it is—

The dream of those days when first I sung thee is o'er,
Thy triumph hath stain'd the charm thy sorrows then
  wore;
And ev'n of the light which Hope once shed o'er they
  chains,
Alas, not a gleam to grace thy freedom remains.

Say, is it that slavery sunk so deep in thy heart,
That still the dark brand is there, though chainless thou art;
And Freedom's sweet fruit, for which thy spirit long burn'd,
Now, reaching at last thy lip, to ashes hath turn'd.

Up Liberty's steep by Truth and Eloquence led,
With eyes on her temple fix'd, how proud was thy tread!
Ah, better thou ne'er hadst lived that summit to gain,
Or died in the porch, than thus dishonour the fane.

'He continues to almost rave at what he considers a most foul attack upon him', wrote Moore's correspondent, and asked for an alleviating explanation. But Moore wrote in reply that the verses 'were wrung from me by a desire to put on record (in the only work of mine likely to reach after times) that though going along heart and soul, with the great cause of Ireland, I by no means went along with spirit or manner in which the great cause was being conducted'. He complained that O'Connell, not only by his talents, was alone, a unit in a legion of ciphers in Parliament. All power was in O'Connell's hands, and 'it was against such abuse of power, let it be placed in what hands it might, I had all my life revolted'.

Moore was uneasy. O'Connell cropped up continually in his conversation. Then came a letter from Con Lyne, who had broached the matter, to say that he had shown Moore's letter to O'Connell, and that it had had a beneficial effect. But O'Connell thought that Moore had 'betrayed great apathy to Ireland since the measure of Emancipation had been effected'.

Moore was ruffled by this; it meant that O'Connell was unaware of his prose writings although he recalled O'Connell's praising his *Life* of *Lord Edward*.

'He little knew the extent of the courage he thus praised', wrote Moore, inviting a smile from one who had defied all the powers of Government in public confrontation since early manhood.

The reconciliation was initiated by O'Connell, who forgot quarrels quickly. Someone was writing to Moore, enclosing a prospectus; O'Connell happening to be present said 'Oh, let me frank the letter to Moore'.

On a subsequent Sunday, knowing that O'Connell was inclined to frequent Brooks's Club on that day. Moore called on chance and found him there. Moore's opening remark seems to have puzzled O'Connell (who hadn't been brooding over the affair, one suspects), but when he woke up to what was being said to him, he shook hands cordially.

MARCH 18th 1835 was a 'wretchedly wet day'. Having worked all morning at the proofs of his first volume of his Irish history at the Longmans' office, and helped young Tom with his exercises, Moore went out to dine with Rogers. Barnes, editor of *The Times*, was expected, and Moore, having failed to collect Lord Lyndhurst, invited J. M. W. Turner, the painter, to make a fourth. Rogers had employed Turner to illustrate his *Italy*, published at his own expense at a cost of £5000.

Moore had an opportunity to talk with the painter after dinner and told him that he, too, had been playing with the idea of 'calling in the aid of the pencil to help me in commemorating, by some work or other, the neighbourhood in which I have now so long resided'. He was interrupted by the artist. 'But Ireland, Mr Moore, Ireland! There's the region connected with your name. Why not illustrate the whole life? I have often longed to go to that country; but am, I confess, afraid to venture myself there. Under the wing of Thomas Moore, however, I should be safe.'

Lord John's editorial asterisks eliminate what Moore said in reply. In any event Turner wasn't with him when he set out in August for Ireland, travelling to Liverpool by railroad—'a grand mode of travelling, though, as we were told, ours was but a poor specimen of it, as we took an hour and a half to do the thirty-two miles, which rarely requires more than an hour and a quarter or twenty minutes'. In Liverpool he found a letter from Lord Lansdowne. With exquisite circumlocution in consideration of Moore's sensitivities he eventually came to the point: would Moore accept a pension from the Government? Once again editorial asterisks remove what it is not unfair to guess was a cry of joy. It was a good beginning to the trip.

Hume, who had appointed himself *fidus Achates*, was in attendance; but Moore left him with his brother in Kildare

Street and went to stay with his own sister, Ellen, at 11 North Cumberland Street. Here he found some rooms prepared for him as 'comfortable as any lord' could have given him. The meeting of the British Association was being held at the Rotunda, and Moore was on the platform 'with the savants'. The past was very much with him on this trip; perhaps he felt that it might be his last.

Accompanied by Hume, he visited the shop in Aungier Street, and when he told the proprietor who he was 'his countenance brightened up with the most cordial feeling, and seizing me by the hand he pulled me along to the small room behind the shop (where we used to breakfast in old times) exclaiming to his wife . . . 'Here's Sir Thomas Moore, who was born in this house, come to ask us to let him see the rooms; and it's proud I am to have him under the old roof".' He led his visitor from the small yard through the little dark kitchen where he used to have his bread and milk in the morning before he went to school. Unlike most revenants he found the front and back drawing-rooms larger than he had expected. They brought back the memory of over-crowded supper parties and Joe Kelly and Wesley Doyle 'singing away together so sweetly'. When Moore came down from the bedrooms—the partition which had marked off his own had been taken down—a decanter of port and glasses had been laid out in the parlour. He drank the health of the proprietor and his wife.

Next morning a note came from Mulgrave, the Lord Lieutenant, asking Moore to come and dine quietly with him at half-past six. On the following day there was a great dinner in Trinity College and then in the evening the ordeal of the theatre. He had called to see who was coming and left his name with the management. When he arrived late, there were shouts of 'Moore' and rounds of applause. 'Tom, don't be shy' and 'Come show your Irish face, Tom; you needn't be ashamed of it' gave him the hint to lean out of his box 'which produced peals of laughter and plaudits in return'. It was all part of the evening's entertainment. But when he moved to the pit box where his sister Ellen was sitting—'Then came the real thunder of the Gods. The people stood up and hurrahed; and many of them threw up their hats, trusting to Providence for their ever

returning to them again.' Moore was called on to speak and
begged to be excused in a graceful little speech. Numbers in the
pit crowded towards the box to shake hands. And all this time
the poor players stood on the stage watching the rival performance.

Then off at full speed to supper at the Viceregal Lodge.

Moore had come to Dublin during the happiest period in
post-Union politics. Melbourne as Prime Minister had come to
an accommodation with Daniel O'Connell. Mulgrave, the Lord
Lieutenant, Morpeth, Chief-Secretary and Thomas Drummond,
Under-Secretary, were engaged on a strenuous policy of
reconciliation, which only ended with Drummond's death and
the return of the Tories to power.

After the Viceregal supper, and having performed at the
piano, Moore was off again to join a party which Nell had
collected at home—Mulvany and his pretty sister and Georgiana
O'Kelly 'and plenty of laughing and soda water'.

Before Moore began his tour of the country another letter
came from Lansdowne to say that the King had made no
objection to an annual pension of £300. It was the first granted
by the present administration, he informed Moore. Another
was to go to Lady Napier whose soldier husband had died in
China; and that exhausted the whole means at the disposal of
the Government.

Having scribbled a few lines to his 'sweet Bess' to inform her
of this good news, Moore set off after breakfast, on a most clear
morning which promised a delicious day, in a landau and four,
for the Vale of Avoca and the Meeting of the Waters. He hadn't
been in this part of the country since he had written the lyric
that begins:

> There's not in the wide world a valley so sweet
> As that vale in whose bosom the bright waters meet.

Was he thinking of Turner's advice when he told himself how
wise Scott had been to connect his poetry with the beautiful
scenery of his own land? He felt this very strongly when his
companions pressed him for details of the spot from which he
had viewed the scene, and he said he preferred 'to leave all
that in mystery. He had been asked for the information before

by an old friend who wanted to put a tablet on a seat in the Abbey churchyard and begged Moore for an inscription of two lines. 'If you can't tell a lie for me in *prose*, you will, perhaps, to oblige an old friend, do it in verse.'

At Gorey, Moore changed vehicles, leaving his companions 'and even Hume' behind. He was bound for Enniscorthy where Thomas Boyse awaited him. He was to be Moore's host in his house at Bannow in the County Wexford.

Mr Boyse proved himself a 'well-informed, off-hand, gentlemanlike person', and dinner was very agreeable. But Moore, so gregarious in town, liked to be alone in the country. Before dinner he had 'a most delicious walk' by himself along the banks of the River Slaney. Only thus could he enjoy Nature thoroughly. 'Men and women disturb such scenes dreadfully.'

In Wexford town Moore walked with Boyse to the corn-market. He was looking for the house in which his mother was born. 'Some old women (entering into my feelings) ran before me to the wretched house I was in search of (which is now a small pot-house), crying out, "Here, Sir, this is the very house where your grandmother lived. Lord be merciful to her".'

Moore couldn't remember his grandmother, but he had 'a pretty clear recollection of little old Tom Codd, my grandfather . . . My mother used to say he was a provision merchant, which sounded well, and I have no doubt he may have been concerned in that trade, but I suspect that he was also a weaver. Nothing, at all events, could be more humble and mean than the little low house which still remains to tell of its whereabouts; and it shows how independent Nature is of mere localities that one of the noblest-minded, as well as most warm-hearted, of all God's creatures (that ever it has been *my* lot to know) was born under that lowly roof'.

These are not the musings of a mean snob. But Moore was not left long to philosophise. As the coach in which he travelled with Boyse neared Bannow it was met by a party of horsemen, bearing green banners and surrounded by people on foot. Carriages 'filled with ladies' were drawn up one either side of the road. A triumphal arch had been erected; and beside it stood a decorated car in which sat the Nine Muses—'Some of them remarkably pretty girls', especially the one who placed a crown on the poet's head. He persuaded her and two of her companions to join him on his coach.

'In advance of the car was a band of amateur musicians, smart young fellows, in a uniform of blue jackets, caps and white trousers who, whenever we stopped at the arches erected along the road, played some of the most popular Irish *Melodies*, and likewise more than once, an air that had been adapted to Byron's *Here's a health to thee, Tom Moore*. As we proceeded slowly along, I said to my pretty Muse behind me, "This is a long journey for you". "Oh Sir!" she exclaimed, with a sweetness and kindness of look not to be found in more artificial life, "I wish it was more than three thousand miles".'

No poet, before or since, has ever been accorded such a welcome in Ireland. For Yeats, after the award of the Nobel Prize, there was a private dinner in the Shelbourne Hotel. Only a cup-winning football team or, perhaps, an Olympic medallist would call out such a crowd to-day.

As the poet moved slowly along in his triumph 'with so many cordial and sweet faces turned towards him', a feeling of deep sadness came more than once into his heart. Whether it was some of the Irish airs calling up mournful associations connected the 'the *reverse* of all this smiling picture', he was not able to determine.

At Graigue House, newly built by Mr Boyse, there were deputations to be addressed; and during the night bonfires were lit in various directions. Next day the crowd reassembled and had to be addressed again. Boyse informed Moore that he had spoken 'much louder and less *Englishly* than the day before'. Moore discovered that the English accent 'which I always had' is not 'liked by the genuine *Pats*'.

There were dinners and dances and visits. Letters arrived, among them one 'written in a very feminine and lady-like hand'. It came from the Superioress of the Presentation Convent at Wexford. 'Permit me, then, to beseech you *not* to leave the country without coming to the convent', she wrote. She knew his sister, she said, and some of her most intimate circle.

Putting the letter away with a bundle of others, Moore proceeded to lay a stone for the erection of a tower to commemorate his visit to Bannow; he received a Mayor, a young musician, and the editors of two liberal Wexford papers. And then he remembered the nun and set off alone to visit her.

'A very fair and handsome person I found her, little more, I should think, than thirty years of age, and becoming her abbess's dress most secularly. Whether she wanted to be complimented on her good looks, I know not; but I felt that it would be bad taste to do so, and, at all events, did not venture it. After showing me the small pretty chapel, the superioress led me to a new organ, which was soon to be put up there, and asked, as a favour, that I would play one short air upon it. If I could ever, at any time, bring myself to *volunteer* my voice, I should have done so on this occasion; and the thought occurred to me that I *ought*. Indeed, if she had but said a word to that effect, I should most certainly have sung; but she asked me only to play, and I played the air, "Oh, all ye angels of the Lord!" which seemed abundantly to satisfy her, as her utmost wish appeared to be that I should have *touched* her organ.'

Nowadays Moore would have expressed himself differently; but even then it may have been as well that he refrained from singing.

The music finished, he followed her to a 'small nice garden (for all was in miniature), where I found the gardener ready prepared with spade, etc., in order that I should plant with my own hands a myrtle there'.

Back in Dublin a letter was waiting for him from his 'sweet admirable Bessy'. It was to ask could it be really true about the pension. How could they be sufficiently thankful to those who gave it 'or to a Higher Power?' If it was true, she wrote, he was to give Ellen twenty pounds and insist on her drinking five pounds worth of wine yearly to be paid out of the pension.

Lord John had his own idea of womanly perfection. Perhaps his editorial exercises have given a too exclusively Marthalike picture of Bessy. And Moore's predictable endearments do nothing to help to dispel what was probably only one side of her nature.

'How you ever will enjoy this quiet every-day sort of stillness, after your late reception, I hardly know', she wrote. 'I begin to want you very much; for though the boys are darlings there is still—'. But what there was Lord John decided not to tell his readers. Three asterisks mark the spot, as they were substituted elsewhere for Moore's entry that Bessy came into his bed at five o'clock one morning when he was about to set out on a journey.

Six years later Moore paid another visit to Dublin with Hume. Before setting out he called at Lacock Abbey where Lady Elizabeth Feilding (Lady Lansdowne's sister) and a group of friends were being 'photogenized by Henry Talbot'. Moore was included in one of the groups (the process takes time), but decided that the portraits were not satisfactory. 'A dead likeness is, in general, the sure, though frightful result of the Daguerre process.'

Ostensibly, his reason for going to Dublin was to look up material for his history in the Trinity College library. But, in fact, young Tom was the cause. It was to be Moore's last visit to Dublin. He had been soothed by the railway journey to Liverpool, 'lolling in a most comfortable arm-chair, and writing memorandums in my pocket-book, as easily and legibly as I should at my own study table, while flying through the air at the rate of thirty miles an hour'.

His first visit was to the Ordnance Survey where he was much struck by Larcom who was in charge. Moore was perspicacious. Larcom, an Englishman, was working strenuously to have the social history of Ireland put on record.

Young Tom came to see him. His regiment was stationed in Ireland and he had fallen into disgrace. He arrived looking very pale and ill. The *United Services Gazette* had published an extraordinary attack, accusing him of having inherited his father's salaciousness and of insulting 'every decent woman he meets'. The mother of a girl he had attacked, the account proceeded, had reported him to his commanding officer. He had been arrested, the *Gazette* said, and confined to barracks for a month. In fact the youth was ill in bed at the time; and other papers came to his aid. It was at bottom an orange and green slanging match and—Tom being attractive—a jealous rival may have given the ammunition to a bigoted editor. The *Gazette* withdrew its story.

Moore does not mention the matter; it must have acutely

embarrassed him, and he doted on his son. He kept Tom close
to him during his stay in Dublin. And, if his spirits had sunk,
they were restored when, seated 'between two very pretty
sultanas', he listened to 'an explosion' of applause at his
appearance in the Theatre Royal. It was a scene to which he
had grown accustomed whenever his coming to a theatre in
Dublin was announced in advance. 'The audience rose as one
man, and again and again the long loud cheer swelled upon the
ear . . . It seemed the madness of joy . . . Mr Moore'—the
report is taken from the *Morning Register*—'repeatedly rose in
acknowledgment of the compliment . . . A call for silence was
then made, upon which the poet again rose and bowed, and
pointing to the stage, where the curtain had been raised, he
resumed his seat'.

But, yet again, the actors were left standing on the stage while
the audience called upon 'the star of the evening' for a speech.

An experience not less familiar was to upset the next day's
pleasure: Moore and young Tom had been invited to dine by
Lord Morpeth in the Chief-Secretary's lodge; getting into the
cab 'driven by an odd fellow named Ennis', Moore directed him
to 'go the the same place you took me to the other evening'.
The length of the avenue to the house raised misgivings and
when they arrived the visitors were told the family had gone
into dinner. After a little delay they were shown into the
dining room where the Viceroy, Lord Mulgrave, his family
and aides were seated at table.

Normanby's manners must have been perfect because
Moore had finished his soup before he realised that he had gone
to the wrong house. 'Good God', he exclaimed.

But all was put right. Messages were sent to Morpeth—the
two residences were in Phoenix Park—Moore finished his
dinner with the Mulgraves, and then went on to the Chief
Secretary's where 'I sung away for them at the rate of a dozen
songs per hour, to make up for my default'.

On the voyage home from Kingstown there was another
memorable incident. 'The day not very favourable for our
passage home; but I cannot expect to be lucky in everything.
Tom danced till two in the morning at the Lord Lieutenant's . . .
Had luncheon at Nell's at three o'clock, and then set off, Hume

and I, accompanied by Tom, to Kingstown. Encountered an odd scene on going on board. The packet was full of people coming to see friends off, and among others was a party of ladies who, I should think, had dined on board, and who, on my being made known to them, almost devoured me with kindness, and at length proceeded so far as to insist on each of them *kissing me*. At this time I was beginning to feel the first rudiments of coming *sickness*, and the effort to respond to all this enthusiasm, in such a state of stomach, was not a little awkward and trying. However, I kissed the whole party (about five, I think,) in succession, two or three of them being, for my comfort, young and good-looking, and was most glad to get away from them to my berth, which, through the kindness of the captain (Emerson), was in his own cabin. But I had hardly shut the door, feeling very qualmish, when there came a gentle tap at the door, and an elderly lady made her appearance, who said that having heard of all that had been going on, she could not rest easy without being also kissed as well as the rest. So, in the most respectful manner possible, I complied with the lady's request, and then betook myself with a heaving stomach to my berth.'

'A strange life mine', he journalises at the end of the year, 'but the best as well as the pleasantest part of it lies at *home*. I told my dear Bessy this morning that while I stood at my study window, looking out at her, as she crossed the field, I sent a blessing after her. "Thank you, Lord," she replied, "that's better than money". And so it is.'

His mother's death, surprisingly, seemed to affect him less than might have been expected. A tribute to Bessy's management. He had been to Dublin and seen Mrs Moore when it was obvious that she had not long to live. When he heard that she had grown worse he spoke of returning there, but was deterred by Bessy, 'full of alarm about the cholera', and then Crampton, the surgeon, wrote and said not to move until he wrote again. Upon this Moore resolved to go; and then Bessy produced a letter giving the news of Mrs Moore's death. He recorded his feelings: 'I had been too well prepared for it to feel anything violent, and the effect it has upon me was rather that of deep and saddened depression, which continued for some days, and seemed more like a bodily indisposition than any mental affliction.'

If Moore was afraid of death, it pursued him relentlessly. After Anastasia's the family was cut down to the two boys, Tom and Russell.

Tom was sent to school at Marlborough and then to the Charter House (as Charterhouse was then called), Moore getting a nomination from Lord Grey. On the first day at school, where young Tom was accompanied by his anxious parents, Sydney Smith's son was produced. He introduced a friend. Moore gave each of the three boys half a sovereign, while Bessy took aside little Tom ('on whom we have always impressed the propriety of not taking money from anyone but ourselves') to explain away the inconsistency. It was a portent.

When Lord John Russell came into office he offered Moore jobs in Government offices which he refused; he then suggested an annuity for the benefit of the boys. Moore delightedly agreed to this. But Melbourne, the Prime Minister and final arbiter, refused to endow Moore's sons, saying that a boy should provide for himself, and settled on Moore the pension of £300 a year for life. Hume, who had fallen out of favour at the time of the duel, had been taken back into friendship. He sought and was given permission to give Tom £100, anticipating a legacy he would otherwise have provided by will.

At school young Tom was admired for his friendliness and sense of fun, but he could not be made to work at his lessons. His father obviously doted on him, calling at the school when in London and sometimes taking him out for the day. He was shocked when a master told him how much he ought to put up for Tom if he went to a university (£250 per annum); but when he paid £450 for an ensigncy in the 22nd Foot for the boy, he embarked on what was going to be a source of recurring expense. He had then to buy a lieutenancy, spending in all £1500.

Tom was first stationed in Dublin; then his regiment was sent to India.

'I can hardly bring myself to send you the enclosed', Bessy wrote when Tom's first bill came home. 'It has caused me tears and sad thoughts, but to you it will bring these and hard, *hard* work. Why do people sigh for children? They know not what sorrow will come with them . . .'

Russell was her favourite; she must have seen the elder boy being indulged, and found herself unable to prevent what was yet another manifestation of her husband's cult of his own personality. He recognised in young Tom a second edition of himself. This adoration can be seen in a diary entry, when Shelley's widow drove out to the Charter House with Moore to visit young Tom. He 'came to me with his bare head all feathered with snow. Mrs Shelley's admiration of him; said she could have sworn he was the image of his mother; "there was all the woman in his face, particularly at the rise of the cheek near the eye".'

'He will, I trust in God, be yet a pride and blessing to us', he wrote down on the strength of a letter breathing 'better feelings towards home and home associations'. There followed the news that he had sold his commission and was coming home. Moore thought of the Austrian army for him, but Tom was by that time in France and deciding to join the Foreign Legion.

Meanwhile his younger brother Russell who had been granted a cadetship* had taken ill in Bengal, soon after his arrival. The Governor General, Lord Auckland, took him into his own house and he was treated with kindness for which Moore was deeply grateful; but the cause of illness was tuberculosis, and the boy was sent home.

Moore describes the arrival at Sloperton of Bessy's favourite, 'the one whom (*next* to myself) she most clings to and loves', how he slowly got out of the carriage 'looking as if the next moment would be his very last . . . Both his mother and myself threw our arms round him . . . the poor boy the only calm one of the three'.

Russell was dying. Moore wrote to Tom to come home before he went to Algiers; but he didn't come.

During Russell's last illness, Lady Lansdowne, according to Moore, 'behaved like a sister' to his wife when he was sent for to help entertain 'the Aucklands, John Russells, Clarendons, Strangways, Lady Kerry and one or two more'. Lady Lansdowne sent Mrs Hughes to stay with Bessy. On the 6th of November, Moore stayed at Bowood and sang in the evening.

* Hobhouse, it is pleasant to record, was the intermediary.

'Lady Lansdowne felt delicate about asking me.' Next day she (and the whole party) urged him to stay on. He compromised by going home, promising to return if all was well. Lord John walked over with him, sat some time with Bessy, and returned alone with a promise that Moore would be back for dinner. He sang earlier that evening so that Lady John didn't miss it—she went early to bed—and after that he finds he can't return to his Journal for a month. Russell Moore died on the 23rd November 1842.

There is a detailed and painful description in the diary of his last day, when he went patiently through all his little possessions, telling his mother to whom he wished each to be given. Painful to read, painful to write, most painful to have witnessed. How could Moore have borne it? The answer is given at the end. 'All this which I have taken down from the poor mother's lips (not being able myself to stand the scene), took place on the morning of the 23rd, about eleven o'clock; and within three hours after our beloved child was a corpse.'

A week passed and then came young Tom's letter giving reasons which seemed 'wise and prudent' why he couldn't come home before he set out for Algiers. In fact there was a lady in the case. A letter of 24th October 1842 from Moore to Mrs Villamil, their close friend in Paris days, agreed to young Tom's engagement to the Villamil's daughter. 'The intelligence . . . would have been hailed by me with the sincerest delight, if so many difficulties do not stand in the way of such a union as my poor sanguine son proposes.'

Usually so sanguine himself, he can rarely be persuaded that there was any future for Tom; he reproached himself for the foolishly indulgent manner in which he brought up the boy. As in his own case the art to please was cultivated to excess. Young Tom was very attractive; Moore was proud to show him off, and would ask to include him at dinners to which he had not been invited. He died in 1845 in Africa, never having come home again.

In 1848 Moore lost his remaining sister, Ellen, after the last of his children. Bessy was the one who, on each occasion, heard the news first and had to break it to him.

These sorrows falling on him—a Lear who had always played

Ariel—found him unable to bear the weight and could explain the decline into which he fell in 1849 when his friends, Lansdowne and Russell, were sitting with him. His last four years on earth could hardly be described as life.

After Anastasia's death, Moore, on a few occasions, broke down at the piano, and had to leave the room in uncontrollable fits of sobbing. He describes one of these seizures after dinner at Bowood, when he sang to a party given by the Lansdownes. In January 1838, he was not having any domestic trouble, but when he began to sing '*There's a song of the olden time*, the state of my spirits not being very good, the melancholy both of the song and my own voice affected me so much that before I had sung the first two lines I broke out into one of those hysterical fits of sobbing, which must be as painful to others as they are to myself . . .'.

Was it to train herself to supply this deficiency in her husband or a form of silent and possibly unconscious reproach that made Bessy rush to assist whenever she heard of illness? This, too, may well have been her way of reconciling herself to her status as an unsuitable wife for a man who went into society. Or was she simply as good as gold?

It must have become rather a joke. When Bessy came to Lacock Abbey with Moore, 'Lady E (Elizabeth Feilding) whispered me on our arrival, "I take for granted there is nobody dying in your neighbourhood or we shouldn't have had Mrs Moore's company to-day".'

But, again, it would be wrong to give the impression of Bessy as one of the stark sisterhood of do-gooders. Young Abraham Hayward writing to his father from Calne in 1840 tells of a visit of two days to the Moores at Sloperton Cottage. He 'almost fell in love with his wife, the Bessy of his songs. Last night he sang for an hour and a half for my amusement, and it is just the sort of singing a man without a musical ear may appreciate—very little voice, but clear, sweet, and expressive'.

THERE IS a special art in choosing the right time to die. Shakespeare, unique in this as in everything, managed the matter perfectly. Keats, undoubtedly, went too soon; Wordsworth, too late; and Moore was another who lingered too long for the reputation of his poetry. But he more or less abandoned verse for prose in his middle years, and sunk eventually under the weight of a four-volume history of Ireland. It was a companion to one on England by Sir James Mackintosh, a great man in his day, now almost forgotten; Sir Walter took on the history of Scotland.

Longmans put out the idea in 1829. Mackintosh was the first to finish his task; then he died. Scott completed two volumes and suffered a stroke of paralysis; Moore's labours can hardly be held responsible for the gradual decline of his faculties; rather, they were symptomatic of his decline.

He was not a highbrow; he avoided the company of pedants; he did not really have a reliable memory; but he had a mania for consulting libraries. Browsing in them was almost a vice. He contracted the habit in Marsh's Library when he was a boy, and indulged it to excess in composing his longer poems; the accumulation of material had the effect on the progress of his history that piling damp rubbish on it has on a bonfire. In 1846, when he delivered the last pages of his 'weary work' to the printers he had so completely run out of energy that he implored Longmans to get someone else to write the preface. Why did he load himself with such a task, for which he was naturally unsuited? Was it to tether himself? His lyrics, which he knew were his best things, came to him as he walked. The composition of these would not have occupied his time sufficiently. How else was he to hold himself at home? Town meant expense and extravagance.

He made himself dull from a sense of duty. For all his praise of the sweetness of domesticity, his ideal home sometimes bored him. He hated to tie himself down. It was not merely a question of money. Although he was ever in pursuit of that elusive commodity, he turned down several good journalistic opportunities; he was jealous of his freedom as an artist, and he knew he was incapable of any form of administrative work. In any business he would only have been safe as a sleeping partner. Moore was one of Robert Louis Stevenson's 'light-headed, variable men who are attracted to marriage by its very awfulness . . . To the end spring winds will sow disquietude, passing faces leave a regret behind them, and the whole world keep calling in their ears'.

He was a wonder child, and there was no place in the world for him when youth vanished. Lady Blessington, who did nothing to help his reputation, describes Byron's account of a visit from Moore: 'the very sight of his face sparkling with intelligence, now lighted up by the very soul of mirth and frolic, and the next instant shaded by a momentary pensiveness, reminding me of a Bacchus recovering from ebriety'. A rather feeble paraphrase of Byron's vigorous style, yet it conveys the impression of Moore's personality; and Sydney Smith caught it when he described him in later years as a 'superannuated cherub'.

And yet, writing to his friend Strangford in 1805, he said he was 'sorry to find that you are not employed in anything better than cyphers and dispatches; though why I should say sorry when there is nothing in the world I pant so much for as release from all drudgery of fancy—this slave of imagination I am bound to . . .'.

Collecting material for his life of Sheridan, he groaned at the thought that he was wasting time he could be using for writing verse; and until his mind collapsed in 1849, he was in the same quandary. Rogers, writing to his sister from Bowood, where he was staying, complained: 'But he is very strange—for when I offered to return with him today to see her (Bessy) he said "Don't come today—and don't talk to me. I compose as I walk".'

Two cranky old men—but the episode shows that even up to the end Moore's true inspiration, the self-generated one, had not altered, even if it could no longer be realised adequately. His Journal notes for this month make all clear.

'The Bowood family arrived, and almost at the same time a kind note from Lady Lansdowne, asking Bessy and me to come and dine there on Monday. So the winter campaign there has opened, and how am I to fight off these kind and agreeable attacks I know not. In my answer declining Monday's dinner, I depicted somewhat more strongly than I had intended, or perhaps ought, the situation between printers' devils assailing me from without, and the cares and wants of home staring upon me from within. Am sorry I let that word "wants" escape me.'

Moore was struggling to complete his most ill-judged literary effort—the fatal Irish history. It preyed upon his mind; he kept on failing to produce copy in time.

Young Tom's ruinous career after the death of Russell, the mother's favourite, in November of the previous year, had robbed the future of hope. The health of both the Moores suffered. Moore made a few efforts to recuperate his spirits in London, staying with the faithful and seemingly immortal Rogers, but to no purpose.

Until Tom began to give serious trouble—as soon as he became a soldier in March 1838—Moore enjoyed his success in London, where he was always in demand; Holland House was only one of the many to which he was able to propose himself as a visitor and cancel and postpone his engagements as he pleased. At home there was Bowood when the Lansdownes were in residence.

Up in town, in September 1842, he noted that he had dined at his own expense alone two days running, 'which in London is a sort of monstrosity. "Base is the slave that pays" says ancient Pistol'. And when he sat down to journalise after dining at Holland House he found himself unable to remember much. 'My knack of reporting, never very good, is nearly gone.' The most lasting impression of the evening was of being irritated before dinner by Allen, the librarian, who criticised Moore's Irish history without having read it. In the same paragraph Moore says the visit ended with Lady Holland trying to nail him down for dinner next day, and his evading her without disclosing where he was going.

Two days later the indestructible Rogers conveyed him to Holland House again. Forgetting his grievance, he asked Allen whether he didn't feel wearied by the effort to keep up conversation during these evenings; and the librarian owned 'that it was frequently a most heavy task'. He seemed to agree with Moore that the Holland House sort of existence, 'though by far the best specimen of its kind going' was the most wearisome of all forms of slavery. Moore found the best result of his visits to town was the relish with which he returned to his own quiet garden and study 'where in the mute society of my own thoughts and books, I am never either offended or wearied'.

And where, it must not be overlooked, Moore had always worked assiduously. If sometimes he gave up all his time to visitors, he groaned at it. A long visit from Sir John Stevenson distracted him; and his usual habits were witnessed by the Griffin brothers who, even when they came from Limerick to see him about entering parliament, were never admitted to his presence until evening.

He was, according to Professor Dowden, who has studied the original Journal, much less pliable than the Russell version suggests, much less fearful of giving offence, and much more given to plain speaking. But there was an ineradicable sweetness at his core. When his troubles were thick about him, a practical joker faked a letter from a Parish Priest in Macroom, Co. Cork, telling him of a legacy of £3000. Moore's comment when the truth came out was 'Alas! Alas! I wish no worse to the ingenious gentleman who penned the letter than an exactly similar disappointment'. (Bessy's 'generous heart' had been 'apportioning out the different presents it would enable her to make to my sister to the poor H's, &c., &c.'.)

Until his health finally collapsed Moore's moods were always evanescent. In February 1840, he had forsworn the world: 'and looking over my Journal, many parts of which brought tears from me, particularly the details of my dear child Anastasia's death. Much struck, too, by the falling off there has been, from various causes, of many of my former friendships and intimacies; people with whom I once lived familiarly and daily, being now seldom seen by me, and that but passingly and coldly. This partly owing to the estrangements produced by politics, and to the greater rarity of my own visits to Town, of late years; but altogether it is saddening'.

Three years later he is driving with Sydney Smith at Combe Florey in a gig. When the horse reared, Moore got out and walked home. He remarks in his Journal that he is the only guest, which suggests that he wished it were otherwise. Smith wrote to him on his return.

August 7th 1843

'Dear Moore,

The following articles have been found in your room and forwarded by the Great Western. A right-hand glove, an odd stocking, a sheet of music paper, a missal, several letters, apparently from ladies, an Elegy on Phelim O'Neil. There is also a bottle of Eau de Cologne. What a careless mortal you are.

God bless you.'

Earlier that summer Moore had been in London, and breakfasting with Lord John was shocked to find that he had promised himself on the previous day 'to Sir Charles Lemon as well as to Bunbury; but if people will not send reminders, what is a many-dinnered gentleman to do? Found myself in another scrape today, having promised my company to *some* Amphytrion or other, but couldn't in the least remember who'.

And when, on the return journey, he arrived in Calne, he 'stopped at the Bowood Gate, and left my luggage, not knowing whether I was to dine with the Lansdownes or at home. Found from my sweet Bess it was to be the former. Walked then to Bowood. Party at dinner only the John Russells and myself'.

Lord and Lady John were both very anxious that Bessy should come with Moore to stay with them at Endsleigh. There was nothing, he wrote in his Journal that he would like better. But Bessy *wouldn't*, 'and even if she *would*, my purse couldn't'.

His marriage excepted, Moore's connection with Lord Lansdowne was the most solid advantage in his life; and without it his marriage might have been less successful. Charles Greville gives an account of a visit to Bowood in December 1841 which shows how attractive the atmosphere was in that hospitable house. He came on from a visit to the Duke of Bedford, and

found a very different party from what he had left at Woburn
Abbey, where there was nothing but 'idle, ignorant, ordinary
people'. Here he met Moore, Rogers, Macaulay . . . The party
included Fanny Kemble with her American husband. They were
joined next day by Dundas and Lord John Russell. Fanny
Kemble gave readings from plays, Moore sang some of his
Melodies. Macaulay 'has been always talking. Never certainly
was anything heard like him'. Only Rogers showed resentment
at the brilliant flow, but he 'will revive tomorrow when Macaulay goes'. Macaulay went, 'and it was wonderful how quiet
the house seemed after he had gone, and it was not less agreeable'. Rogers perked up, the host—a different talker—likewise.
'It does not do', Greville reflected, 'for more than two or three
days; but I never passed a week with so much good talk, almost
all literary and miscellaneous, very little political, no scandal and
gossip.'

That was the tone the Lansdownes set, and it must be said of
Moore's Journal that for all the gossip in it, there is very little
scandal. Greville lamented the difference between the company
at Bowood and that which he usually kept. With 'shame and
sorrow' he had to admit that he had wasted by far the larger
proportion of his time, when he could have lived with the
'cultivated and the wise'. But a few days, he had said, was
enough; and if Moore complained that he was called upon so
often, he lived under no servitude to the big house. He came
and went as he pleased.

We have his recollections of that Bowood party. 'The plot
again began to thicken at Bowood, and I was again accordingly brought into play.' But he is not complaining; not a word
of adverse criticism escapes him. Rogers had given 'the natural
sweetness of his disposition fair play'. Macaulay was 'a wonderful
man', and he rejoiced at the prospect of a history of England
from his pen. He refers to Fanny Kemble's visit—she stayed for
a fortnight—and he had sung some of his songs with her. He
noted that Charles Greville was much impressed by the beauty
of the house.

Fanny Kemble gives the visit a generous space in her
Memoirs. Bowood was 'a home of terrestial delights. Inside . . .
all tasteful and intellectual magnificence . . . outside a charming

English landscape . . . They are good, pleasant, and every way distinguished people, and I like them very much. He . . . a man of the finest taste and cultivation. Lady Lansdowne is a specimen Englishwoman of her class, refined, intelligent, well-bred, and most charming'. She mentions Rogers and Moore in that letter by name among 'a parcel of choice *beaux esprits* . . . so incessantly clever, witty, and brilliant that they every now and then give me a brainache'.

Whenever she looked into the morning-rooms she saw Macaulay in the same position on the hearth-rug, always talking, always answering questions. The volume of his voice— 'full and sonorous'—gave him an immense advantage in sound as well as sense over his adversaries. Sydney Smith's humorous and good-humoured rage . . . was very funny. Rogers, of course, was not good-humoured; and on this very occasion, one day at breakfast having two or three times uplifted his thread of voice and fine incisive speech against the torrent of Macaulay's holding forth, Lord Lansdowne, the most courteous of hosts, endeavoured to make way for him with a "You were saying, Mr Rogers?" when Rogers hissed out, "Oh, what I was saying will keep".'

When Fanny Kemble was about to leave and was passing through the hall, she met Lansdowne and Moore talking together. Moore picked up Fanny's daughter and kissed her. 'Pray, mamma, who was dat little Gentleman?' she inquired when she was alone with her mother. She thought she had been 'taken a liberty with by some enterprising schoolboy'. But her mother reflected that 'if one of her own Irish rosebuds of sixteen had received that poet's kiss, how long it would have been before she washed that side of her face! I believe if he had bestowed it upon me, I would have kept mine from water for its sake, till—bedtime. Indeed, when first *Lalla Rookh* came out, I think I might have made a little circle on that cheek, and dedicated it to Tom Moore and dirt for ever . . . But, you see, he didn't kiss my stupid little child's intelligent mother, and this is the way that fool Fortune misbestows her favours'.

Lansdowne was described by Guizot as bearing some resemblance to his London residence: 'capacious, imposing, well-furnished, but somewhat cold in the nature of its ornaments'.

To a Frenchman there may have been something a little distant in his manner—perhaps he was shy. How little he must have touched on personal matters with Moore is illustrated by the fact that having lived beside him so closely he could, even as late as 1823, not know what Moore's religious beliefs were. But his treatment of Moore was unfailingly undemanding and kind. He never showed any sign of regretting the impulse that, at one of their very first meetings, made him suggest the poet should come and live in his neighbourhood.

Moore kept to the resolution of his college days never to be a pedant or a bore. He had the 'simple and unaffected manner of behaving and expressing himself' which Scott recognised as all that was necessary to make a man of talent a success in 'the best society'. Mulvany, the Irish artist, who knew him well in later years, praised his buoyancy, ready wit, wish to please and —as important—aptitude to be pleased, his musical voice, 'clear, ringing laughter', love of fun 'without a taint of low or gross humour'. 'I have mixed with all grades of Society . . . Tom Moore was the best table companion I ever met.' His tiny stature did not depress Moore. When a tall friend asked him if he found the day cold, he answered 'Why, rather so. How is it up there with you?'

*　　*　　*

There was no bigotry in the Lansdowne circle. But a certain type of Irish Catholic bigot has always been on Moore's tracks, and it was asserted that he had been persuaded by his firmly Protestant wife to adopt her faith; she was also—inevitably— accused of refusing to let a priest see him in his last hour.

The Rev. Mr Edgell, the rector of the parish, wrote many years afterwards to Daniel Ambrose, a member of Parliament, denying these rumours. Moore used to come to church with his wife, but did not attend the service. Mr Edgell regretted the rumour; he did not see Moore during the last two years of his life. The person chiefly responsible for the misunderstanding was S. C. Hall who, with his wife, wrote a three-volume Irish travel book. Hall was said to be Dickens's model for Pecksniff.

Moore ended his *Travels in Search of a Religion* with 'Hail, then, to thee, thou one and only true Church . . .'. So we must accept that public declaration—by no means to his interest—as his final position. Elsewhere in this strange medley of theological pickings and stealings he describes how after studying the early tradition of the Mass he felt himself 'drawn back to old Mother Church'. In Dublin he 'went to attend Mass in Townsend Street Chapel as a peace offering to the name of my venerable old confessor Father O'H— . . . So ashamed I felt even on this slight hankering after my former faith which this visit to the old church betrayed, that I took care to place myself where I should be least likely to meet with persons who knew me and even there cowered in my corner so as to be as much as possible concealed'.

He had, he said, 'by nature very strong devotional feelings and from childhood had knelt nightly to my prayers with a degree of trust in God's mercy and grace'.

The story of the priest being refused admission had this basis in fact; the priest in the English mission which included Sloperton met Moore out walking and invited him to take communion at Easter. Before that he would have to make a good confession. Moore said that he had long desired to do such a thing and invited the priest to call next day. When he did he was met by Bessy. 'Oh my God!' she exclaimed. 'What have you done on yesterday to cause the present state of my poor husband? For, since he told me he met you, he has been almost in a constant state of delirium, and he is now in bed, too ill to see any person.'

Nevertheless, she did allow the priest to come in.

The parson, Mr Edgell, in his letter to Daniel Ambrose, wrote that 'Moore was devoted to his wife and children (whatever Croker may have said or written) and was himself one of the most *lovable* men I ever knew. Hall knew from me that I had buried Moore in our churchyard, and so may have jumped to the conclusion that Moore had died a Protestant . . . I can only repeat that I never told Mr Hall or Lewis any such thing, and that Moore *died as he lived a Catholic*'.

Moore's accounts of his marriage sometimes sound almost too good to be true. Did Bessy's perpetual martyrdom not try his nerves? Was she never nasty when he ran up bills in town while she eked it out at home? Was her perpetually being unwell to some extent a safety device? Or were they so firmly knitted to each other that their respective foibles were between them laughed away? Was ever incompatability more cheerfully recorded than '19th August 1837: Took Bessy to hear Mass at Wardour: the first time she ever saw Catholic service performed. The music as usual (when it is so good) raised me to the skies, but the gaudy ceremonies and gesticulations of the Mass shocked my single-minded Bessy, and even the music, much as she feels it, could not reconcile her to the old garments of the priest'.

'I am sinking here into a mere vegetable', Moore wrote to Rogers on 23 June 1847. His helplessness which had always been a marked trait and his forgetfulness increased to the point of embarrassment. He had to abandon his Journal, and as early as 1842, having dined out in London, he could not remember the name or face of any of the guests. Even his old enemy Hobhouse, who in Byron's lifetime had referred to Moore as his aversion, found himself so moved by Moore's plight that he had to forgive him. He even had his ancient enemy to stay at Erle Stone and noticed with affectionate concern how he found it almost impossible to get to bed, having to return to each room after he left it to look for something he had left behind, and in the process becoming quite bemused as to his whereabouts. Having announced his departure on a certain morning, he forgot all about it. 'I was very glad of it for he is very agreeable.'

That was in 1844, and Moore had still eight years to live. Three years later he suffered what must have been a stroke and was unable to write his name. In 1849 when Russell was staying at Bowood, he came over with his host to pay Moore a visit. He collapsed that evening. Russell gives the date as the 20th December. It was the beginning of a living death, advanced senility, but interspersed with brief recuperations. He inquired for friends and sang a little up to the end.

From that time on Mrs Moore, who was herself often very unwell, and was never in good health, nursed him, stayed with him and read to him. He had flashes of coherence, asked that she should read the Bible to him. She kept people away because she did not want them to see the fallen idol.

The Halls, who may have spread untrue rumours about Moore's religious attachments were, nevertheless, kind friends to Mrs Moore at this time, and Hall wrote a testimony to her angelic treatment of her husband. It was all deserved; and whatever may be said about the superficiality of Moore's emotions, his praise of Bessy was only her due. He knew what a treasure he had; she lived for him, shielding him as far as she could from the sorrows which piled up on them in the last years.

Whatever defects there were in her formal education, she was rich in the intelligence of the heart. She used a word about her husband which was so well chosen that it might be accepted as the final verdict on his elusive character. Writing to Rogers, who was always an admirer of hers, and who never let her feel his acerbity, she said: 'My mind is full of fears, but God gives me the great comfort of nursing him; he knows me, talks of you and other friends, his evanescent temper is now a blessing to himself and me . . .'.

Evanescent is exactly the right word to describe the essence of Moore. Superficial will not do; not merely because it is worn thin from over-use; it is too pejorative. He was a song bird; not an eagle, not a dove; and he was untrue to his essential nature when he tried to be an owl.

Bessy took him for little walks. In 1851, she even essayed a trip to Bath; but he was lost there.

'Lean upon God, Bessy; lean upon God', he sometimes said to Bessy, who had no one else certainly to lean upon.

He died on 26th February 1852, sinking without pain. There was a demand in Ireland for a funeral there; but Bessy preferred to bury him in the vault in Bromham with the two children. Only one coach followed the funeral. The admirable Thomas Longman, the younger, came down from London. No celebrity was there. Nobody else thought to make the journey to Wiltshire. The Lansdownes were not at Bowood when Moore was buried on March 3rd, and Russell in London was at a critical moment in his political career.

In later years, Bessy gave Moore's library to the Royal Irish Academy; she had a small pension; and her only employment until she joined Tom and Anastasia and Russell in their resting place was to keep up the little charities which Rogers used to help her with. Lady Lansdowne was kind.

But Bessy, suffering from some undefined complaint, became unable to move beyond the terrace where Tom used to walk in the morning, catching inspiration in the air. Lord John gave her a suitable pony, and agreed to carry out Moore's charge that he should publish a memoir. Thomas Longman offered £3000, which provided Bessy with enough to enable her, with what she had, to keep on the house. She used to rise at half past five every morning; her care was to see that the gardener kept the terrace weeded; she sat herself all morning in Tom's room.

She tried as best she could to help Russell with his task; but he was far too busy—Foreign Secretary in Aberdeen's cabinet in 1852, President of the Council 1854—and he should not have undertaken it.

Russell's botched job has not helped Moore. It led to notices favourable and otherwise—more favourable on the whole in Ireland where Moore's reputation stood higher than ever; in England he had simply gone out of fashion. Unfortunately the *Quarterly Review*, the graveyard of so many reputations, was still in business; more unfortunately it gave the first volumes to John Wilson Croker to review when they appeared in 1853.

Croker was not a pleasant man; at this time he was a dying one. He had crossed swords with Macaulay early in their career in the House of Commons. Macaulay took his revenge in his review of Croker's edition of Boswell's *Life of Johnson*. Croker bided his time and joined battle again when Macaulay's *History* came out. Macaulay described him as that 'impudent, leering Croker'. Mr Wenham (cockney for venom) 'the abject parasite of the infamous Marquis of Hertford' is how Thackeray portrays him in *Vanity Fair*. He is Counsellor Con Crawley, a grovelling, Irish place-hunter in *Florence MacCarthy*, one of Lady Morgan's novels of the time. The Duke of Wellington, in old age, accepted his attentions; but, then, he was too self-sufficient to have bothered himself very much with character analysis so long as he enjoyed Croker's gossip, and he spoke up and minded his manners. Greville in his epitaph described him as occupying a high place among the second-rate men of his time. 'His stores of general knowledge made him entertaining, though he was too overbearing to be agreeable.'

Croker had no reason to believe Moore disliked him. Moore spoke of cultivating his acquaintance in early Dublin days; he solicited Croker's help in the Bermuda affair. Croker, founding the Athenaeum Club, invited Moore with Scott and Lord Lansdowne to form the nucleus. Moore would have liked Croker if anyone could have liked him. He did not quarrel with people.

Croker took up the first instalment of the eight indigestible little volumes with no animus against Moore (whose bust stood in his house) but, of course, as a political opponent of Lord John's. He was going to have a field day at the editor's expense even if there had been nothing in Moore's text to annoy him personally. His opening expression of sympathy for 'the reputation of poor Moore', put in jeopardy by this ill-judged publication, was a trifle condescending, but he can be pardoned for repeating Sydney Smith's quip about 'his Lordship's readiness to undertake *any* thing and *every* thing—to build St Paul's— cut for the stone—or command the Channel fleet'. And his general criticism of the slovenly way the work was done was thoroughly deserved. The publication did nothing to help Moore's claims on the good opinion of posterity. There is far too much trivia; even if Moore was the most restless of men— 'for we neither of us bother chairs much', he said of Rogers and himself—no effort was made to remove an impression of superficiality, due largely to Moore's impatience as a diarist. For Moore's eye and ear were not selective; he rarely expanded; the Journal consists largely of jottings. But what did most serious damage to Moore's reputation was the editor's failure to make clear that it was kept when Moore was on the wing; he hardly ever records his thoughts and doings when he was at home; he did not, in any event, go in for *pensées*. On the cover of the Journal for 1823, Moore wrote, 'It is not my wish (in case of anything happening to me) that this Journal should be published or shown to any one. T.M. It may be made use of by the person who shall be employed to write a Memoir of me'.

Cutting, Russell did in plenty, leaving loose ends—references to entries that don't appear. He put a blank for Croker's name where it required very little effort by anyone, and none by Croker, to recognise to whom Moore was referring when he wrote: 'Met —, who walked about with me and made me take a family dinner with him at his hotel. I have not seen so much of him since we were in college together, and I find that his vanity is even greater than has been reported to me, and his display of cleverness far less than I expected. He is undoubtedly a good partisan, a quick skirmisher in reviews and newspapers; and a sort of servant of all-work for his employers; but as to the higher sort of talent, I am greatly mistaken if he has the slightest claim to it.'

This, no doubt, inspired Croker (who was genuinely hurt to discover Moore disliked him) to write seventy-one pages which, if they do allow Moore many recommendations, build up into a devasting criticism of him as a man, a husband, a scholar, and —to a large extent—as a writer. The attack, like all long attacks, eventually boomerangs. One ends up tired of it, disliking Croker, and infinitely preferring Moore, whatever his short-comings might have been. Croker never discloses his own motive —it emerged in a subsequent and tedious correspondence with Russell in *The Times*. Russell's behaviour is consistent with his reputation as a person of monumental awkwardness in human relations. When defending himself, for example, he says that he had suppressed even more hurtful references to Croker. This explains the dying Croker's unseemly correspondence with his namesake (Thomas Crofton Croker) who was raking up dirt with which to bespatter Bessy in the good cause of maligning her husband and the circumstances of his marriage.*

Croker alludes to the hugger-mugger nature of that transac-tion at the outset of his essay. Moore's disparaging remarks about him were made after a meeting in Paris. Croker was then with his wife. They had recently lost their only son, and she was in no mood to make new acquaintances. In consequence she neglected to pay any special attention to Mrs Moore. This, Croker satisfied himself, vexed Moore and explained his momentary irritation. He was in a constant fidget about the way people received Bessy.

'Spiteful slyness' was Croker's explanation of Russell's elision

* Croker was one of several to whom Moore had suggested writing his biography.

of his name, letting the hurtful paragraph stand. But Russell was not sly; he was tactless; his references to suppressed passages compounded Moore's offence in Croker's eyes. It was extraordinarily clumsy. No wonder Russell's handling of the Famine crisis left the Irish under the impression that he wished to starve them, that his handling of the papal claims to English dioceses left the impression of a hardened bigot. He was nothing malevolent; he was a Russell.

A 'delirium tremens of morbid vanity' is how Croker describes Moore's longing for praise and the childish pleasure with which he records it. But if, as Croker admits, it was never present in his manner in society—nobody who met Moore ever came away without a pleasant impression—and if Croker, even in a revengeful mood, can still describe him as 'a most agreeable companion', remembers his 'joyous and sanguine temper', deems him 'naturally kind and loving', there must have been an underlying sense of insecurity, a deep psychological need, to explain it. Vanity, yes; but as Gladstone (a greater man than Croker) said of O'Connell's, 'an innocent and sportive vanity'. A child's delight in itself is not hidden. Moore matured sufficiently to reserve his displays for his mother and his wife and his women confidants and those who depended on him, as some men boast to their barbers.

Having dealt at length with Moore's amiable weakness, Croker proceeded to make out, with the thoroughness of a police report, a detailed list of Moore's social engagements in Paris and in London to show the extent to which he neglected Bessy. Night after night, he dined out or went to the theatre or stayed away from home when she was ill.

'Next after his own self-worship—if indeed it was not a branch of it—there is nothing so prominent throughout the volumes as his adoration of his wife . . . We can have no doubt of the sincerity of Moore's attachment to and admiration of his wife, but we must observe that these ultra-uxorious expressions occur with peculiar emphasis just before and just after some *escapade* from home; they are the honey with which he sweetens the edge of his absence. It is evident that Mrs Moore saw the Journal . . .'

Croker goes on to list typical references to the 'dear girl', 'my darling Bessy', 'dear generous girl'—and then details the circumstances which evoked them. In Paris, to begin with:

'If his friends in England could have guessed what the Diary has now revealed to us of the life of the Exile of Erin, they would not have thought it any great hardship . . . and what ladies were the companions of these flights—strange ones, we think, for a father of a family aged forty-three . . .'

Descended three times 'in the cars' with each of the Miss Kingstons, four times with Mrs Story, ten or twelve times with the young Scotch girl, and then 'with Lucy'.

Croker's jackdaw's eyes did not catch all the references to Lucy Drew or he would certainly have asked how any married man could explain them to the entire satisfaction of even the sweetest and most understanding of wives. But Croker does not hint at more than frivolousness; and he was probably aware that there was no emotional entanglement in Moore's life. He had no need of one. He was always the pursued; and Lucy may have run only more determinedly than the rest. None of his letters to friends before his marriage suggest that he was ever very deeply in love. He aroused affection; he did not know what it was to look for it. Witness the ultra-respectable, highly serious Fanny Kemble's feelings when she met him, aged sixty-three, at Bowood.

But how answer Croker's charges of neglect, leaving Bessy alone, ill or in pain, while he went out and enjoyed himself? There is, I am afraid, no answer. He could not endure pain or suffering. He threw it off as a dog shakes off water, coming out from a dip. He avoided the deathbeds of his children; Anastasia's dying eyes were fixed on the door through which he never came; he avoided funerals and, after Byron's, took the Story girls out to Vauxhall to get his spirits back. He could forget Bessy's illness at the opera. He brought this aptitude to such perfection that he never let his company see that he was under any pressures. For the time being he had always shrugged them off. It explains why he never stayed long anywhere or with anyone if he could help it. It explains why he preferred the company of women. So far as feeling went he concentrated his capacity for emotion into his performances at the piano. In them Croker acknowledged 'a charm of manner the most graceful, the most natural, and the most touching that we have ever witnessed'. And with this 'singular and seductive talent . . . perfect good manners and lively conversation'.

Croker leaves us still with awkward unanswered questions, and all that can be said about them is that Moore's wife did not love him any less on their account. Once she seems to have pursued him to London, but when she got there he did not alter his programme, and saw comparatively little of her until he entered in his Journal 'up at five. And *saw my TREASURES safe in the coach!*'

Mrs Moore was suffering from some unspecified illness— perhaps the consequence of child-bearing—and she went to Cheltenham for two months for a cure. In all that time he seems to have spent only two days with her. There was also a sudden trip to England with young Tom that Bessy made on her own initiative when the Moores were living in France. What was the motive for this? Was it on account of Lucy Drew?

Who was she? The index to the *Memoirs* is faulty; but we find her in it and she often turns up—where we are not directed— sometimes as 'L'. Could she have been the young woman Miss Rennie described waiting outside Moore's lodgings in a coach? Bessy knew her; in Paris and in London, Moore mentions that they had gone out together; but on most occasions when she is referred to Moore is seeing her alone.

In March and April 1823, she is in town, and Moore is driving about in a hackney coach with her. She is with him on the morning of the Monkhouse dinner. Moore solicits a box in the theatre for her from Lady Holland. Sometimes when Bessy is in town, Lucy drives out with her; but she sees Moore alone even on these occasions. He meets her at her friends, the Montgomerys, and coaches down to the Charter House where she has a friend, a Mr Barber. Sometimes he keeps Lucy's carriage all night. He refers cryptically to meetings with 'L' in Bury Street, and once when he has been in Brighton, the diary entry ends: 'Got to town at 7. Saw L. Packed up.'

Mademoiselle Drew is on the publisher's list for an author's copy of *Sheridan*. She would appear to have been well-to-do, delicate ('Poor Lucy'), and frequently on Moore's mind, if not his conscience. It was in all probability an innocent affair: persistence on one side; weakness and vanity on the other. She was almost certainly pretty. She disappears from the Journal in 1829.

The entry in Greville's diary for 6th September 1857 rounds off the story of Moore's life neatly. Greville reads the Honours List, notes that the most conspicuous of the new peers is Macaulay. He had not seen or heard of any complaints at his elevation. Lansdowne had declined the offer of a dukedom. Greville regretted the decision. It would have been a 'graceful and becoming' public recognition of his character and services.

'While Macaulay is thus ascending to the House of Peers, his old enemy and rival Croker has descended to the grave, very noiselessly and almost without observation, for he had been for some time so withdrawn from the world that he was nearly forgotten. He had lived to see all his predictions of ruin and disaster to the country completely falsified. He continued till the last year or two to exhale his bitterness and spite in the volumes of the *Quarterly Review*, but at last the editor (who had long been sick of his contributions) contrived to get rid of him.'

'What a bitter unfeeling man he is' was all Bessy said about Croker at the time. Afterwards she held her peace. She joined Tom and the children in Bromham churchyard on 8th September 1865.

BIBLIOGRAPHY

I have restricted this to the books I have used as sources. Periodicals are cited in the text. Moore, throughout, unless otherwise stated, is quoted from his own *Journal* or letters. I have drawn on the material in the National Library of Ireland (including the Joly collection) relating to Moore. This is set out in the admirable catalogues of Irish source material in manuscript and Irish periodicals, edited by the late Dr Richard Hayes.

Ambrose, Daniel. 'Thomas Moore: the Religion in which he died.' *Irish Ecclesiastical Record*, 15 (1895), 18–26.

Berlioz, Hector. *Memoirs of Hector Berlioz from 1803 to 1865*. Macmillan, 1874.

Berry, Mary. *Extracts from the Journal and Correspondence of Miss Berry*, ed. Lady Theresa Lewis, Longmans, 1866.

Betjeman, John. *High and Low*. John Murray, 1966.

Bowles, William Lisle. *A Wiltshire Parson and His Friends*, ed. Garland Greeve. Constable, 1926.

Carlisle, Henry E., *A Selection from the Correspondence of Abraham Hayward Q.C.* John Murray, 1886.

Clayden, P. W. *Rogers and his Contemporaries*. Smith Elder, 1887.

Cockburn, Lord. *Life of Lord Jeffrey*. Edinburgh: Black, 1852.

Coleridge, S. T. *Collected letters of Samuel Taylor Coleridge*, ed. E. L. Griggs. Oxford: Clarendon Press, 1956–59.

Croker, J. W. *The Croker Papers*, edited by Louis J. Jennings.

Croker, J. W. *Correspondence between the Rt. Hon. J. W. Croker and the Rt. Hon. Lord John Russell on some passages of 'Moore's Diary'*. John Murray, 1884.

Croker, T. C. *Notes from the Letters of Thomas Moore to His Music Publisher, James Power*. New York: Redfield.

Davis, Thomas. *Essays Literary and Historical*, ed. D. J. O'Donoghue. Dundalk: Tempest, 1914.

Dowden, Wilfred S. *The Letters of Thomas Moore*. Oxford: Clarendon Press, 1964 (2 vols.).

Dowden, Wilfred S. 'Let Erin Remember.' *A re-examination of the Journal of Thomas Moore*. Rice University Studies. Winter 1975.

Greville, Charles C. F. *The Greville Memoirs*, edited by Henry Reeve. Longmans Green & Co, 1888 (8 vols.).

Griffin, Daniel. *The Life of Gerald Griffin*. Dublin: Duffy, 1874.

Gwynn, Stephen. *Thomas Moore*. Macmillan, 1905.

Hall, S. C. *A Memory of Thomas Moore*. Virtue, 1879.

Hall, S. C. *A Book of Memoirs of Great Men and Women*. Virtue, 1877.

Hobhouse, John Cam. *Recollections of a Long Life*. Scribner's, 1910.

Hunt, Leigh. *Autobiography*, ed. Edmund Blunden. Oxford, 1928.

Ilchester, G. S. H. Fox-Strangeways, 6th Earl of. *Elizabeth, Lady Holland to her Son.* 1821–45. Murray, 1946.

Jordan, Hoover H. *Bolt Upright: The Life of Thomas Moore.* Salzburg Studies in English Literature under the direction of Professor Erwin A. Stürzl. Austria (2 vols.). 1975.

Joyce, James. *Letters of James Joyce,* ed. Richard Ellmann. Faber & Faber, 1966.

Kemble, Frances Anne. *Records of Later Life.* Richard Bentley, 1882.

Keats, John. *The Letters of John Keats,* ed. M. B. Forman. Oxford, 1935.

Kelly, Michael. *Reminiscences of Michael Kelly.* Colburn, 1826.

Lockhart, J. B. *Life of Sir Walter Scott.* Adam and Charles Black, 1893.

Marchand, Leslie A. *Byron* 3 vols. John Murray, 1957.

Lovell, Ernest J. *His Voice and Very Self.* Collected Conversations of Lord Byron. Macmillan, 1954.

Marchand, Leslie A. *Byron's Letters and Journals.* John Murray (5 vols. in 1976).

MacManus, M. J. *A Bibliography of Thomas Moore. Dublin Magazine,* 8 (1933) 55–61.

Martineau, Harriet. *Autobiography.* Smith Elder & Co. (1877).

Moore, Doris L. *The Late Lord Byron.* Murray, 1951.

Morgan, Lady. *Lady Morgan's Memoirs: Autobiography, Diaries, and Correspondence.* Allen, 1862.

Mulvany, G. F. *Recollections of Moore. Dublin University Magazine,* 39 (1852), 477–96.

O'Connell, Daniel. *The Correspondence of Daniel O'Connell,* ed. Maurice O'Connell (1973). Irish University Press.

O'Hagan, Lord. *Occasional Papers and Addresses.* Kegan Paul, Trench, 1884.

O'Hanlon, John Canon. *The Catholicity of Thomas Moore. Irish Ecclesiastical Record,* 15 (1895), 249–58.

O'Sullivan, Donal. *Charles Dickens and Thomas Moore. Studies,* 37 (1948), 169–78, 342.

Poe, Edgar Allan. *The Works of Edgar Allan Poe,* ed. John H. Ingram. Edinburgh, 1875.

Rennie, Elizabeth. ('A Contemporary') *Traits of Character.* Hurst Blackett, 1860.

Robinson, Henry Crabb. *Diary, Reminiscences, and Correspondence of Henry Crabb Robinson,* ed. Thomas Sadler. Macmillan, 1872.

Rogers Samuel. *Recollection of the Table Talk of Samuel Rogers,* ed. Morchard Bishop. Richards, 1952.

Russell, Lord John. *Memoirs, Journal and Correspondence of Thomas Moore,* ed. Lord John Russell. Longmans, 1853–56.

Scott, James. *Recollections of a Naval Life.* Bentley, 1834.

Scott, Sir Walter. *The Journal of Sir Walter Scott,* ed. W. E. K. Anderson. Oxford, 1972.

Shelley, Percy Bysshe. *The Letters of Percy Bysshe Shelley,* ed. Frederick L. Jones. Oxford, 1964 (2 vols.).

Strong, L. A. G. *The Minstrel Boy.* Hodder and Stoughton, 1937.
Trench, W. F. *Tom Moore.* Dublin, Three Candles, 1934.
Young, Julian Charles. *Last Leaves from the Journal of Julian Charles Young.*
    Edinburgh, Edmonston, Douglas, 1875.

INDEX